A History of Religious Rules

A legacy of Piety and Coercion

CLAUDE VARNER

SECOND EDITION

REVIEW OF *A HISTORY OF RELIGIOUS RULES*

"In his ambitious survey, Varner compares the three great monotheistic faiths, Judaism, Christianity, and Islam, in their rules for behavior, giving history and a typology. He views these rules in one of four categories: Moral Rules, General Admonitions, Organizational Rules, and Religious Rules. Moral rules cover basic principles of living together, such as admonitions against murder or lying, while general admonitions are principles without specifics. These two categories of rules are often shared across religious traditions and can be derived by reason. Organizational rules determine how societies govern themselves, and they are rare in religious texts themselves. Varner focuses on religious rules, the specific details revealed to prophets, of how to be holy.

Perhaps since Varner anticipates his readers to be less familiar with the Qur'an and Hadith than other religious texts, he spends significantly pages discussing Islam's relationship with religious rules than Christianity and Judaism, taking care to show the broad scope of legal and faith traditions within Islam and including a helpful appendix with extensive quotes from the Qur'an and Hadith, plus extensive bibliographic notes. He also touches on Hinduism, Buddhism, and Taoism but doesn't deal with those traditions in as much depth as the monotheistic traditions.

A History of Religious Rules is well researched and respectful of all the different traditions it discusses, even in its occasional tangents—in a discussion of the "Woke' narrative" debated in contemporary U.S. politics, he strives to present complex positions and contested history evenhandedly. Varner is well aware of diversity within and between religions and attempts to sketch them out for an educated lay audience. Throughout, Varner endeavors to spread tolerance by making it easier for people to communicate about where they disagree. His typology provides a valuable tool for that communication. Readers of any faith will appreciate Varner's care as he lays out different types of rules within religions and how they serve our societies or sow dissent."

Booklife (Publisher's Weekly)

With many thanks to my lovely wife, Tina, for supporting me through this. She was always there with the right word and some of the world's best scones.

To paraphrase George Orwell,

"We live in a time when it is the duty of concerned people to repeat the obvious."

Contents

Introduction

The prophets and founders of the great monotheisms: Judaism, Christianity, and Islam, have given us many rules and much advice in their holy scriptures. This book is an outline, a classification, and a history of some of the effects of the rules found in the great religious texts. It is written by someone who likes to study and has had a lifelong interest in religions and tolerance. By using a different classification of the monotheisms' rules, I hope to present a way of looking at them, and the religions of the East, that will allow for a better approach to the difficult issues between and within the different religions. I told a good friend of mine that I was writing a book about religions. He responded, "Organized religion has been around for about 2400 years and has about 5 billion adherents, and you think you know something they missed?"

Hopefully, this different way of looking at the prophets' and founders' messages will improve understanding and help answer Rodney King's poignant question that applies inside and outside the religions, "Can we all just get along?" Problematically, we will have to want to get along and compromise to do so. Many religious and political actors are vested in keeping us separated.

The belief that religions can be reconciled and live together labels me as a syncretic. This label comes from the assumption that, at their moral and emotional core, the great monotheisms are almost exactly alike.

I gave this book to my wife to read. She noted that lots of people are interested in "Saving the world" by writing books like this. I suppose I am joining the list of these writers. I will also discuss some of the questions of racism and inequality. They are not necessarily formal religious issues, but they do overlap.

To avoid favoritism, throughout the book I will present each section of my observations about the monotheisms in historical order: First Judaism, then Christianity, and then Islam. Frequently, all three will be addressed in the same paragraph.

There is a lot of emphasis on "reason", and many references to "reason". Reason can mean almost anything. "Reason" has been used to justify all sorts of crimes and atrocities, from Nazi genocide to chattel slavery. In the broadest sense, every decision is "reasonable" from someone's point of view or another. "It seemed like a good idea at the time."

The results of reasoning depend on one's premises. Is one interested in getting along better and the compromises that that entails, or is domination one's goal? For the purposes of this book, I propose that an action or belief is "reasonable" only if it clearly increases people's ability to live together peacefully and productively. This still leaves broad areas of disagreement culturally and economically. To be 'reasonable" an idea or project must not only support harmony but also support the individual human rights of free speech, free religion, free press, the vote, and habeas corpus (access to impartial justice). Some compromise is almost always necessary to any reasonable approach.

It will be important to remember throughout this work that assuring the individual freedoms of religion and speech will separate church and state. Also, we are speaking of "freedom", not "license" to do or say anything. Freedom comes with responsibilities, and it demands personal patience and concern for the "other". Freedom of speech does not include lies and threats.

I have assumed that most of the readers of this book will be Westerners who are somewhat familiar with Judaism and Christianity and their principal texts, the Tanakh (Old Testament) and Talmud for Jews and the whole Bible, the Old and New Testaments for the Christians. I have also assumed that many will not be very familiar with the Muslim texts. Consequently, I have included in the appendix a small list of

Qur'an verses. Many Qur'an verses are presented in two or three different translations so that the reader can see how the translations differ. I highly recommend reading the Qur'an if you have not already done so. It is often said by Islamic scholars that the only real way to understand the Qur'an is to read it in Arabic. For Muslims I have also included in the Appendix brief summaries of the Tanakh (Old Testament), the Talmud, and the New Testament. The Penguin Classic Publications contain a very readable translation for Westerners.

Many reformers attempt to solve organizational problems with a "scientific" approach involving statistics and polls. Concerning "science", there is a distinct difference between the hard sciences such as chemistry, physics, biology, geology and astronomy and the "soft" sciences such as sociology, psychology, political science, history, and economics. Medicine and engineering are applied hard sciences. All the sciences use statistics to make their points. The hard and applied sciences can predict actions and plan events very well. The softer sciences can be helpful but are not nearly so precise in predicting. Their narratives are much more subject to manipulation, polarization, and conflict. Today many government decisions concerning culture and sharing resources depend on soft and hard science statistics. Unfortunately, all science statistics can be manipulated to support almost anything. "Lies, damn lies, and statistics."- Disraeli or Mark Twain.

My hope is to promote a charitable and forgiving look at all the monotheisms. Humans are sometimes harsh to each other. Fundamentally I think that the God of all wants us to treat each other well and forgive each other frequently.

It is true that almost any broad statements about religion seem shallow and are often wrong in whole or in part. I submit that that is just the nature of the subject. This is not an academic thesis; it is a collection of observations about religions that seem self-evident to an interested citizen immersed in Western culture.

Chapter 1

The Rules

Before the maturation of the hard sciences, almost all of nature and life were mysteries. Humanity dealt with these mysteries through religious faith and ritual. Religion was at the center of life, and prophets informed us about our place and how to approach life and God. Then science explained natural disasters, demystified disease, and described our origins. Scientific knowledge and technology also gave us enormous power over our environment and health. Einstein and Heisenberg showed us that the universe was not precisely what we thought it was, and Darwin, Freud, and Jung showed us that we are not exactly who we thought we were. The fundamentals of life, death, salvation, and fulfillment are mysteries and remain articles of faith.

Besides the great spiritual messages, the religious prophets and founders of the three great monotheisms, Judaism, Christianity, and Islam, have brought us many Rules. I have divided the Rules into four types:

1. Moral Rules – don't lie, steal, murder, or commit adultery.

2. Organizational Rules -governmental laws.

3. General Admonitions.

   a. "Love your neighbor as yourself"- Moses and Jesus.

   b. "Do unto others as you would have them do unto you." – Jesus.

   c. "There should be no coercion in religion." Muhammad.

   d. "No man is a true believer unless he wishes the same thing for his brother as he does for himself"- Muhammad.

4. Religious Rules -pious or holy actions to please God.

Enlightened reasoning can provide a good set of the first three types of rules. The Moral Rules and General Admonitions are almost exactly alike in all the great religions. The Organizational Rules are political and swing between the poles of socialism, capitalism, democracy, and autocracy. A good ethical system can result from combining these three types of rules. The fourth category, Religious Rules, is completely idiosyncratic, has nothing to do with morals, and would not necessarily be arrived at by enlightened reasoning.

Additionally, reason is concerned with finding the "truth". There are many narratives about any situation. Most of these narratives may have at least some part of the truth. Out of all the narratives defining the "truth", I have tried to find common areas of justice and tolerance. The General Admonitions, such as "Do unto others as you would have them do unto you", are found in all the monotheisms and must be considered in any model for the "truth". Very importantly these General Admonitions which are present in the principal monotheistic texts clearly promote a tolerant narrative.

Religious Rules are revealed by God to various prophets and founders. They concern piety or holiness. For some people the prayer and ritual actions in the Religious Rules are associated with profound spiritual experiences and a serene sense of security in a difficult and dangerous world. The Religious Rules are not essential to the moral and spiritual message of the prophets. While the piety that they encourage is a source of great pleasure for many, imposition of Religious Rules on others can cause much difficulty with individual human rights and freedoms. Their imposition on others can result in oppression and violence. The General Admonitions in all the monotheisms promote kindness and tolerance. Is this promotion more important than the religious rituals? If one can say "Yes" or "Possibly", there is room for this discussion.

Today, almost everyone recognizes that despite their great progress relative to the rest of the world, the African Americans population in the US was put at a disadvantage economically and educationally. To rectify these, there are many programs of affirmative action requiring racial quotas were put in place to produce a more equitable place in society for African Americans and minorities. These have recently been weakened by court rulings. The conservatives says that some are excessive, unfair to whites and Asians, and create an unpleasant confrontational atmosphere in African American-white relations. The progressives say that they do not go far enough.

Context effects everything. One needs to consider who the speaker is addressing. Was the community in danger? Was it God or the prophet speaking? Have findings in the hard sciences changed our world view? Have experiments in democracy altered our fundamental understandings about government? Is this consistent with the prophet's overall message? Proper contextualizing will require a patient and tolerant reading of texts. Most of the punishments and violence in the texts were proposed when the existence of the tribe and the religion were at stake. That is no longer the case. The violence and punishments are no longer needed to assure the continuation of the great monotheistic religious communities and their rituals.

The Religious Rules are almost completely concerned with pieties and holiness. If the pieties described in the Religious Rules help one through life, that is a bonus. Pious rituals are, as one of my editors said, "Good reminders of God." Piety and prayer help to make a place for peace and harmony in many lives. Many get upset when their ideas of a pious atmosphere and actions are disturbed. My thoughts are that God will take care of judgment and punishments for impieties in our relationship to God. We don't have to worry about policing or judging levels of piety in others. Demanding that others become pious can only be disruptive. Interfering with the personal pieties of others is inexcusable.

The Categories of Rules

1. **Moral Rules.** There are essentially four Moral Rules in all the scriptures: don't murder, don't bear false witness, don't steal, and

don't commit adultery. The "don't murder" rule includes don't bully, torture, rape, or assault. "Don't bear false witness" means don't lie in a legal or serious sense. Harmless "white lies" that smooth over social problems or diminish unnecessary conflict are fine. "Stealing" includes confiscation and any benefiting from the work of others without appropriate compensation. These Moral Rules are very similar in all the great monotheisms. All the prophets bring these Moral Rules. They can be arrived at by compassionate reason without revelation.

All the monotheisms clearly condemn adultery as a divisive and disruptive practice. Because of improvements in medicine, birth control, safety, and women's empowerment, most of the rules concerning sexual morality will be addressed in the Organizational Rules.

2. **General Admonitions.** The General Admonitions are the most important rules involving applied religion. They give us the attitude that we need to have in approaching any question. Especially religious and interpersonal questions. They do not tell us exactly how to act. They just give us the approach to take in our actions. They broadly tell us to be kind to each other, be compassionate and tolerant. If we would consider the General Admonitions in our interactions with others, life would be easier. They are very similar in the three monotheisms.

The General Admonitions consist of sayings such as:

"Love your neighbor as yourself" -This is first stated in Jewish scriptures in Leviticus 19:18. This admonition is also stated by Jesus in the Christian New Testament. Matthew 22: 35-40

"Do unto others as you would have them to do unto you", The Golden Rule. Jesus states it in the Bible's New Testament in the Book of Luke 6:31.

"There should be no compulsion in religion". Muhammad, Qur'an 2:256.

"Requite evil with good." Qur'an 23:95 and 41:34

"No man is a true believer unless he desires for his brother what he desires for himself". Muhammad, Hadith, Bukhari 1:2:13

"Do not do unto others what you would not want done to you." Confucius' Silver Rule.

3. <u>**Organizational Rules.**</u> The Organizational Rules are the "law", and they concern the particulars about how a state, tribe, or nation is to function judicially, economically, and governmentally. They are the stuff of politics. There are very few specific Organizational Rules in the major texts, but "Justice" is mentioned prominently and repeatedly in all the texts. The use of reason in a framework of the Moral Rules and General Admonitions given by the prophets can deduce all the best Organizational Rules (laws) and promote justice. Separating temple/church/mosque and state avoids all sorts of problems.

The Organizational Rules may be supported by prophets, but they do not require divine revelation. Religious Rules and Organizational Rules do not necessarily have anything to do with each other. They become comingled when people use the government to enforce the Religious Rules or when politicians use charges of heresy and sacrilege to discredit, punish, or defeat others.

There is a large discussion about Organizational Rules in this book in Chapter 4. Organizational Rules are political rules governing rights, racism, capitalism, socialism, slavery, education, division of wealth, property, taxes, marriage, divorce, punishments, freedom of individual actions, and the relationship of religion to the nation. Our stances on all these issues are affected by the Moral Rules, a concern for justice, and the General Admonitions given by the monotheisms. Religious Rules do not necessarily impinge on any of these issues if temple/church/mosque and state are separated.

To Jews and Christians living in a Western style democracy, the best Organizational Rules are run under the guidance of the Moral Rules, the General Admonitions, and a desire for justice. Very importantly democratic Organizational Rules separate church and state [2]. This is probably the largest difference between democracy and current conservative theocratic thought.

"Islamist" is a word used to describe politicians and scholars who want Islamic Law (Sharia law) to inform the foundations of government. The Islamists believe that God has given us knowledge in the Qur'an and Hadith that is sufficient to run society. They essentially ask "Why would people ignore God's instructions about governance?" They believe that the essential issues about government are covered in the Qur'an and Hadith, and that proper study will reveal them. It appears that these scholars see the separation of religion and state as theological error.

As far as following blending the religion with the state, Abdul Maududi, founder of Jamaat-e-Islami (an Islamist political movement in Eastern Islam) said it this way, "You (Christians) separate religion from your policies, contradicting the pure nature which affirms absolute Authority to the Lord and your Creator." He is essentially asking, "If God has given you instructions, why won't you follow them?"

It turns out that that, as with all things involving humans, there are many religious scholars and many Islamic law schools with different interpretations. The problems occur because there are seemingly contradictory passages and definitions. "There should be no coercion in religion" (Qur'an 2:256) competes with "If they leave the faith, kill them" (Hadith Bukhari 9:84:57). Contextualizing the instructions in the texts will be very important. Chapter 3 is entirely devoted to the issues around contextualizing.

The Organizational Rules include the constitutions, governmental rules, business laws, taxes, domestic laws, and criminal laws. They concern morality, safety, industry, commerce, property, leadership succession, marriage, divorce, justice, and punishment. They may support various forms of capitalism or socialism, often a combination of the two. Among the most important types of Organizational Rules are those concerning the individual human rights of speech, religion, press, vote, and habeas corpus. As mentioned, they first were codified in the US Constitution's Bill of Rights. These Individual Rights are so important that they will be mentioned repeatedly and discussed at length in Chapter 4, on Organizational Rules. They cannot exist if church and state are connected. Corruption cannot be controlled, minority voices cannot be heard, and humanitarian progress cannot be sustained without these individual rights. These rights come with responsibilities.

Any discussion of Organizational Rules will be dominated by two factors.

1. Is the organization a "Group" oriented government? Or is the organization an "Individual" oriented government? What is most important: Group cohesion or Individual rights?

2. Does the state, nation, tribe, religion, or organization enforce the piety recommended in the Religious Rules?

Group oriented entities are interested in the preservation of the group and its ethos. The group can be tribal, monarchical, ethnic, racial, religious, socialist, democratic, dictatorial, fascist, elitist, or mafia-like. Groups punish or ostracize members who do not support the group. Groups usually become nepotistic and promote their own. Also, if the group or dictator thinks that it helps the group, they tend to tolerate forms of corruption and inequality. Groups formation also makes everyone else an "other" who can be treated differently. Group organizations do not grant individual rights of freedom of speech, freedom of press, or freedom of religion. The voting process and habeas corpus (impartial police and courts) are dominated by concerns for group security. Most group societies only allow vetted candidates to run for office. Group ethos has been the principal form of government since the dawn of civilization. Individual oriented nations are historically very recent.

Individual cultures are interested in individual expression and promote rights concerning speech, press, religion, assembly, the vote, and habeas corpus. They are today's liberal democracies. Historically there have been many small republics with some partial rights, but individual oriented liberal democracy did not get codified in a large nation until 1791 when the amendments called the Bill of Rights were added to the US Constitution. Current Progressives point out that there is much hypocrisy imbedded in the U. S. Constitution. They observe that liberty, equality, and justice for all are proposed, but in truth that slavery was tolerated, and voting was restricted to property owning white males. This is obviously true. It took a bloody Civil War and another 200 years to correct the injustices of slavery in codified law. We are still working on the residual effects of racism as manifested in poverty, poor schools, institutional bigotry, and legal inequities. However, the Constitution did provide a framework that has allowed for continual progress. This progress proceeds by fits and starts and is usually achieved under pressure of liberals or progressives. The religious prophets and founders did not give many clear Organizational Rules about individual human rights.

I will paraphrase Senator Russel Long who was paraphrasing Fisher Ames, Massachusetts' first Congressman, "Authoritarianism is like a sleek craft, it sails along well until some bumbling captain runs it into the rocks. Democracy, on the other hand, is like a raft. It never goes down but, it is slow, difficult to direct, and damn it, your feet are always wet." All parties, particularly the radicals, are always unhappy with the pace of change. Our "feet are always wet".

Some thinkers have noted that haste might be the biggest problem in evolving democracies. It is wise to bring the people to understand the desired changes rather than cramming very "progressive" ideas down the throat of an unready populous. Impatience with political institutions because they are not perfect can be an unwise recipe for revolution and destruction of very useful and functional governments that are capable of change. Liberal radicals and progressives are always unhappy with the rate and extent of change. Conservative reactionaries are always upset with limits on their prerogatives. If, however, radical progressive minorities gain power and move too far ahead of the people, the more traditional masses may be willing to get rid of the entire democratic system by supporting some demagogue who seems powerful enough to oppose the radical progressives. The public must be brought along before big changes can be made.

The Jews are group oriented, and their scriptures, the Tanakh and the Talmud, have laws emphasizing this. However, the laws are for the Jewish nation only. They are not imposed on others. The Hebrew scriptures have some Organizational Rules that recommend punishments for Jews who violated Religious Rules such as working on the Sabbath or leaving the religion (apostasy). Organizationally, in the Jewish scripture, the Tanakh (The Christian Old Testament), there are some passages advising Jews not to install a king. [1] They did it anyway. There are few other Organizational Rules in the Tanakh.

The Christians are generally divided into Catholics, Greek Orthodox, and Protestants. Under the term Protestant, I will include all the other Christian sects. There are roughly 2,000 to 10,000 Protestant sects depending on definitions. The Catholics and the Greek Orthodox are highly codified hierarchal organizations with strong central authorities. The principal Protestant sects are not very hierarchical, and many are centered on each individual or church. Protestants do not have strong central authorities.

All Christians share the group oriented scriptures in the Jewish Tanakh (Old Testament) but they do not enforce any Organizational Rules from the Old Testament. In the New Testament part of the Christian Bible Jesus gives almost no Organizational Rules other than to separate church and state. Jesus' statement, "Render unto Caesar what is Caesar's and unto God what is God's" (Matthew 22:21, Luke 20:23-26), has been taken to separate church and state. This statement occurs when Jesus is asked by Jewish elders whether the

Jews should pay taxes to Rome. The Jewish religious critics were trying to trap and silence him. If he had said not to pay, he would have upset the Romans. If he had advised payment, he would be going against the prevailing Jewish political resistance to Roman rule. In responding, Jesus asked for a coin and then held it up. He asked, "Whose picture is on the coin?" They answered, "Caesar's". Jesus then said, "Render unto Caesar what is Caesar's and unto God what is God's." He was speaking to the ages. Theologians repeatedly debate the implications of this verse, but functionally, in Christianity, it has been almost universally accepted as separating church and the modern state. If church and state are connected, everyone including politicians and the public are subject to the approval of religious bodies or individuals. Individuals and politicians can be influenced or oppressed by religious charges of heresy, blasphemy, and apostasy.

When I use the term "West" or "Western", I am referring to the liberal capitalist democracies that arose out of the Protestant Reformation and Enlightenment in Europe and were first put into practice in the US. It includes most of Western Europe, Canada, Australia, New Zealand, and countries who have generally adopted the Western Democratic governmental institutions such as Japan, Taiwan, Singapore, South Korea, Uruguay, and numerous other nations.

In the West, the organized religions are not involved in judgment or punishment for transgression of Moral Rules or Organizational Rules. Because of the separation of church and state, enforcement of Religious Rules concerning apostasy, heresy, and blasphemy are not governmental issues. Jesus separates church and state in Matthew 22:21, "Render unto Caesar what is Caesar's and unto God what is God's". More on this below. Paul and Peter, two principal founders of the Christian church, clearly accept this separation of church and state. Paul's letter to the Romans 13:1 says, "Let everyone be subject to the governing authorities, for there is no authority except that which God has established. The authorities that exist have been established by God." In 1 Peter 2:13, Saint Peter states "Submit yourselves for the

Lord's sake to every human authority: whether to the emperor, as the supreme authority."

Muhammad is leader of a threatened tribe and, of necessity, gives Organizational Rules. The Qur'an and Hadith (the sayings of Muhammad) advise defending the tribe, obeying the leaders, and some punishments for fornication, apostasy, and blasphemy. Many current Islamic scholars support freedom of religion and have clear support for their stance in the Qur'an 2:256, "There should be no coercion in religion." Other leaders *(imams)* want the government to punish apostates and blasphemers. Islamists dream of a day where everyone is a Muslim and piety is enforced. In many Muslim majority areas, hard line theologians can urge punishment for those who are deemed to be apostates, heretics, or blasphemers.

Islam supplies a judicial and legal system based on the Qur'an and the Hadith that is called Sharia law. There are numerous Sharia law schools, eight of whom have significant authority in different Muslim majority nations today. They are involved in Organizational Rules such as government organization, domestic law, and in Religious Rule infractions involving charges of heresy, sacrilege, and apostasy. The five major goals of the Sharia are:

a. The protection of orthodox religious practice

b. The protection of life.

c. The protection of sanity.

d. The protection of the family.

e. The protection of personal and communal wealth. (IslamiCity)

According to all Islamic schools of law, the adoption of sound local customs throughout the world is encouraged by Sharia.

The differences between "group" and "individual" cultures, and the importance of the separation of church and state are addressed at length below in Chapter 4 Section 3 under "Organizational Rules".

4. **<u>Religious Rules.</u>** The Religious Rules given by the prophets are completely idiosyncratic. They are different in every religious sect. They tell people how to be pious or holy. They can describe what to wear, eat, how to worship, how to style your hair, how often to pray, etc., and very importantly, what to believe and say about God. They also include a lot of things not to do such as: don't curse God, don't work on the Sabbath, don't change religions, etc.

Transgressions of Religious Rules are called heresy, sacrilege, blasphemy, or apostasy. These labels can be very dangerous in oppressive cultures.

a.   Heresy is a wrong belief.

b.   Sacrilege is violation or ill treatment of sacred objects, places, or persons. Done verbally it is called blasphemy.

c.   Apostasy is leaving one's faith.

If one has a wrong belief, does that mean that they are apostates? It depends on how rigorous one is in defining the terms. Conservatives can escalate charges of heresy to charges of apostasy, which is much more serious and dangerous. More on this below.

Considering today's science and knowledge, Religious Rules would not necessarily be arrived at by reasoning. The only real meaning that Religious Rules have is that meaning given by the group of believers. They have no other significance. Some rules concerning beards, haircuts, clothes, and hats seem particularly bizarre to outsiders.

Prayer or meditation are recommended by almost all religions. The ritual recurrent practice of prayer, meditation, or contemplation probably has real benefits in psychologically and emotionally nurturing us. However, people regularly rise from daily prayer or meditation and do very disturbing things.

The Religious Rules are not a problem if they are followed by the individual. If used personally by an individual, the Religious Rules simply instruct one on how to be pious enough to please a God. A society must separate church and state to avoid forcing Religious Rules on others. In fact, the only reason to join the temple/church/mosque with the state would be to enforce Religious Rules of one sort or another.

Theoretically Religious Rules, if not observed, can affect one's relationship with God. In some messages, prophets and religious texts advise that everyone must do the same pious rituals and openly express the same beliefs. They also recommend punishments to be carried out for violations of the Religious Rules. The recommended punishments in the Tanakh or Old Testament include stoning people to death for working on the Sabbath in the Book of Numbers 15:32-36 and killing witches in Exodus 22:18. Jesus and Paul in the New Testament recommend no punishments on earth. Their God will take care of violations later. Muhammad was governing a tribe and his holy texts, the Qur'an and the Hadith, have numerous and sometimes conflicting statements about punishments. Frequently the punishments seem to be protective measures for the tribe when it was threatened.

The Qur'an is God's word spoken by Muhammad when pressured by the Angel Gabriel (Jabril). The other Islamic holy scriptures, called the Hadith, are a record of Muhammad's sayings, actions, and rulings as a tribal and spiritual leader. The Sunna or "way" is the recommended path which is generally outlined by following the Qur'an and Hadith under the guidance of Sharia law. Muhammad did not write the Hadith and Sunna down. They were actions and sayings which were reported and written by numerous others who were around Muhammad, including at least one of his wives. Some Hadith, or sayings, were not written down until one to two hundred years after Muhammad died. They can be controversial. The different sects of Islam such as Sunni and Shia use different sets of Hadith.

The differences in the Qur'an and Hadith have created multiple law schools (Sharia law) consisting of Islamic scholars who give guidance to the faithful. Today there are five to eight schools of Sharia law that are followed in different areas of Islamic majority. Prominent Sunni schools of law include the Hanafi, Maliki, Shafi'i, Khariji, Zahari, and Hanbali. Ja'fari is a principal Shia school. These schools can be called *madhhabs*. Each is most prominent in different geographical areas of Islam. The groups of scholars (*ulema*) study the Qur'an, the Hadith, the Sunna, ancient Arabic, previous rulings, and Islamic history. The prominent scholars (*muftis*) issue rulings called fatwas. Almost all the law schools recommend harsh treatment for apostacy and blasphemy. Punishments for leaving the religion range from disenfranchisement, to taking away one's children, to execution. In the Qur'an there are penalties for apostasy, but death is not mentioned. Death is recommended in the Hadith. The texts do allow for mercy with repentance.

Unfortunately, any transgression of a Religious Rule can cause a person to be labeled a heretic, blasphemer, or apostate. When the texts recommend punishments for transgressions, the problems can become much more dangerous and acute. Even if the government is not involved, zealous mobs and vigilantes frequently want to enforce them. (3)

One of the greatest concerns is that forced imposition of Religious Rules immediately eliminates the possibility of individual freedom of speech, press, religion, and habeas corpus. All these freedoms are essential to protect the individual from harassment by the state or religious bodies. The rights are also essential in the control of corruption and nepotism in a society. Only a confident and safe citizen protected by individual rights and impartial courts can or will report corruption and nepotism.

Importantly, Religious Rules written into the texts do not go away. One generation may come to good terms with them, but the next generation may use them badly. Each generation must deal with them. They are recurrent issues forever.

To Summarize

This book explores the following propositions:

1. Enforcement of Religious Rules about pieties cause most of the current problems with religions. To avoid oppression, the individual human rights of speech, press, religion, and the vote must be included in any Organizational Rules.

2. If we keep the General Admonitions in mind, human interactions would be much better.

3. "There should be no compulsion in religion". (Muhammad, Qur'an 2:256) This statement from Islam's holiest of books would be a great standard for all religious discussion, reformation, and conduct. In short, if you want to be pious, fine, but keep it to yourself.

Chapter 2
Sacred Texts

The sacred texts contain a lot of controversial and contradictory passages.

1. <u>The Tanakh and the Talmud.</u> These are the Jewish holy scriptures. They are almost the same as the Old Testament in the Christian Bible. The Tanakh is the story of the Jews, their laws, their prophets, their history, and their wisdom. It has around 35 to 40 authors including prophets and historians. It was written down between 1200 B.C. and 165 B.C. The first five books of the Tanakh are called the Tora (law) and are attributed to Moses although he may not have written them down. God in the Tanakh says that a leader will come who "I will put my spirit in him and he shall bring justice to all the nations" Isaiah 42:1-4. This leader is called the messiah by many believers. Christians believe that Jesus is this messiah.

    The *Talmud* is a very extensive commentary on the Tanakh by Jewish scholars and teachers. For many years it was passed down orally. It was written down between 250 B.C.E. and 500 C.E. and consists of 2,711 double sided folios. Jewish scholars and rabbis study it constantly. The Talmud is a principal text in Jewish schools studying Jewish law. (*yeshivas*).

2. The <u>Christian Bible</u>. The Christian Bible has two distinct parts, the Old Testament (39 books or chapters) and the New Testament (27 books). It has about 10 authors. The Old Testament is almost exactly like the Jewish Tanakh. There are

seven books called the Apocrypha describing the time between the Old and the New Testaments. They are included in most Catholic Bibles, but not all Protestant Bibles. They are considered questionable or "secret".

The second, and shorter part of the Christian Bible, is called the New Testament. The first four books of the New Testament are called the Gospels. They are biographies of Jesus by four different authors and contain his teachings, miracles, and history.

The Gospel of Mark probably dates from c. CE 66–70, Matthew and Luke around CE 85–90, and John CE 90–110. The authors of the Gospels have been the disciples' names, however some of them may have been anonymous. It is also possible that none of the authors were eyewitnesses. Some very credible scholars think that one or two of the Gospel's authors actually witnessed Jesus' ministry.

There are seven miracles mentioned in the Gospels. The virgin birth is mentioned in Matthew and Luke. Jesus is said to have walked on water in Matthew, Mark, and John. Not in Luke. Mark's is very brief. Jesus performs many healings and raises two people from the dead. The Resurrection from the dead by Jesus is reported in all four gospels, and it is different in all of them.

Christians believe that Jesus is the Messiah described in Tanakh who is bringing justice, peace, and salvation.

In the Book of John 4:25-26 Jesus is talking to a Samaritan woman. "The woman said to him 'I know that a Messiah is coming. He is called Christ. When he is come, he will show us all things.' Jesus said, 'I who speak to you am he'". Christians say that Jesus' will show us that, in the end, all is fulfilled for those who are kind to their others and believe that Jesus is the Son of God, the Christ.

The other New Testament books contain thirteen letters from Paul to various churches and individuals, a few letters from other disciples, and a final mystical book called Revelations.

Farther below I will divide the New Testament into two parts. Jesus is central to Christianity and for my purposes the most important part of this division consists of the first four books, the Gospels, where Jesus' teachings and actions are recorded. The New International Version (NIV) translation for Bible verses is used unless otherwise noted.

3. The Qur'an and Hadith are the principal Islamic texts. They differ from the Judaic and Christian texts in that they are both from one person, Muhammad. The Tanakh and Bible were written by about 45 authors. Muhammad speaks the Qur'an when pressured by the angel Jabril (Gabriel), and the Hadith are a list of his rulings and sayings. In evaluating the uses of these sacred texts, it is very important to remember that Muhammad had two distinct roles. He was leader of a tribe that was under attack from other tribes, and he was delivering a timeless spiritual message of compassion and mercy. In the first role, he had to promote and deal with the safety, cohesion, and discipline of his followers. In the second role, he was bringing a timeless spiritual message of hope, salvation, and brotherhood.

a. **Qur'an.** This is the word of God spoken through Muhammad when pressured by the angel Gabriel. It is not a story as such, but a series of revelations on various subjects. The revelations are organized based on length. The longest is the first. Some believe that the Qur'an exists on golden tablets in Heaven. What we have on earth is a copy. Muhammad knew about Judaism and Christianity and their texts. Adam, Abraham, Moses, Ismail, David, and Jesus are discussed in the Qur'an and are included in various lists of the prophets preceding Muhammad.

Muhammad is recognized as the final prophet. There will be no more. His message puts a seal on the messages from God.

Unless otherwise noted I have used the Penguin Classic translation of the Qur'an or Koran. (Koran translated by N. J. Dawood. 1990 Edition.) Qur'an is the current more popular spelling in English. For those who are not very familiar with the Qur'an, one could use Dawood's translation or one of the following: Al-Qur'an translated by Ahmed Ali, Princeton Press. Qur'an.com on the internet. Thenoblequran.com also on the internet.

It is often said that the only real way to understand the Qur'an is to read it in Arabic.

Here are some of the initial lines from the Qur'an translated by Ahmed Ali from the Princeton Press translation.

All Suras begin with the following statement:

"In the Name of God, The Compassionate, the Merciful.

2:2-6. This is The Book free of doubt and involution, a guidance for those who preserve themselves from evil and follow the straight path, Who believe in the Unknown and fulfil their devotional obligations, and spend in charity of what We have given them; Who believe in what has been revealed to you and what was revealed to those before you, and are certain of the Hereafter. They have found the guidance of their Lord and will be successful. As for those who deny, it is all the same if you warn them or not, they will not believe.

2:176-177 Righteousness is not that you turn your faces toward the east or the west, but [true] righteousness is [in] one who believes in Allah, the Last Day, the angels, the Book, and the prophets and gives wealth, in spite of love for it, to relatives, orphans, the needy, the traveler, those who ask [for help], and for freeing slaves; [and who] establishes prayer and gives zakat; [those who] fulfill their promise when they promise; and [those who] are patient in poverty and hardship and during battle. Those are the ones who have been true, and it is those who are the righteous.

b. **Hadith** These are the personal sayings, actions, and rulings of Muhammad as leader of the religion and the tribe. The *Sunna* is the "way". It is a compilation of actions and sayings of the early Muslim community under Muhammad. The Hadith and the *Sunna* will be included in the term "Hadith" throughout this book. Muhammad did not write the Hadith down. Several of his followers and wives wrote them down later. Some Hadith were written down around the time of Muhammad, others from about 70 years after Muhammad's death until about 200 years after his death. Some felt that the Hadith should not be written down because they would seem to be competing with the Qur'an.

There are 1,400 to 10,000 Hadith depending on the source. Islamic clerics and scholars have debated their authenticity and promote different sets and interpretations of Hadith. One of the first and most respected collections was done by Bukhari in the 800's. Many of the controversial Religious Rules, punishments and statements in Islam are in the Hadith.

The two principal Islamic sects are Sunni (87%) and Shia (13%). Shortly after Muhammad's death, they divided over the question of who should be the leader. The Sunni thought the leader should be chosen by the elite. The Shia said that it had be a relative of Muhammad's. Arabs and Indonesian Muslims are predominantly Sunni. Iranians and Kurds are mostly Shia.

There are six canonical Sunni collections of Hadith. *Bukhari, Muslim, and Dawood* are probably the three most widely accepted collections. There are about 30 other Sunni collections. There are four principal Shia collections of Hadith and about 20 other collections.

The Hadith cause much controversy because of doubts about their validity and the often occasional conflicting messages. Because of this there have been recurring efforts within Islam to focus exclusively on the Qur'an.[4] Ahi al-Kalam was a movement in early Islam (around 800 C.E..) that rejected the importance and validity of the Hadith. Shortly thereafter, a group named Mu'tazili worked to reconcile Greek reason with Islam. At that time, they too felt that the Hadith were too subject to prejudice and error to be authentic guides.

Recent proponents of using the Qur'an alone, include Aslam Jairajpuri, Distinguished Professor of Arabic and Persian and Ghulam Ahmad Parwez, a pioneer of Qur'anic doctrine from pre-Independence India. They explored Qur'anic themes, by challenging established Sunni doctrine that considers the Hadith to be important. These recent Islamic scholars hold the position that the Hadith should not be considered canonical since Muhammad did not write them down. Many others reported the Hadith at various later dates. These scholars feel that the Hadith are too subject to distortion and manipulation.

I will use the adjectives "modern" "reform", "conservative", "orthodox", and "fundamentalist" for the different religious approaches to scripture within Judaism, Islam, and Christianity. Others use these terms, and they seem to be descriptive without being too judgmental. "Reform", "modern" and "moderate" are all used to describe more liberal worshippers. Some Muslims feel that these terms are offensive, in that the terms imply that they are not devout, or that they imply that Islam is divided and not inherently pure and consistent. (5)

Orthopraxy is about doing the right thing (Ortho= straight, praxis= action). Orthodoxy is about believing correctly (Ortho=straight, dox= doctrine or belief). When the word "orthodox" is used alone in this book as an adjective, it generally refers to a conservative approach to belief and action. The great monotheisms have some of each in very different amounts. Protestant Christianity is almost exclusively an orthodoxy.

I am quoting a lot of scripture to illustrate certain points. Much of it is in the Endnotes. Quoting scripture to make one's point is a practice that has been going on for several thousand years. It is well known that one can use scripture to promote almost any position. The fact that there are numerous translations of each text increases the variables. In choosing scripture or interpreting scripture, I try to keep the General Admonitions foremost in mind. They encourage us to use a positive and charitable attitude to the reading and contextualizing of the great texts. Inclusion, tolerance, and forgiveness are encouraged. With that optimistic approach in mind, my questionable selections and interpretations of scriptural quotes may be better understood.

Sacred Texts: Which are most important to whom

For this book concerning Religious Rules, I am dividing the great monotheistic texts into four groups:

1. Jewish texts: The Tanakh and the Talmud.
2. The whole Christian Bible, Old and New Testament.
3. Jesus' teachings in the four Gospels. These are biographies of Jesus in first four books of the New Testament (Matthew, Mark, Luke, and John).
4. The Qur'an and Hadith.

   This will result in four different sets of Religious Rules.

1. **Jewish Texts** The Tanakh is the title of the principal Hebrew scripture. It is almost identical to the "Old Testament" in the Christian Bible. The first five books of the Tanakh are attributed to Moses. They are called the Torah, which means "the Law". He is the prophet, historian, and tribal leader who led the Jews out of Egyptian bondage into Israel. Other chapters include histories, stories, prophecies, proverbs, poems, and songs (Psalms). There are 613 Rules in the Hebrew Scriptures. However, these rules are for the Jewish community and do not necessarily involve non-Jews. Many are Religious Rules. A list is easily available on the internet.

   Extensive priestly and scholarly commentaries on the Hebrew Scriptures are known as the Talmud which is divided into the *Mishna* and *Gemara*. The Talmud is considered the source of Jewish law and background of Jewish culture by many scholars, and it is constantly consulted. As noted before the Talmudic texts were oral at first and cover an era beginning about 800 B.C.E. until redacted about 500 C.E. Depending on degree of orthodoxy and orthopraxy, the Jewish believers can generally be divided into reform, conservative, orthodox, and extremely orthodox or fundamentalist adherents. Some fundamentalists are called Haredi.

Judaism is not a monolithic religion. There is no central authority or hierarchy within Judaism. Jews call themselves Reform, Conservative, Orthodox, Reconstructionist, or ultra-Orthodox. They generally enjoy debate and dialectic. Concerning Judaism, "It has been said that if you bring two Jews together you are likely to get three different opinions." Jews can be universalistic and almost wholly involved in the affairs of the world. Others are very sectarian and insular.

There are two principal impulses driving Judaism. One is concerned with the preservation of Judaism. The other is a commitment to be an example to others in the building of a better world for all.

2. **Christian Texts** This includes Catholicism, Eastern Orthodox, and all the Protestant sects. They generally use the whole Bible (Old and New Testament) with an unstated emphasis on the New Testament and Jesus. Jesus' teachings are contained in the first four books of the New Testament and are called Gospels. They are biographies of Jesus. In addition to Jesus biographies, Paul's thirteen letters in the New Testament are particularly prominent in Christian teachings.

Catholics and Eastern Orthodox worshipers generally look to the organized church for guidance. Eastern Orthodox will be included in the general term "Catholic" for the purposes in this work. Eastern Orthodox pieties, liturgy, and ceremonies differ, but both look to a highly structured and centralized clergy for Biblical guidance.

Protestants have no central structure, and in general, think that each person must study the text and decide how to act individually. *Sola scriptura* is a position identified by Martin Luther. Basically, it states that the Bible is the final source for guidance [6]. It implies that every

Protestant is responsible before God and must follow the scriptures as s/he sees them. The idea that all Protestants must read the Bible put an enormous push behind literacy. Many Protestant preachers have claimed that they offer the best interpretation of the scriptures. This is more fully discussed in the history section in Chapter 9. Mormons have an additional text, *The Book of Mormon*, describing some activities of Jesus in North America and the teachings of some latter day prophets. There are several Gospels that were left out of the commonly used Bible including the Gospel of Thomas and the Gnostic Gospels.

3. **Text containing Jesus' Teachings.** This title, "Jesus' Teachings", is purely a functional grouping that I will use in this work when I discuss the effects of Religious Rules. This selection is intended to separate Jesus, the philosopher, from the mysteries of divinity, miracles, healings, and Jesus' resurrection that are central to much of Christian faith and belief. All Christians value Jesus' teachings. The vast majority accept the mysteries and the resurrection. Belief in the mysteries is personal and does not necessarily affect one's response to the teachings. The questions of divinity and miracles will remain articles of faith and mystery.

    Jesus' teachings are in the Bible in the four biographical Gospels: Matthew, Mark, Luke, and John. Almost all his teachings concern Moral Rules and General Admonitions. They are primarily directed to the individual and concern how people should treat each other and God. There are a very few Religious Rules and even fewer Organizational Rules.

    I will use the name "Jesus" for the philosopher. "Christ" is a title describing Jesus as the divine son of God who sacrificed himself to "atone for the sins of mankind". His sacrifice made it possible for Christians to be forgiven their sins and to enjoy eternal life. The writings concerning the resurrection from the dead and Jesus' sacrifice to save humanity are striking beautiful stories concerning salvation and eternal life. This book is not about salvation and its mysteries.

Outside of these divine events, Jesus' teachings concern how we should treat each other in this life. He recommends that we pray, fast, donate money, and approach God in private. (Matthew 6:1-18) [7]. Instruction on actions and lessons can be learned at the church which is out of the public view. Jesus seems to know that public demonstrations of piety can at times create confusion and coercion.

The number of people who approach Jesus mainly as a philosopher is probably very small. Thomas Jefferson. [8], being one of the most prominent, produced a philosophical Jesus by cutting out all the miracles from the Gospels. The resulting text made Jesus a philosopher and spiritual guide. It avoids the questions concerning a divine savior. Approaching Jesus' as a philosopher can be roughly thought of as a deist, humanist, or Unitarian approach.

This grouping includes Christians who value Jesus as a principal philosophic source and spiritual inspiration. For them, the Old Testament and Paul can be inspiring but allow for some confusion and misuse of the principal Biblical message. It would seem that all Christians should look primarily to Jesus as the final authority. However, Christian clerics, theologians, and others spend large amounts of time contextualizing and quibbling over all sorts of obscure, contradictory, confusing and sometimes inspiring writings by others in the rest of the Old and the New Testament.

Jesus' teachings are particularly demanding in that they recommend a primary role for service, forgiveness, and avoidance of judgment of others. To paraphrase G. K. Chesterton, "Jesus' teachings have not been tried and found wanting. They have been found difficult and left untried." Jesus allows the state to pass judgment on crimes. Jesus' forgiveness is directed toward interpersonal relations and does not necessarily mean that one should forget. In dealing with crimes, forgiveness is very important, and. punishment and reparations are often essential.

Certainly, there are groups that describe themselves as Christian who are racist, sexist, or brutal. The racist Ku Klux Klan is a prominent recent one. In the Old Testament and some of the New Testament, they can find Biblical sanctions or suggestions for their actions or beliefs about slavery and racism (9). No such sanctions can be found in Jesus' teachings.

Although the Bible has many Religious Rules, Jesus himself gave almost none. The principal exception is the Religious Rule that Jesus presents in several verses in the Gospel of John. This Religious Rule says that we must believe that Jesus is the son of God to get to heaven or have eternal life. John 3:14-15 says, "… so must the Son of Man be lifted up, that whoever believes in him may have eternal life." John also quotes Jesus as saying, "I am the way and the truth and the life. No one comes to the Father except through me." (John 14:6). Also, "I am the resurrection and the life, he who believes in me, though he die, yet shall he live." (John 11:25-26)

Organizationally Jesus repeatedly tells his followers to spread his teachings. He also asks his followers to remember him by having bread and wine in a group ceremony celebrating his last supper with his disciples. This is called mass or communion. Basically, Jesus gives three Religious Rules: Believe Jesus is the son of God, baptize believers, and celebrate communion or mass. Baptism is done with water and symbolizes washing away one's sins and dedicating the rest of one's life to Christian values. He never recommended any punishments on earth for anything. God will take care of heretics, blasphemers, and apostates.

Other than baptism and communion Jesus gave almost no specific information on how his church was to be run. He clearly recommends service to others and separation of church and state. He does say that the purpose of the church is to teach the people to love God, and that they should treat others the way they want to be treated.

When the holy Temple was in Jerusalem, sacrifice of animals was a central part of Jewish worship. Animals for sacrifice including birds, sheep, and cattle. They were for sale in the Temple courtyard. Also, there was a religious tax collected at the temple. It had to be paid in Jewish money, so the money changers changed Greek and Roman coins for Jewish shekels. The money changers and sellers of animals for sacrifice were known to demand hard bargains. Jesus, in his one act of force, drove the money changers and sellers of sacrificial animals out of the Jewish temple. "And making a whip of cords, he drove them all out of the temple, with the sheep and oxen. And he poured out the coins of the moneychangers and overturned their tables. And he told those who sold the pigeons, 'Take these things away; do not make my Father's house a house of trade'" John 2:13-16. It is recorded in all four gospels. When specifically addressing sacrifice Jesus says in Matthew 9-13, "…I desire mercy and not sacrifice". This possibly refers to animal sacrifice at the temple.

Those prioritizing Jesus' philosophic teachings can include deists, Unitarians, agnostics, and humanists. They generally recognize in Jesus a vision that brings compassion to human interaction. However, they probably do not think that a God does miracles in response to prayer.

What has kept Christianity viable? It appears that the transcendent nature of Jesus' compassion, his profound example of sacrifice, his emphasis on forgiveness, and the possibility of eternal life have been enough to keep Christianity alive.

4. **Muslim Texts.** Almost all Muslims accept the Qur'an and various collections of the Hadith as holy scriptures and guides to follow. Abraham, Moses, David, Noah, Jesus, and various others are all considered to be lesser prophets bringing parts of God's word. Muhammad is the final prophet who in the Qur'an completes God's message for the world. As stated before, he puts the seal on the revealed word of God.

It is important that one consider the context of Muhammad's message. Many of the controversial verses refer to Muhammad's instructions as defender of his tribe at a time of conflict. (12) The other parts of Muhammad's message don't need contextualizing. When he wasn't organizing the tribe or doing tribal business, Muhammad was "speaking to the ages" about:

a. Tolerance: "There should be no compulsion in religion" Qur'an 2:256.

b. Forgiveness: "Requite evil with good," Qur'an 23:95. *"And the retribution for an evil act is an evil one like it, but whoever pardons and makes reconciliation – his reward is [due] from Allah. Indeed, He does not like wrongdoers" Quran 42:40.*

c. Mercy: There are many verses in the Qur'an that extol the value of repentance. Muslims who stray from the faith will be forgiven by God if they repent. God's mercy for apostates who repent is frequently noted. Qur'an 3:89, 9:5, 25:69, 39:54.

d. Compassion and generosity: "No man is a true believer unless he desires for his brother that which he desires for himself," Muhammad, Hadith, Bukhari 1:2:13.

Historically, all these important interpersonal principles were already present in the teachings of Jesus, and the Muslims respected him as one of the great prophets. Muhammad made these principles relevant and important to the 7th century Arab world. His teachings put the never ending blood feuds in the Islamic courts thereby uniting the Arabs in a more moral and secure society. Thereby His message and skills created a beautiful and powerful civilization.

Islam means "submission". Submission to a complete way of life. It comes with instructions on every type of action, from ways to worship, to personal hygiene, to clothes, to food, to domestic law, to social mixing of the sexes, etc. Today the decisions on all these issues have become legal opinions made by various Islamic legal scholars and courts. These legal opinions are parts of Sharia law, and they are based on the Qur'an and Hadith.

Islamic law schools study the texts and issue opinions and directives on every type of human action. A prominent Islamic scholar and politician, Kurshid Ahmad, said it this way in his book, *Islam: Basic Principals and Characteristics.*

> "For the proper development of human life, man needs two elements: (a) the resources to maintain life and to fulfill the material needs of the individual and society, and (b) knowledge of the principles of individual and social behavior to enable man to fulfill himself and to maintain justice and tranquility in human life. The Lord of the universe has provided for both in full measure. To cater to the material needs of man, He has put all of nature's resources at his disposal. To provide for his spiritual, social, and cultural needs, He has raised His prophets from among men and has revealed to them the code of life that can guide man's steps to the right path. This code of life is known as Islam, the religion preached by all the prophets of Allah".

This "code" is the law as described by Sharia *law* scholars (*mufti*). It contains Moral Rules, General Admonitions, Organizational Rules, and Religious Rules. Muhammad is the final prophet who brings the final word, the seal on revelation from God.

The Qur'an and the Hadith mix tribal governing rulings with a sublime spiritual message of salvation, tolerance, and mercy. The comingling of punishments with pious recommendations and mercy exposes the texts to misuse by driven zealots. Mixing governmental and judicial advice with a magnificent spiritual vision allows violent fundamentalists and militant despots to pick and choose verses that justify their actions. The verses extolling compassion and justice impart a beautiful hope of a harmonious spiritual community. While demagogues and zealots extol Islamic dreams of a highly controlled community, they invoke tribal rulings from the 7th century to justify their rules and desires for cultural and political power.

Today the poverty and the recent violent history of colonization of many Muslim lands produce intense young men demanding rapid change. Some think that the situation is so desperate that suicidal bombing is seen as a reasonable option. Some think that all the problems are outside of Islam. Other more liberal followers think that the problems are inside where intolerant and overly zealous scholars have distorted Muhammad's central message of brotherhood, tolerance, mercy, and hospitality. Fundamentalists of various types have claimed textural sanction for their intolerant and militaristic actions and have produced a world in which many borders of Islamic nations are tense or dangerous.

Hinduism, Buddhism, Confucianism, Taoism, Gnosticism, and Atheism

Hinduism, Buddhism, Taoism, and Confucianism are not religions in the same sense as the three large monotheisms. Hinduism and Buddhism are very much concerned with spirituality, enlightenment, and mysticism, but they have no historical prophets who give Religious Rules directly from God. They have no articles of "faith" in a prophet's message. They don't believe in the accuracy or divinity of prophets who are giving us direct instructions from the God of the zBuddhism, and Taoism recommend that one focus inwardly to experience "enlightenment" or the "truth" of the universe. This experience will answer all your questions and concerns.

Buddha was not a god. He was an enlightened being who brought a clear message of compassion and understanding. He was not a god who created the heavens and the earth and worked miracles.

Confucianism is not generally thought to be a religion. It is not concerned with salvation or eternal life. It is considered a collection of mores, wisdom, and ethics derived by reasoning. The reasoning is guided by General Admonitions such as the Silver Rule, "Do not to others what you don't want them to do to you". It has been pointed out that the Golden Rule, "Do unto others as you would have them do unto you," can be an invitation to utopian intervention in other's affairs. The Silver Rule's double negative does not easily promote imposition on others.

Taoism is principally Chinese and is very similar to and compatible with Confucianism and Buddhism. Tao means the way or path. Living in harmony with the essence of life, the Tao, is central. Essentially there are no revealed rules of any kind. There are no references to governmental issues. The book, *Tao Te Ching,* contains the teachings of Lao Tzu and is the principal text. The "Three Treasures" of Taoism are compassion, frugality, and humility. [13]

The deists and agnostics think that compassionate reason answers most of the practical and scientific questions of life, but reasoning is unable to answer the "first cause" questions such as: How did the universe get here? These seekers generally think that there is some sort of intelligence at the foundations of the universe. Atheists apparently reason that there is no underlying intelligence to the universe, and we are just here and conscious by random luck through the pathway of evolution. They seem to think that if one has rocks, heat, gasses, lightning, and water long enough, evolution will produce DNA, human consciousness, science, and art by sheer random long term association. That seems a stretch to me. The universe is incredibly orderly and scientifically elegant. It obeys very strict laws, many of which have been discovered by human intellect through science. The fact that all these countless discoverable laws result in creation is a miracle itself. Evolution is enough of an answer for some, but the question of origin seems to be ultimately unanswerable using reason. Perhaps it can be "experienced". Experience is explored below in "Mysticism", Chapter 8.

In the search to understand this universe and our existence, one could say generally that the Eastern religions, Hinduism and Buddhism have looked inward. Encouraged by Jesus' emphasis on compassion, reasoning, and empowering the individual, the Judeo-Christian West has looked outward through science. Islam has pursued understanding through God's revelation in its holy scriptures. In about 1200 C.E. there was a fundamentalist encouraged shift to deemphasize human reasoning in the pursuit of wisdom and understanding. They felt that more emphasis on the texts was in order. This slowed scientific and technical evolution in Muslim lands. It is further discussed below in Chapter 9: Historical Issues with Religious Rules.

It is interesting to note that the East looked inward and found that the fundamental essence of all phenomena was a wave form, Om or Aum. The West looked outward with science and found that, essentially, the fundamental state of all matter is energy, and energy is a wave form. This is very a simplistic observation that has no significant meaning. It is just a delightful example of the similarity of some findings of outward exploration in the science lab and inwardly focused personal exploration.

Heaven, Paradise, Eternal Life

There are, I think, generally three duties of Religion.

1. It should engender a sense of joy, fellowship, and fulfillment through ritual and community.
2. It should address and relieve the problems and mysteries of suffering on earth.
3. It should provide a path to or some understanding of heaven, death, paradise and/or eternal life.

All the prophets generally agree that to live some sort of good life, one must obey the Moral Rules and the General Admonitions. Both are similar in all the great monotheisms. The Organizational Rules are political and deal with keeping order, the treatment of others, justice, and the distribution of goods. They are not spiritual.

The prophets and founders also proposed various numbers of Religious Rules that must be followed to produce an atmosphere pleasing to God so that one can be "saved", go to paradise, or receive enlightenment. Moses, the Jewish prophets, and Muhammad had a lot of Religious Rules. Paul had a few. Jesus taught a very few.

Jewish heaven or afterlife is not clearly explained in the texts. In Genesis 15:15 God says to Abraham, "You shall go to your fathers in peace." Many Jews think that there is something like a divine spark that lives on after worldly death. In the *Mishna* it says that good Jews will "have a place in the World to Come." Maimonides, a great scholar from the 12th century, adds an additional stipulation. He writes that "the world to come is reserved for those who do good because they know that this is what Gd wants from them. Those who do these things simply because it makes sense to them, he writes, are not righteous, they are just wise." [14]

There's a Jewish joke that says there is no Heaven or Hell. Everyone goes to the same place when they die. There, Moses and a prominent rabbi give constant and everlasting classes on the Tanakh and the Talmud. For the righteous this is eternal bliss, while for the wicked this is eternal suffering.

Many orthodox Christians believe that if they are good in God's eyes, they will be resurrected and go to a heaven. There they will be joyous in God's presence. The followers are not worthy, but Jesus' sacrifice made it possible. He cleansed everyone of all their sins. He redeemed every believer.

Muslims who follow the Five Pillars of Islam and the Six Beliefs will go to a paradise described as a "beautiful garden". They are not worthy, but God is merciful. There they will be served wonderful, non-intoxicating drinks and sit with beautiful youths and virgins. (Qur'an 37:46-48)

The Way or Path

Religious believers generally give more importance to their religious texts than they do to human ability to reason well. For them the "path" or "way" (*Halakhah* to Orthodox Jews, *Sunnah* to Muslims) derived from the holy texts gives much better advice than simply reasoning. The path or way is the collection of laws and regulations derived from their texts. These laws and regulations guide their life, politics, and relationships. However, within religions, the interpretations of a divinely revealed path can vary greatly.

The Jews have a covenant with God. God offers protection and land to Abraham and his descendants. In return the Jews are to follow the path and rules of God. The Tanakh gives us the history of their early relationship with God. As mentioned above, The Talmud is an exhaustive study and interpretation of the Tanakh that contains the teachings and opinions of many rabbis. It is a compilation of Jewish legal opinion and discusses who is a Jew and how Jews are to live together and singly. There is a wide range of interpretations. Today Judaism is generally divided into Reform, Conservative, and Orthodox. The division is loosely based on the importance given the Jewish Religious Rules. The Halakha or path for Orthodox Jews involves adhering to the many Religious Rules found in the Tanakh. In general, they believe that to be a Jew one must be born of a Jewish mother, but one can become a Jew through rigorous study and adherence to the Religious Rules. In Israel some very doctrinaire Orthodox Jews think that Conservative and Reform Jews should not be considered Jews at all. Reform Jews believe in religious pluralism. They are generally liberal and see Conservative and Orthodox Judaism as valid forms of the religion. They think the Orthodox Jews are too focused on tradition, and that they make insufficient allowance for the findings of modern science. Most Reform believe that a Jewish father qualifies one as an ethnic Jew. The Conservatives are somewhere in between. All of the Jews from Reform to very Orthodox have shared the same historic fate. The Holocaust being the most horrific example.

The "consecrated life" in Catholicism is a way of life followed by those called to approach Jesus and God in a more exacting way. It can vary from a private personal approach to taking formal orders as a Catholic nun, priest, or monk. For Catholic and Eastern Orthodox Christians, the organized Church gives interpretation of scripture. The church tells how Catholics should live with others and God. Protestant Christians are generally advised to go to the Bible directly as a guide on how to relate to God and others. This can be called *sola scriptura* (only scripture). It roughly means that one must go directly to scripture and use rational thought guided by the General Admonitions concerning tolerance and inclusion for direction. One's pastor can be very helpful, but the choice is yours.

The "way" in Islam is called the *Sunna* and is closely tied to Sharia. It is a collection of instructions from the Qur'an and the Hadith outlining the traditions, sayings, and practices of Muhammad. It describes a model life that a Muslim should follow. Islamic law schools decide how the *Sunna* should be carried out through adherence to Shari law.

Sharia is Islamic law based on the principles found in the Qur'an and the Hadith. Sharia is very prominent in Muslim life and thought. Sharia is not a codified text of law or laws written down in a holy book. To follow Sharia means to live and write governmental laws that conform to the instructions and admonitions presented in the Qur'an and the Hadith. In a sense, Sharia can be compared to a Christian using the Bible as the final authority for law. Because of differences, numerous Sharia law schools have formed to decide exactly what the law is. There are distinct differences in Sharia between the modernists and fundamentalists. Today the more conservative schools of Sharia law are most prominent, and they often issue legal opinions (*fatwas*) on how the codified laws in governmental constitutions or organizing documents are to be obeyed.

Various schools (*ulemas*) of scholars (*mufti*) and clerics study the Qur'an, the Hadith, ancient Arabic, and previous rulings. The study is called *Ijtihad. Jihad* means "struggle" and can mean the internal struggle to be a better person, or the outer struggle for a better society, or it can mean active holy war. As mentioned above, legal scholars can use their knowledge and prominence to issue their opinions on all parts of the law. The schools often disagree. Courts are run by judges (*qadi*), and their opinion is usually final. In some instances, rulings can be appealed to a higher court. There are no juries. Sharia law concerning Moral Rules, General Admonitions, and Organizational Rules is very much like Judaism and Christianity. The punishments associated with the Religious Rules involve charges of heresy, sacrilege, and apostasy under Sharia. They are presently unique to Islam.

Sharia law is not codified or written down in a constitutional form. Due to differences between the numerous Sharia law schools, lack of codification, and various ways of contextualizing, there is significant disagreement over the exact application of Sharia. Contextualizing becomes very important. Despite the lack of clear codification and serious disagreements between Sharia scholars, many Muslims think that any proposed conformity to some form of Sharia is the best means to improve society. Today the more fundamental schools are dominant, and they feel that many of the problems in Islamic nations occur because a strict Sharia is not followed. Modernists note that deference to Sharia would impose the opinions of clerics on government and those are variable. Some clerics would like Sharia to apply only to domestic law such as divorce and inheritance and avoid other areas of organizational law. That would be much less controversial. Confining Sharia to domestic law has occurred in Egypt to some extent. (A detailed explanation of these nuances is available on the internet from the *Carnegie Endowment for International Peace* entitled "Egypt and Islamic Sharia, a Guide for the Perplexed." by Nathan J Brown on May 15, 2012.)

Jewish law is principally in the Talmud and is studied at *yeshivas*. It only applies to very orthodox Jews and there is no enforcement agency. For Christians there is no such thing as a Christian "law" school comparable to the schools of Talmudic and Sharia law. Christians separate church and state, and Jesus was not forming a government. As mentioned before there are eight prominent law schools of Sharia law, five of them are most influential, four Sunni schools and one Shia school. The Sharia law schools are generally more conservative concerning Religious Rules than the various constitutions and documents that form the basis of the law in many modern Muslim majority nation states.

While not demanding that Sharia is to be the actual law, some constitutions and other organizing documents in Muslim majority nations often state that the rights and laws in the text "shall not conflict with Sharia" or something similar. [15] This caveat means that the law will be subject to interpretation by Islamic religious organizations or courts. This statement effectively leaves out any assurance of individual freedom of press, speech, religion, or habeas corpus. The <u>Cairo Declaration on Human Rights in Islam (1991)</u>, adopted by the Organization of Islamic Cooperation (OIC) includes this caveat. [16] The OIC is the most recent and largest international body representing Islamic nations.

The differences in the great monotheisms' texts explain some of the difficulties. The Judaic and Christian texts were written by many authors, and they offer many different views of God and community. The adherent and reader of the Bible is forced to choose between very different points of view. "An eye for an eye" (Leviticus 24:19–21) is very different from "Forgive your brother seventy times seven." (Matthew 18:21-22). Islamic texts have only one source, Muhammad. His prophecies, rulings, and advice are paramount. However, his instructions must be contextualized to distinguish between his different roles as leader of an endangered tribe in 7th century Arabia and as the final spiritual prophet speaking to the ages. "There should be no compulsion in religion." (Qur'an 2:256) is very different from "Allah's Apostle said, "The blood of a Muslim who confesses that none has the right to be worshipped but Allah and that I am His Apostle, cannot be shed except in three cases: In *Qisas* for murder, a married person who commits illegal sexual intercourse and the one who reverts from Islam (apostate) and leaves the Muslims." (Hadith, Bukhari 9:83:17) People tend to pick what they want in the texts. Contextualizing will be very important.

Chapter 3
Contextualizing

Contextualizing is often essential to the understanding and application of religious texts. Was the tribe under war like threat? Was the very existence of the religion threatened? Is the religion under existential threat today? Had the people become proud, selfish, and self-righteous, lacking compassion for others? All the great monotheistic scriptures require some contextualizing. Science and democracy have changed our understanding of the natural world and how governments function. The changes that they have pointed out must be considered.

The less contextualizing is needed, the less confusion there is, but some statements demand contextualizing. Once you start "contextualizing", who will be the authority that decides the context? Whomever is stronger? Hopefully, the most tolerant scholars who value the compassionate General Admonitions will prevail. Historically, tolerant proponents have frequently been silenced by more militant fundamentalist approaches, particularly in difficult economic and political times. The miracles will remain mysteries.

The Jewish Tanakh tells the story of a tribe through eras, good and bad. The commands and advice of the Hebrew God and the prophets varied depending on the times. Sometimes the Jewish God was violent, sometimes demanding, often moralizing, occasionally forgiving, seemingly contradictory, and usually protective of his people. One must contextualize to get any consistently compassionate intercultural advice from the Hebrew Scriptures. The Ten Commandments are mixed in with such things as God's demands for obliteration of every Canaanite (Deuteronomy 20:16) (Joshua, 6:21). Also, God sends a bear to kill children who were irritating the Prophet Elisha. (II Kings 2: 23-24). Some observant figure, I don't know who, said, "The Tanakh (Christian Old Testament) is the story of God before He became a Christian."

The Christian Bible has about forty authors whose advice varies widely, so contextualizing and picking and choosing are obligatory. Jesus in the New Testament is somewhat of an exception. One almost never has to pick and choose because he essentially "always speaks to the ages" even though he had four different biographers. He avoids punishments, and consistently presents a message of compassion, equality, and forgiveness mixed with warnings concerning the fate of sinners. He allows the state to deal with punishments for crime. His advice is generally timeless.

The other principal character in the New Testament is Paul. Like Moses and Muhammad, Paul was very involved in building a church and ordering a religious community. Often his statements must be contextualized to that time and his task. Fortunately, Paul's statements that seemingly condone slavery, belittle women, and disapprove of gay people have no counterpart in Jesus' teachings. Neither Paul nor Jesus recommends punishments.

Contextualizing must also consider differences in translations. There are many translations of the Qur'an and The Bible. The Hebrew, Aramaic, and Greek of the Bible are arbitrary at times. The Qur'an is thought by some to be untranslatable and only truly understandable in ancient Arabic. This can mean that everyone gets something different from the texts. The fact that the sacred texts can be interpreted in many ways means that they will be. Louis Armstrong says about music and life, "You blows what you is." Translation is personal, and religious text translations can be a very personal. One usually reports what one wants. Relations seem to be better when the translators are guided by the General Admonitions.

As stated earlier, there are also groups that describe themselves as Christian who are racist, sexist and/or brutal such as the Ku Klux Klan. They can find biblical sanctions or suggestions for their actions or beliefs in the Old Testament and some of the New Testament. Pro-slavery forces used Biblical scripture to condone their support for chattel slavery. The Book of Numbers, Chapter 31, describes God telling Moses to kill all the Midianite men, boys, and sexually active women and keep the virgins and female children for themselves, presumably as slaves. The Book of Exodus 21:20-21 states, "When a slave owner strikes a male or female slave with a rod and the slave dies immediately, the owner shall be punished. But if the slave survives a day or two, there is no punishment; for the slave is the owner's property."

There are two verses quoting Jesus in Matthew that racists have used as some of their justification. These verses are:

"A disciple is not above the teacher, nor a servant (slave) above the master." (Matthew 10:24),

"Who then is the faithful and wise servant (slave), whom his master has put in charge of his household, to give the other servants (slaves) their allowance of food at the proper time? Blessed is that servant (slave) whom his master will find at work when he arrives." (Matthew 24:45-46)

When thinking of Jesus' approach to most issues, one would think that "servant" would be a proper translation to convey the spirit of Jesus' teachings. However, racist scholars and some sincere scholars have insisted that "slave" is the correct translation of the Greek word recorded by one of Jesus' biographers. In Matthew 10:24 above, "disciples" are voluntary, so "servant" would seem to be the appropriate translation. The second quote allows for more controversy. Most translations today use "servant". Paul's and Peter's letters in the New Testament seem to condone a form of slavery and lesser roles and status for women.

The Qur'an in verse 2:85-86 says "Can you believe in one part of the scriptures and deny another? Those of you that act thus shall be rewarded with disgrace in this world and with a grievous punishment on the day of Resurrection." A strict literal interpretation of these verses complicates discussion and seems to make any discussion difficult.

Mercy and forgiveness are constant themes in the Qur'an. Their application varies from sect to sect. Compassionate contextualizing under the guidance of the General Admonitions can resolve most problems. At times Muhammad was busy protecting and organizing his newborn religion's followers. Other times he was speaking to the ages. If one is interested in harmony the verse stating that "There should be no compulsion in religion", Qur'an 2:256, must be considered when discussing religious issues. Most people don't think that Islam is under existential threat. Some Islamic clerics think otherwise. If the text was arranged chronologically the contextualizing might be easier. It might be clearer about which statements were in times of existential danger.

Jews, Protestants, and Muslims are ultimately alone before God and must make their own personal contextualizing decisions. Jews have texts and extensive commentaries in the Talmud. Catholics are advised to go to the church for clarification. Catholics can get some absolution for their sins by confession to a priest. Most Protestant doctrine allows for forgiveness with repentance. Forgetting is not mentioned. Muslim fundamentalists can find verses that support their excesses.

Grace is an interesting Christian concept. It has two areas of application. In some ways grace is like mercy. Mercy means that one has been spared the consequences of one's negative actions or sins. In another sense grace is like enlightenment in the Hindu or Buddhist sense. In that sense "Grace" can mean that one has been lucky enough to be granted insights and understandings about the mysteries of life. These insights can provide consolation and lead them on the best path. Grace allows one to see the truth, and, as Jesus says in John 8:32, the "truth" has made them compassionate and set them free from sin and worry.

Mostly, believers must read and decide what Moses, Isaiah, Paul, Jesus, and Muhammad have to say. Listening carefully to what each says in several different translations probably gives one a general tone of their message. Is one doing the right thing? Leading a pious life as described in the texts is felt by many individuals to offer a better chance for forgiveness and grace. In picking a path, it might be good to remember that "You shall know a tree by the fruit it bears" (Jesus, Matthew 7:20). What are the characteristics of the governments and people who follow a particular path?

"Close reading" describes in depth study and research on a subject or text and its origins. So much depends on intent, translation, definitions, and context that there can be huge differences between a "charitable" close reading and an "ideologic" or "critical" close reading. Close reading can arrive at almost any opinion about the subject being discussed. Results depend on the goals of those reading. Charitable close reading can produce more harmony and understanding. Peaceful interactions frequently require forgiveness.

People can be censored and judged depending on someone's "close reading". Today, close reading is often used to evaluate the opinions and finding of others. It can be used to attach labels to speakers and authors such as racist, sexist, blasphemer, apostate, fascist, Orientalist, Islamophobe, communist, white supremist, Western exceptionalist, etc. This form of labeling can have consequences for freedom of speech and, hopefully, will be used judiciously. "Close reading" of the texts by Moses, Jewish prophets, Paul, Jesus, and Muhammad, can produce a wide variety of results. A compassionate and tolerant approach can produce harmonies among competing positions.

Some groups, especially in educational settings, can "cancel" the statements or opinions of others. Cancelling can avoid giving a forum to bigots, liars, irresponsible conspiracy theorists, and racists. It can also serve to stifle discussion. Both sides may need to compromise. What can be done to eliminate those that blatantly lie? What about irresponsible conspiracy theorists who undermine the institutions of government? Difficult questions.

Anecdotally, Ali Rizvi, a self-described ex-Muslim atheist and secular humanist author, recites an encounter with a young Muslim woman. "I have a friend who calls herself a "feminist Muslim". 'What does that mean?', I asked her, "Like a meat-eating vegetarian?" "Well," she said, "of course there are passages that discriminate against women in the Qur'an that I take issue with, but everyone cherry-picks, and so do I." Charitable "Cherry picking" might be seen as a form of contextualizing or close reading.

As mentioned above, in as least two verses the Qur'an clearly says that one cannot pick and choose what parts to believe. One must accept the whole Qur'an, or God will be very displeased (Qur'an 2:86, 15:89-90). By contextualizing these statements to a time and place in the security and defense of a beleaguered tribe, one can avoid applying force and labels inappropriately. In times of attack, unquestioned unity without quibbling may be necessary. It seems that some clerics think that Islam is continually under threat. Others feel that now Islam is secure and working out multiple internal differences. Universal conformity to one single vision of Islamic unity is always in question. Diversity of approach is common, and multiple sects and political entities such as Sunni, Shia, Sufism, Salafism, the Wahabis, etc. are forming and competing all the time. Salafism arose in the 19th century and advocates a return to conservative practices and values that it feels were present in the first three generations of Muslims. Salafism has spawned several subsequent sects including Wahabism, the Muslim Brotherhood, ISIS, the Taliban, Al Qaeda, and others.

As mentioned before, Hinduism, Buddhism, Taoism, and Confucianism have essentially no revealed Religious Rules that require contextualization. They have no Prophets bringing "the word" from God. They are not even "religions" in the great monotheistic tradition because they have no articles of supernatural faith. Hindus and Buddhist are searching for an enlightening experience or union with God. They are all mystics of a sort, and in mystical terms, these experiences could fulfill them completely. Such an experience would hopefully take them to a consciousness of truth that is "beyond hope and fear". Broadly speaking, this state has several names or attributes in all religions. For

Jews the Kabbalah is a text and area of study concerning mystical efforts to contact God. Other religious terms include grace (Christian), Fana Fillah (annihilation of the self in God in Sufi Islam), moksha (Hindu), nirvana or passionless peace (Buddhist, Sikh, and Hindu), Samadhi (Hindu, Jainism), and Satori (Japanese Zen Buddhist). The Taoist seeks harmony with the universe as it is.

Eastern dogma is so fluid and undemanding that one could that one could probably be a Hindu, Buddhist, or a Confucian and a liberal Protestant or a Sufi at the same time. The morals, ethics, and hands-off attitudes are very similar.

Finally, contextualizing, charitable close reading, optimistic cherry picking, and good will are essential to harmony in politics and religion. In other words, we will have to want to get along if we are to do so. Compromise will be necessary and contextualizing essential.

Unity. Is religion one sect or many? There are a lot of groups out there

Jews readily separate into different groups such as reform, conservative, and orthodox. Christians label themselves as one of the thousands of sects. These labels give a general idea of their doctrines. Christians generally identify as Catholic, Eastern Orthodox, Presbyterian, Lutheran, Baptist, Methodist, Anglican, Mormon, Coptic, Jehovah's Witnesses, etc. Descriptive classification makes discussion, socializing, and communication much easier. Then again, if a person says they are Jewish or Christian, they are usually not primarily interested in coercion or political unity. Any discussion of Islam runs into the question of unity. Obviously, there is a very wide spectrum of beliefs and practices under the label "Islam".

Many prominent Muslim clerics and politicians including Imran Khan, the former Prime Minister of Pakistan, and Recep Erdogan, president of Turkey, insist that Islam is only one thing, "a beautiful compassionate way of life". This is clearly true to the vast majority of Muslims worldwide. To them every other description of Islam is uninformed or possibly Islamophobic. In a speech in 2017 at a program hosted in Ankara by the Organization of Islamic Cooperation (OIC) on women's entrepreneurship Turkish President Erdogan said "Islam cannot be either 'moderate' or 'not moderate'. Islam can only be one thing." Erdogan went on to say, "Recently the concept of 'moderate Islam' has received attention. But the patent of this concept originated in the West... They are now trying to pump up this idea again. What they really want to do is weaken Islam ... [17]. It appears that Erdogan thinks that any definite recognition or codification of the differences within Islam would lead to the formation of various sects who approach culture or God differently and consequently would "weaken" Islam politically. He is not interested in diverse personal approaches to community and God. Unity is politically necessary.

Conservative theologians of all religions and sects, Judaism, Christianity, and Islam, think that a religious base to politics would benefit the people culturally and spiritually. All religious leaders dream of a world where their ideas of justice and piety would be permitted to inform the government on all sorts of issues including economics, justice, recreation, foreign policy, culture, and education. They act as if an enforced piety of some extent would work best for cultural and economic success, and it is their duty to promote their vision of that piety. These preachers and clerics worry that if individual adherents are allowed to construct their own visions that they would splinter into many groups. This has proven to be true. Jewish and Christian leaders have generally given up trying to control political issues, but they regularly vocalize their concerns about politics and cultural issues. Some forms of Islam are more controlling in politics, particularly in Iran, Pakistan, Saudi Arabia, Afghanistan, and recently Turkey and Indonesia.

From the outside it appears that conservative religious leaders fear that if the members are not tightly controlled that their vision will splinter like the Protestants, and the unity needed for power and a pious environment will be lost. They act as if unified adherence to a strict pious orthopraxy is essential to realize their vision, maintain their power, and, as importantly, to please God. For orthodox Jews, the Tanakh and the Talmud outline the piety. For Catholics, it is the church. For Protestants, it is the reasoning individual. For Muslims, Sharia law defines the piety.

Unity concerning the Moral Rules and the General Admonitions does not need to be forced. Unity comes easy because most rational people agree on these issues. Adultery will be determined by the culture. Organizational Rules concern the politics around democracy vs autocracy, capitalism vs socialism, and public piety vs individual piety. These Organizational Rules will be debated and changed continually. The maintenance of individual rights can avoid persecution of religious minorities by unified fundamentalists. Unity increases power in any political situation.

Reform and moderate religiously oriented people seem to think that the elimination of coercion concerning Religious Rules will allow everyone to practice as they see fit and coexist in their search for earthly and spiritual fulfillment. Individual choice will also allow the state to be flexible enough to become economically, educationally, and culturally successful. Everyone does not have to be forced into some vision of conformity. Muslims with these liberal ideas such as the Muslim Reform Movement in the US are just beginning to become organized.

The Muslim Reform Movement (MRM) in the US says that parts of Islam have been taken over by a few repressive conservative factions. These factions are the "Islamists." MRM's public statement on Meet the Press Dec. 6, 2015, says, "... we are opposing a very real interpretation of Islam that espouses violence, social injustice, and political Islam ... The problem is sitting in the birthplace of Islam, in Mecca, Saudi Arabia, where (a conservative) interpretation of Islam has gone out into the world over the last four decades (through the fundamentalist *madrassas* funded by the Saudis), creating militant groups from Indonesia to San Bernardino, California, the scene of a vicious attack. (14 killed, 22 seriously wounded, Dec 2, 2014) We must take back the faith. And we must take it back with the principles of peace, social justice, human rights, women's rights, and secularize governance ... we've had enough.".

A limited survey of British Muslims revealed that they did not like to be called "moderate". Even if they were moderate in their approach to punishments, culture, and politics, they did not identify as "moderate" in their devotion to the pieties of Islam. They felt that the label "moderate" described them as lacking serious devotion. They love the pious rituals, ceremonies, strict sexual morality, and family closeness so central to Islam. Being devout and rigorous in carrying out all the individual and group rituals pleased them very much. They did not want the rituals or pious obligations changed in any significant way. There seems to be no single term that describes those who dislike punishment and coercion yet want to preserve the group warmth and pieties. "Modern" may be a better word than "Moderate". Moderate isn't always working well everywhere.

Muslims already identify as Sunni and Shia, but these identities concern Organizational Rules dealing with leadership and ethnicity. The two sects are generally interested in the same Religious Rules about piety. Sufis identify clearly as Muslims, but they are mystics, generally tolerant, and not as political and culturally doctrinaire. Their veneration of saints has made them the target of fundamentalist Muslims who see them as polytheistic apostates. Sufis are intermittently murderously attacked by fundamentalist Islamic zealots. In 2017 over 300 Sufis were killed by ISIS fundamentalists at a mosque in the Sinai. The worst attack in modern Egyptian history.

Because Islam does not separate mosque and state, there are two forces in play most of the time among the religious elites: a political drive for power coupled with a desire to have the community follow Religious Rules concerning piety. In any corrupt economically stressed Islamic nation there is usually a movement by conservative factions demanding stricter pieties. A stricter Islam is their answer.

Organizing Islam as one entity could give too much power to violent extremist groups. In a unified system, the fundamentalist can intimidate the leadership, take over the agenda, and stifle reform. This has happened in numerous Muslim countries including Pakistan, Saudi Arabia, and Iran. A clear labeling of multiple diverse groups might be more difficult to intimidate. The smaller entities could seek refuge within their group or alliances with other groups.

One advantage to a generally unified Islam is that it could possibly condemn and perhaps lessen the brutalities perpetrated by violent smaller sects such as ISIS, al-Qaeda, Boko Haram in west Africa, and Al-Shabab in Somalia. However, there might be fundamentalist factions like the Muslim Brotherhood that would turn a blind eye to the violence if the terrorists are spreading Islam. They act as if the brutal excesses would be eliminated later.

If the dissenting sects were labeled, people approaching Muslims would know what sort of doctrine and practices they support. As it is, when someone says that s/he is a Muslim, others are not sure what they mean. There are lots of different kinds of Muslims. The more orthodox they are, the more they want unity. What sort of Islamic doctrine and practice do they espouse? How rigorous are they? The labels Sunni and Shia don't give much information about how they stand organizationally and politically. Both support adherence to Sharia law. Do they support female "circumcision" (Female Genital Mutilation, FGM) [18], honor killings [19], homophobia, and dowery deaths?

Culturally Muslims vary in support for female genital mutilation (FGM) or "female circumcision"? "Female circumcision" is the same as FGM under another name. Labeling it "circumcision" is an attempt to avoid criticism [19a]. Incidentally FGM is almost completely unknown in Shia Islam. FGM is closely associated with Sunni Muslims in parts of the Middle East, Africa, and Indonesia. It is completely unnecessary and causes many health problems when done to women. It is an example of coercion and control concerning women. More on this in Chapter 5, under "Sexuality and Marriage".

I know several Muslims who describe themselves as "modern Muslims". They seem to be interested in none of these problems. Like many Muslims they enjoy the family and cultural ties, but don't adhere strictly to the pious Religious Rules concerning mingling, FGM, intolerance, and conformity.

A significant problem is that any internal debate about Islamic practices can be misconstrued by extremists on both sides. If Islam is only one thing, it is difficult and potentially dangerous for moderates to speak out or define themselves as different. If they openly state that public punishment concerning some Religious Rule is not necessary, then radicals can label them as heretics, blasphemers, or apostates. Some Islamic governments have tolerant constitutions, but, in practice, they are lax in suppressing and controlling the dangerous non-governmental elements and mobs that threaten potential apostates or moderates. Between 1987 and 2017 at least 1,500 people were charged under Pakistan's blasphemy laws which include the death penalty. Although the state hasn't executed anyone, at least 75 people involved in accusations of blasphemy were killed by religious vigilantes. [20]

Politics in much of the Middle East follow religious lines. If one asks a Westerner for a one-word self-description, the answer is usually, "I am an American, Brit, Frenchman, etc." A Muslim citizen will likely reply, "I am a Muslim". 79% of Pakistanis see themselves as Muslims first as do 70% of Moroccans, 63% of Jordanians, 43% of Turkish citizens, and 39% of Indonesians. ("Islamic extremism: Common Concern for Muslim and Western Public. How Muslims See Themselves and Islam's Role." *Pew Research*. July 14, 2005)

At the end of WWI in the secret Sykes Picot Agreements most of the Middle East was divided by British and French colonizers into arbitrary national boundaries. These borders did not take ethnic and religious concerns into account. Some of the resulting nations do not have a history of democracy or financial success that lends itself to patriotism. All these failures tend to make some people identify politically with a branch of their religion rather than a nation state. The lack of geographic patriotism tends to make politics in some Islamic nation states more subject to sectarian religious pressures. The violence between the Sunnis and Shia in Iraq following the US invasion has been a recent example

When the US invaded Iraq in 2003, many Muslims viewed it as attack on their religion. From that point of view the whole enterprise in Iraq is suspect and deplorable. The US did not think it was attacking Islam. The US government, rightly or wrongly, was worried about the possibility of Weapons of Mass Destruction (WMD) in the hands of fanatics. WMD's were a very serious concern due to the recent 911 al-Qaeda attacks. The US saw the invasion as the overthrow of a dangerous and murderous tyrant who, besides abusing his people, posed a serious threat concerning nuclear weapons or dangerous gases. To show Saddam Hussein that they were very serious in their demands for inspections, the US and its allies had put an army in the desert. Initially Hussein seemed willing to cooperate, but he changed, and acted as though the recent objections to invasion by France, Germany, and Russia would deter any US action. Summer was coming to the desert. The US and its allies could not wait long for Saddam to decide, and they attacked. They were misinformed. No WMD were found. [21] Many Iraqis died, and critics said the invasion was a grab for oil.

It is estimated that through war and internal terror, Saddam Hussein oversaw the violent deaths of approximately 42,000 of his citizens yearly for his 23 years in power, many by torture, over 960,000 in all. During the two month invasion of Iraq and defeat of Saddam's Army, over 7,000 Iraqi civilians and 10,000 Iraqi military died because of US action. Over the next five years of internal fighting, mainly between Shia and Sunni, almost 400,000 Iraqis were killed in a civil war, mostly by "unknown assailants". A fragile democracy has been installed. Iraq has a democratic constitution, and, as of today, Iraq continues to elect its leaders. An ORB (British opinion polling service) poll in Iraq in 2007 showed that despite the remaining violence only 26% of Iraqis preferred life under

Saddam Hussein's regime, while 49% said that they preferred life under the current political system.

Many Muslims say that all of Islam is one entity and that all Muslims are bound together in one way of life. On the other hand, they say that many things done by other Muslims in the name of Islam are not "true Islam". "One Islam" conflicts with "True Islam". There is one Islam in that probably all Muslims embrace the Five Pillars and Six Articles of Faith of Islam.

Five Pillars:

Belief in one God and Muhammad is his final prophet.

One should pray, possibly five times a day. (There is no clear number in Qur'an)

Go on Pilgrimage to Mecca if possible.

Fasting at some point. The month of fasting called Ramadan is highly recommended.

Give money for the poor.

Six Beliefs or Articles of Faith:

Belief in Allah as the one and only God.

Belief in angels.

Belief in the Qur'an

Belief in the Prophets. e.g. Adam, Ibrahim (Abraham), Ishmael, Musa (Moses), Dawud (David), Isa (Jesus), Muhammad

Belief in the Day of Judgement.

Belief in Predestination.

"True Islam" seems to be in the eye of the beholder. True Islam appears to mean following some group's particular interpretation of the Qur'an very closely. True Islam for conservative Islamists is not just a personal relationship with God but involves a group push for unity, power, and a strict public adherence to many pieties.

In much of Islamic religious thought, particularly in conservative Islamist circles, the idea of an attainable world peace means that all nations will be Islamic and ruled under Sharia law. Osama Ben Laden clearly stated this in his letter to the West. (21a) The Muslim Brotherhood and all the fundamentalist groups also state this. "Islam is the answer." On the other hand, Western ideas of world peace involve a world of nations functioning as liberal democracies with individual rights for all where government is changed by voting, corruption is controlled by impartial courts, and everyone worships as they wish.

Since Islam is a highly structured complete way of group and public life, it can become heavily involved in politics. Organizations such as the Muslim Brotherhood run for office in Egypt, Iran is under clerical rule, Pakistan's laws demand conformity to Sharia law, ISIS proclaimed a caliphate in captured lands, Boko Haram tries to establish harsh Sharia standards in lands in West Africa. It seems obvious to those outside Islam that Islam is many different things to people who are united in valuing the Five Pillars and the Six Articles of Faith.

Most Western Muslims appear to value the security and protection of the liberal democratic nations. Additionally, many Muslims seem to want to live a religious life unconcerned with the fundamentalists who are interested in world domination, dangerous *fatwas*, and violent jihadist visions of conquest and revenge. In August 2017, Pew Research published an article entitled, *Muslims and Islam: Key findings in the US and around the world.* [22] Pew Research reports that 65% of US Muslims say religion is very important in their lives. Of these, 43% say traditional understandings should be reinterpreted vs. 46% who say traditional understandings are all that is needed. Of those Muslims in the US who say religion is less important, 70% express the view that Islamic teachings need to be reinterpreted. Of those asked in Egypt, Saudi Arabia, Jordan, and Kuwait only 20% think any change is needed. Since the Reformation and the Enlightenment, Christians wanting reform have simply changed denominations or created new ones. This sort of splintering is perhaps what worries many prominent Muslims. Clearer group differentiation would lead to better communication, but less unity and political power.

Fundamentalist (radical, Islamist, or puritanical) Muslims generally support militant jihadist thinking. They comprise less that 5% of Muslims (Pew Research), and most of them reside in nations that are predominantly Muslim. They can be misogynist, anti-modern, triumphalist, intolerant, violent, and/or terroristic. World domination, imposition of serious orthopraxy, and violent revenge seem to dominate their thinking and discourse. These views appear to have been encouraged through a vast network of fundamentalist *madrassa* schools set up over the Muslim world by the Wahabis from Saudi Arabia in the last 50 years. "Madrassa" means "school" and in the past referred to all sorts of schools. Lately it has become associated with fundamentalism. These schools emphasize memorization of scripture, and a conservative Islam. They frequently neglect math, science, history, and literature. In 2015 it was estimated that the Wahabi influenced Saudi government has spent $100 billion on *madrassas* since the 1970's. There are 30,000 *madrassas* in Pakistan alone, most funded by the Wahabis. As of today, there are 140,000 in Indonesia. Historically Indonesia had been home to a tolerant branch of Islam. It is generally felt that the recent increase in fundamentalist pressure and intolerance in the Indonesian Islamic community is a result of these schools. Recently a *fatwa* proposing death for homosexuals was issued. Also another death fatwa was issued on a prominent leading liberal Indonesian Muslim, Ulil Abshar Abdalla, and several suicide bombings involving Indonesian youths have demonstrated this fundamentalist trend [22a]. In the last few years, the new Saudi leader, Muhammad bin Salman, has begun to be more tolerant. The schools are still in place. All religions harbor some adherents with fundamentalist views. In Judaism and Christianity most religious fundamentalists are not highly politically organized or generously funded.

In addition to the spread of Wahabi fundamentalist education, the internet has allowed political terrorists and fundamentalists of all sorts to find and support each other. Before the internet, many fundamentalists probably led solitary lives and were unable to find others professing similar violent or oppressive views. The connectivity of the internet has allowed them to find each other and organize. Unscrupulous violence and modern weapons have made some of them, such as ISIS and Al Qaeda particularly dangerous. [23]

The adoption of an adjective like "reform" or "modern" might give moderates solid Islamic credentials but separate them from such things as FGM, honor killings, the need for unity, and the threatening accusations of heresy, blasphemy, and apostasy.

In an attempt to unify religious Islam and clarify the issues around charges of apostasy, a group of 200 scholars from 50 countries organized by the King of Jordan under the auspices of the Grand Mufti of Jordan put forth the Amman Three Point Message in 2004. It was a statement encouraging unity in Islam. The Amman Message focused on defining who is a Muslim, who speaks for Islam, and who can be excommunicated or determined to be an apostate. All these issues involve Religious Rules. Recently relatively large numbers of people in the Islamic world have been threatened by deadly *fatwas* labeling them as apostates. Many were labeled by Islamic clerics for political and cultural reasons. The Amman Message seems to be a genuine attempt to stop the excessive use of unapproved threatening *fatwas* and increase unity among Islam's different scholarly organizations and Sharia law schools. Below is my shorthand summary of the Message. The full text is under Endnote (24)

The First and Second Points essentially say that everyone who believes in God, his messenger, Muhammad, the Five Pillars of Islam, the Six Articles of Faith, and who "does not deny any self-evident tenet of the religion" is not an apostate. They should not be labeled as such. This obviously allows a large degree of latitude. How does one define "self-evident"? Charges of apostasy and blasphemy against Muslims and non-Muslims can be arbitrary and dangerous. A list of famous *fatwas* can be found easily online.

The Third Point says that the only people who can issue *fatwas* are those who have been approved by one of the recognized Sharia law schools. There are eight prominent schools and numerous others.

The questions of control, unity, and identity in Islam are very similar to the ones debated by strongly orthodox Jews and the Catholic Church. In Judaism, the debates take place in the orthodox yeshivas and do not affect the reform Jew. In Orthodox Judaism, apostates can be shunned or excommunicated. Today the Catholic Church is more tolerant of internal dissent, but the Vatican still has the last say. Catholics who are considered heretics can be excommunicated from the Catholic Church. Protestantism has no central authority. Apostasy is not a significant issue, and worshipers change sects frequently. Every Protestant is an individual who must relate with God based on his or her understanding of the biblical teachings. Protestants can be excommunicated by their different sects, but it is extremely rare.

Chapter 4

Rules: Detailed Definitions of the Four Categories of Rules

1. Moral Rules or Laws

The four Moral Rules or Laws (Don't murder, bear false witness, steal, or commit adultery) are primarily about safety, justice, and good order. They involve things that are better "not" to do. Murder would include brutality of all sorts such as bullying, rape, torture, and assaulting. False witness covers any serious questions of honesty such as lying and cheating. White lies concern minor issues, and they are often very useful in social dealings. The Qur'an clearly states that such things as inconsequential lying about beauty to make one's wife happy is acceptable. Stealing would include all illegal ways of getting money or goods. These rules can be arrived at by rational thought. They are fundamental in all the great political and religious organizations. They do not require a revelation from God through a prophet. It does help a lot when God lists and emphasizes them clearly like the Jewish/Christian God does in the Ten Commandments and the Qur'an does in *sura* (chapter) 17:22-39 [25]. If the leaders of a society transgress the Moral Laws, it is the definition of corruption or oppression. If the Moral Laws are not justly enforced, corruption, in the forms of bribery, nepotism, graft, or extortion will become a way of life. This will destroy faith in and cooperation with the government. That corruption can drown any hopes of a society becoming a land of opportunity.

Adultery is a poor choice because of serious betrayal and loss of faith and intimacy. Judaism, Christianity, and Islam are firmly against it. Muslim approaches to adultery are different in that a man can have multiple wives and sex with female slaves is permitted. As for fornication, the availability of birth control, modern healthcare, LGBTQ issues, and lessening of paternalism effecting women's rights have completely changed the issues around extramarital sex. Consequently, fornication will be discussed under Organizational Rules.

Courts and police are involved in judging and enforcing Moral Rules or Laws. Many people think that, if these Moral Rules are disconnected from their organized religious roots that they will lose their force and central place in society. In the case of Christianity, this is being tested in Europe. European governments have adopted the Moral Rules and charity. They have also recognized the equal value of every individual. The people are, however, discarding formal Christianity. Measured by church attendance, organized Christianity is declining. Fortunately, there seems to be a Christian "legacy effect" in that the populace has generally maintained an honest, charitable, and law-abiding attitude.

Historically the assimilation of peoples from tribal or group societies with different value systems has always been difficult. The US government has in the past treated indigenous people and immigrants badly and occasionally brutally. Treaties were broken regularly. This all occurred in a time when every nation in the world was taking what it could. The US was not exceptionally bad. The rough people on the frontiers exploited the good will and economic naivete of the Indians. Also, many Americans, including the government, took land from tribal areas. No stone age people has fared well when meeting a more powerful culture. These were no exception. When I use the term "stone age", I am referring to a culture's technologic development, not their moral or governmental development. *A People's History of the United States* by

Howard Zinn is a very critical look at the difference between America's stated goals and its actions. Lately the government has become more sensitive and conciliatory.

It is helpful to remember that up until the 20th century's international organizations such as the United Nations, most national borders were defined by conquest. In fact, the Treaty of Westphalia in 1648, ending the 30 Years War, was the first time that a significant number of nations had agreed on any boundaries, and even these agreements were soon broken. When the Western hemisphere was colonized by Europeans, the world standard for action was one of conquest. If a country or group was stronger than another, it usually took it over, by force if necessary. This was true of essentially every tribe, group, and monarchy in history. Often the conquering peoples felt that they were bringing benefits to the conquered. Most conquerors have felt that their religion was a benefit to the conquered people.

In Judaism these Moral Rules are included as four of the Ten Commandments. All Ten Commandments are generally endorsed by the practicing Jewish community. After the destruction of the Second Temple around 70 C.E., the Jews were powerless to impose Rules on others until the creation of modern Israel. They have installed a liberal democracy.

Jesus does not address each of the Ten Commandments individually. Jesus says we must follow "the commandments" to get to heaven. When asked by a young man, "Which ones?" There are a lot of them. Jesus replied, "You shall not murder, you shall not commit adultery, you shall not steal, you shall not give false testimony, honor your father and mother, and love your neighbor as yourself." (Matthew 19:16-19) None of these are Religious Rules. They are Moral Rules, Organizational Rules, and General Admonitions. In the New Testament, a very conservative orthodox Jew asks Jesus, "What is the greatest commandment of the law?" Jesus responds, "Love the Lord your God with all your heart, with all your soul, and with all your mind. This is the greatest and most important commandment. The second is like it: Love your neighbor as yourself. All the Law and the Prophets depend on these two commands." –Matthew 22:37-40 . Both are General Admonitions.

In Islamic law, the Qur'an and Hadith also support the four Moral Laws. According to the Qur'an, murder of anyone of any faith is a serious sin. However, some Hadith texts say killing a Muslim is worse than killing an infidel. [26] Stealing has been treated severely in Islamic societies. They used to cut off the hand of a thief, but this is almost never done now.

Islam is very detailed about lying. Lying is condemned except in three circumstances that are summarized in two Hadith, Muslim 45:130, and Tirmidhi 27:45.

1. One may lie to one's wife to make her happy.
2. One may lie to bring about a peaceful solution to a problem.
3. If someone is going to harm a Muslim for his/her beliefs or hurt the Islamic community, as in oppression or war, lying is acceptable.

This last concept of protective lying is called *taqiyya*. If the individual is seriously threatened for their religion, lying is permissible. This is perfectly reasonable. Shia Muslims used it frequently because they were in a minority and often persecuted by Sunni Muslims. The concept of sanctioned lying because of a perceived threat can create opportunities for scoundrels of all sorts. Who decides what is a threat? How much lying could be excused as a response to some sort of threat? Is lying permissible if a nation is under threat. After signing a peace treaty with Israel, Yasir Arafat, President of the Palestine Liberation Organization, was criticized as he spoke in a mosque in South Africa. He responded by that his signing was only *taqiyya*, a pause until they were more powerful and able to defeat Israel.

Moral transgressions: Sins of Commission and Omission

Offences against the Moral Rules are called sins. They are punished by the state. Offenses against General Admonitions are commonly sins of omission and are not concerns of the state. When ignoring the General

Admonitions, one feels guilty for not having been kind, considerate, or respectful. Offenses against the Religious Rules are also called sins. The government is usually involved in punishing transgression of the Moral Rules and Organizational Rules. Transgressions of the General Admonitions are usually personal failures. The offenses against the Religious Rules can be active sins or sins of omission. The active sins against Religious Rules usually come under the headings: "heresy", "sacrilege", "blasphemy", and "apostasy". The sins of omission are usually less prominent and involve omitting something that is recommended such as fasting, going to ceremonies, covering, praying, ablutions, etc. Today violations of Religious Rules are dealt with by the state only in some Muslim nations.

Here is a brief definition of the types of sins against Religious Rules. They are discussed in considerably more detail below.

1. **Heresy** is a wrong belief. Religious leaders and scholars can decide who is a heretic. A *fatwa* is a ruling by an Islamic legal scholar or *mufti* that can label someone a heretic or worse. No one can know for certain what another believes. Recitation of various creeds can outwardly express one's beliefs.

2. **Sacrilege** is the violation or ill treatment of sacred objects, places, or persons. Done verbally it is called **blasphemy.** Jesus says that blaspheming the Holy Ghost is the only unforgivable sin. Matthew 12:30-32 [29]. It is not exactly clear what this means, and no punishment on earth is recommended. If Christianity had courts and police, religious lawyers could make it mean almost anything.

   Ill treatment of Muhammad verbally or in drawings is a very serious sin in Islam. Pakistan law since 1990 has supported the death penalty for blasphemy. Imran Khan, when running for office as Prime Minister of Pakistan, vigorously supported the law and wanted the Western nations to prosecute blasphemy against Muhammad. Ironically, he is now being accused of blasphemy in Pakistan.

3. **Apostasy** is the abandonment or disavowal of one's religion. Some

authorities equate heresy and sacrilege with apostasy. To them, if you profess the wrong thing (heresy) or blaspheme, you are an apostate and can be persecuted as such. Punishments for apostasy can be draconian and are mentioned in some parts of all the founding texts.

Discussions about sin can involve forgiveness and/or punishment. In Islam, some sins are labeled "*hudud*". They are sins against God's laws written in the Qur'an. Generally non-hudud crimes are sins against other people. Hudud crimes concern unlawful sex, apostasy, drinking alcohol, or theft. If one commits one of these serious *hudud* sins, one can be forgiven, but nevertheless the perpetrator may be given the prescribed punishment. [29a] Sexual crimes must have four witnesses. They are almost never invoked because the requirements for proof are so extensive.

Potentially Hudud crimes.

Theft

Highway robbery

Illegal sexual intercourse

False accusation of intercourse.

Unlike the first four offenses listed above, not all jurists consider the following two to be hudud offenses:

Drinking alcohol

Apostasy including blasphemy.

Blasphemy and Apostasy can be punished by death in most Muslim majority states, but it is almost never done by the state today. Fundamentalist vigilantes do it more often. [30] The fact that punishment is recommended in the holy texts can be very intimidating.

2. General Admonitions.

All the great prophets and teachers from the monotheisms give General Admonitions to their followers. The General Admonitions differ from the Religious Rules and Moral Rules in that they include no specifics as to how the recommended actions are to be carried out. The General Admonitions include "Deal justly" (Micah 6:8). "Love your neighbor as yourself" (Leviticus 19:18 and Mark 12:31. "Do unto others as you would have them do unto you" (Matthew 7:12). "Love God" (Matthew 22:37). "Honor your mother and father" (Exodus 20:12). "Requite evil with good," Qur'an 2395. "No man is a true believer unless he desires for his brother what he desires for himself" (Muhammad, Hadith, Bukhari 1:2:13). Help the poor and disadvantaged (Matthew 25:34-36). "Don't do to others what you do not want them to do to you," Confucius, the Silver Rule. They are from the principal prophets in all the major texts. They are essentially the same in all religions. They describe good attitudes to be taken in one's approach to life. They delineate no specific actions and therefore do not qualify as Religious Rules. They don't tell one exactly how to love, honor, or treat others. They just outline the compassionate attitude that one should take in the effort. All General Admonitions recommend alms or largess for the poor and unfortunate.

The success or justice of all large decisions concerning equality, welfare, or equity will ultimately be dependent on the degree to which the compassionate General Admonitions are embraced by all sides. The details of any agreement are always subject to rational criticism from more than one viewpoint or narrative. Conservative and liberal narratives must both be considered, and the Moral Rules must be obeyed. Fiscal limitations on charity and the amounts of adequate welfare will always be questioned and criticized from all sides.

As mentioned before the General Admonitions do not necessarily require religious revelation. However, it certainly does help when God is very clear about them. All the monotheistic texts are very clear.

"Enlightened self-interest" is a term that describes one's state of understanding when one realizes that helping others helps oneself. Reason leads us to understand that we are happier if our neighbors are happier. If everyone would "love your neighbor" and be reasonably sensitive to their needs, things would work out better. Everyone would have to participate. All participants may have to forgive a lot of transgressions to get to that state. "Requite evil with good," (Qur'an 23:95) and "Turn the other cheek" (Matthew 5:38-40) are good options.

Forgiveness is a difficult approach, and Jesus' advice to Peter is perhaps the most difficult. In Matthew 18: 21-22 the following conversation occurs. "Then Peter came up and said to him, 'Lord, how often will my brother sin against me, and I forgive him? As many as seven times?' Jesus said to him, 'I do not say to you seven times, but seventy times seven.'" A difficult standard which brings up the question, "What is the nature of forgiveness?" Moral crimes such as murder, lying, and stealing all demand justice of some sort. The perpetrator must pay a price. When it is paid, those involved can be forgiven. In interpersonal disagreements and quarrels, often forgiveness alone may provide an end to the problem without the need for punishment or retribution.

Very importantly, the pursuit of compassionate reason ultimately leads one to conclude that being honest is the best way to live. If one doesn't have to remember one's lies or worry about the people that one has cheated, life is better. Society will function better. One's family will be treated better.

This exchange between a young man and Jesus is recorded in Matthew 19:16-21, " Then someone came to him and said, 'Teacher, what good deed must I do to have eternal life' And Jesus said to him, 'Why do you ask me about what is good? There is only one who is good. If you wish to enter into life, keep the commandments.' He said to him, 'Which ones?' And Jesus said, 'You shall not murder; You shall not commit adultery; You shall not steal; You shall not bear false witness; Honor your father and mother; also, you shall love your neighbor as yourself.' 'All these I have kept', the young man said. 'What then do I lack?' Jesus told him, 'If you want to be perfect, go, sell your possessions, and give to the poor, and you will have treasure in heaven. Then come, follow Me.' When the young man heard this, he went away in sorrow because he had great wealth."

The Tanakh, New Testament and Qur'an/Hadith all stress charity to the poor and disabled. Helping the disadvantaged is continually emphasized as one sure thing that one can do to please God in all the monotheisms. Individual acts of compassion are highlighted. Visiting the jails, helping the stranger, healing, and giving food to the poor are wonderful actions. Should everyone do it in person? The people have voted to give money to the state to help the poor and unlucky through organized welfare. This is much more efficient. In effect, the governments are so embedded in religious doctrine that they are trying, a least to some extent, to fulfill the admonitions.

Jews, Christians, and Muslims are all encouraged or required to give money to the needy. Some verses recommend ten percent of one's wealth. Judaism has had care for the indigent population as a goal of its religious community for 2,400 years. Both charity and help for the poor are also emphasized in Islam. Islam requires hospitality for the stranger and alms (*zakat*) for the poor. The government or the local Imam may collect the money. Many who encounter Islam in peaceful times remark at the extraordinary hospitality they receive. Charity is also considered virtuous in Hinduism, Buddhism, and Confucianism.

3. Organizational Rules

The texts give very few Organizational Rules. As outlined previously, Organizational Rules are the laws and constitutions governing society, rights, politics (democracy or autocracy), economic structure (capitalism or socialism), commerce, infrastructure, defense, domestic law, welfare, and justice. Where religion is concerned, the most important Organizational Rules are those separating church and state. In democracies the Organizational Rules deal with infractions of the codified laws. The Organizational Rules can all be arrived at by reasoning with the Moral Rules and General Admonitions as guides. They do not require religious revelation. When dealing with the Organizational Rules, it is very important to keep the General Admonitions in mind. Today they are codified in constitutions or other organizing documents. In Islamic nations many of the codified laws and constitutions contain a phrase saying that "these laws shall not conflict with Sharia."

The texts present the Moral Rules that underlie the Organizational Rules, but the Moral Rules say nothing concerning democracy, economics, governance, voting, or individual human rights other than to suggest that we treat all others justly.

The Organizational Rules have several goals:

1. The first job of government is safety and personal security from invasion, thuggery, assault, and injustice (habeas corpus).

2. The second job is assuring that the citizens have access to the essentials: food, shelter, and healthcare. A good government provides the opportunity to attain them with reasonable effort, or it provides them as welfare for the disabled or unlucky.

3. Thirdly, a particularly good government will provide the opportunity to improve one's lot without having to become brutal or corrupt. Advancement should be possible through a true meritocracy that recognizes personal hard work or education. Education in this discussion refers to the ability to read, write, develop a skill, learn to interact with others, and have some understanding of government. It is not recommending college for all. The residual effects of racism including poor schools have put some minority individuals in the US at a disadvantage in educational achievement. More below.

4. Fourthly, an excellent government will protect reasonable freedom of individual speech, press, and religion in the pursuit of happiness.

5. Importantly, the Organizational Rules will also provide a way to change leadership and policy through voting within a framework including the individual rights.

Discussing Organizational Rules takes us into morals, politics, and culture, not necessarily into questions of faith, spirituality, Religious Rules, or orthodoxy. The Organizational Rules determine if the country is a democracy, a monarchy, a dictatorship, a republic, fascist, mafia-like, or some sort of oligarchy. Organizational rules can be capitalist or socialist and are usually a combination of the two. A good set of Organizational Rules does not require divine revelation, compassionate reason will suffice.

The domestic laws deal with marriage, divorce, and inheritance, and they can vary depending on religious influence and culture.

Inheritance is discussed in the Tanakh in Deuteronomy 21:15-17, it says that the firstborn son gets a double share. In the book of Numbers 27:8-11 daughters get a share only if there are no sons. Today in Israel, only people of the same faith can marry. To divorce in Israel today, the husband must consent. Jesus says divorce should only be allowed in cases of adultery. He did not address inheritance. The Qur'an outlined inheritance for women and gave them many clear rights to their money that they had not previously had. In Islam women cannot marry outside the faith. Islam did give women in Arabia more power and justice in divorce situations. Usually, the husband must consent to the divorce, but there are exceptions. The Prophet Muhammad said, "Of all the lawful things, divorce is the most hated by Allah.".

Types of Organizational Rules: Group and Individual

As mentioned previously Organizational Rules promote or spring from one of two types of culture: a **group** culture or an **individual** culture. Below is a definition of each of these two types and a discussion of their different effects on government and rights. The principal difference between group culture and individual culture is that people in individual culture have codified rights. The individual rights of freedom of speech, freedom of press, freedom of religion, habeas corpus, and the vote are not necessarily included in "Group" organizations. Historically, these individual rights were not codified in an organizational document until the first ten Amendments were added to the US Constitution in 1791.

Group: Organization and Culture

The oldest type of Organizational Rules are "group" rules. They have been the standard since the dawn of human organizations. They have covered every sort of human governing organization throughout all of history. The group rules promote the safety and prerogatives of one group or another. The group can be tribal, monarchical, ethnic, racial, religious, socialist, dictatorial, fascist, or mafia-like. Unfortunately, group type organizations tend to be nepotistic, become corrupt, and rely on power rather than the law. They also produce a category of "others" who are not in the group and can be treated differently.

Monarchies or aristocracies are run under group rules and have been the dominant forms of organization for most of history. The monarch or aristocratic leaders determined the laws and reserved final say for themselves. Maintenance of a good impression on the monarch has been the only assurance of position and property. One's birth status meant almost everything. Without constitutions and enforced codified rights, one's reputation with the powerful, or power itself, was most important. A few exceptional lower class individuals could work their way up into group hierarchies.

All the monotheisms taught that every individual was equal before God. However, in this life, Jewish leaders, the Catholic Church, and Muslim imams have felt that the preservation of their group or tribe was existentially important. To survive, the group or tribe demanded loyalty and viewed everyone else as "others" who were less important and unequal. They were not greatly interested in the promotion of individual rights, opinions, and options. Loyalty, orthodoxy, and conformity were valued and enforced.

Individual: Organization and Culture

The other type of Organizational Rules highlights the "individual" and is generally involved in a liberal democracy. It grants the individual human rights of freedom of speech, religion, press, the vote, and habeas corpus (justice) to all citizens. Historically, it is very recent. As mentioned previously the first codification of individual rights occurred in 1791 with the addition of the Bill of Rights. The effort was incomplete and hypocritical due to slavery, racism, and the lack of voting for women and minorities. It did set a standard to work towards and provided a mechanism to get there.

Individual type culture thinks that a protected and enfranchised individual will control corruption, help ensure justice, support fair markets, and defend the enterprise. Additionally, the individual is allowed to pursue personal ideas of happiness within mutually agreed cultural restraints. For the purposes of this paper the most important aspect of Individual Rights is the separation of religion and state. The state should not allow a religious group to harm its citizens for perceived religious infractions.

The Monotheisms and Organizational Rules

The Jews are very group oriented. They have about 613 various types of rules or laws in the Tanakh and Talmud. They are a mixture of Moral Rules, General Admonitions, a few Organizational Rules, and many Religious Rules. Jewish scholars have been studying their meaning and application for several thousand years. Very importantly Judaism refers only to Jewish people. They don't plan on ruling the world. They are charged by their God to maintain their faith and serve as an example, not to dominate world government. Today in the state of Israel orthodox religious guidelines are only followed in domestic law such as marriage, inheritance, and divorce. The male must consent to divorce, and people can only marry people of the same religion. Other than these domestic laws, the state is not involved in enforcing Religious Rules.

The most important Christian Organizational Rule is Jesus' separation of church and state. All Christians use the Old Testament (Tanakh) and the New Testament as guides with an unstated emphasis on the latter. The New Testament has relatively few Organizational Rules.

Christians think that a nation composed of Christians is the best form of government because the citizens will honor and support an honest approach to government and a tolerant approach to each other. They try to convert the world to Christianity. They are not interested in coercion concerning religion. Separation of church and state is fine with most of them.

Jesus advised his followers to be kind and forgiving toward each other, to believe that he was the Son of God, to separate church and state, and to spread his message of brother/sisterhood. Besides requiring belief, Jesus' Religious Rules included instructions that his followers baptize people, pray the Lord's Prayer (78), and observe communion (Catholic Mass). There were no punishments on earth for neglecting these actions. That is just about the entire extent of Jesus' Organizational and Religious Rules. The pieties of prayer, fasting, and alms giving were generally personal and are observed in private. (Matthew 6:1-18) (7)

Jesus' Organization Rules instructed his followers to spread the "good news" of forgiveness in his teachings. These teachings encouraged tolerance, prioritized forgiveness, helped the disadvantaged, and avoided judging "others". Rome would take care of political matters, criminal law, and personal safety. God would take care of religious issues. For Jesus, the kingdom of heaven was close, and the experience of this truth could eliminate fear and set us free. "The kingdom of heaven is within." (Luke 17:21), and "You shall know the truth, and the truth shall set you free" (John 8:32).

Islam is more group oriented and has some Organizational Rules in the Qur'an and even more in the Hadith. Very importantly the Qur'an clearly states that "There should be no compulsion in religion" (Qur'an 2:256). Most modern Western Muslims share this approach. However, according to Pew polling, many Muslims worldwide hope for a world where Islam is in the majority and the nations are under some form of Sharia law which includes some degree of public piety conforming to Religious Rules. (31)

Organizationally one can generally say that Jews are advised to maintain their faith and be an example, Christians are advised to spread their faith [32], and Muslims are advised to defend their faith [33].

The various religious texts give the following Organizational Rules.

1. Usury (charging interest when lending money). The Hebrew Scriptures, the Old Testament Christian scriptures, and the Qur'an forbid usuary. Usury at that time meant the charging of any interest. Today it more commonly means charging excessive interest. [34] There is no mention of usury in the New Testament, and, in the Parable of the Talents in Matthew 25:14-30, Jesus seems to condone profit making in loaning money. [35]

2. Private property. All the texts recognize, endorse, and protect private property. [36]

3. Justice. Equal justice for rich and poor is clearly and repeatedly emphasized in all the monotheistic texts.

4. Women's status. There are several rules in the Tanakh, some by Paul and Peter in the New Testament, and a few in the Qur'an that limit women's freedom of action [37

   Jesus doesn't mention any limitations for women.

5. Homosexuality. Some verses in all the texts advise against it. The Tanakh or Old Testament in Leviticus chapter 20, verse 13 reads "If a man has sexual relations with a man as one does with a woman, both have done what is detestable. They are to be put to death; their blood will be on their own heads." Paul says that they will not go to heaven. Jesus doesn't mention it. The Qur'an says that they are degenerate. The Hadith are much harsher. [38]

6. Proselyting. Jews don't try to convert others. Christians are charged to spread their faith and baptize everyone. Many Islamic states forbid proselyting of Muslims. Muhammad does not emphasize it.

7. Political leadership. Jews were advised to obey their elders. Jesus, Paul, and Peter in the New Testament texts recommend that one

respect the nation's laws and leaders. The Qur'an 4:59 recommends obeying leaders who follow the Qur'an.

8. Voting. There are no clear rules about leadership succession. Some passages in the Tanakh (Old Testament) do advise against selecting a king. [1]. The Pope is selected by Catholic clerics. Jesus says that Peter will be the founder of his church. The question of succession divided Islam into Sunni and Shia sects. There is no overall leader or Caliph at present in Islam.

9. Habeas corpus is implied in some places, but it is not clearly spelled out except in repeated admonitions to be "just". True justice would resolve disputes fairy, provide speedy trials, and avoid excessive punishments.

Separation of religion and state

For the purposes of this book, temple/church/mosque- state separation is a most important issue. The Jews in the formation of Israel followed the example of liberal democracy that came out of the Western Enlightenment. Today in the Jewish state of Israel, the religion and the state are mostly separated. The Israelis are not interested in prosecuting heresy, blasphemy, or apostasy. The incoming government currently is much more religiously conservative than any previous government. Some things may change, but the Israeli constitution generally separates temple and state. The Israeli state is charged with judging and enforcing the Moral Rules in a constitutional framework of individual rights. Domestic law concerning marriage and inheritance follows rather strict Jewish religious lines. There are some recent Israeli laws that forbid attacking another's religion. These were designed to decrease friction between Jews and Muslims. In Israel the different treatment of the Palestinians concerning land and citizenship are separate and complicated political matters. They are not directly concerned with Religious Rules.

In the 4th century, the Christian Church was embraced by the Roman Empire. Christianity became the official religion. It was formalized and installed in Western Civilization by the Catholic Church. The Catholic

74

Church was a central political power in Europe for about 1200 years until changes in the 16th century caused by the Reformation and Enlightenment finally began to install Jesus' advice to separate church and state, Matthew 22:21.

Muslim majority nations have large numbers of clerics and citizens that want to join mosque and state by having religious review of all laws under some form of Sharia law. There are numerous political parties such as the Muslim Brotherhood which are clearly religious. The effects of Sharia law play out differently in the various Muslim majority nations. 16 nations have laws stating that the head of government must be a Muslim [39].

Group Organization and Rules in the Monotheisms

In a group oriented society or nation, everyone else is an "other". The Jewish texts are very group oriented and are speaking to the Jewish community exclusively. The "others" are not to be persecuted, but rather guided by the example set by the Jewish nation. The Jews are not interested in converting others. They are called by their God to do two things: preserve the tribe and serve as an example to the world. In the Book of Isaiah 42:6 in the Tanakh it states, "I the Lord have called unto you in righteousness, and have taken hold of your hand, and submitted you as the people's covenant, as a light unto the nations". And in Deuteronomy 14:2, "For you are a people holy to the Lord your God, and the Lord has chosen you to be a people of his own possession, out of all the nations that are on the face of the earth". Some recently elected religiously conservative Israeli politicians agree with Meir Kahane and think that all Arabs in Israel should go, and if they stay in Israel, they should have no vote. [39a]

Paul in the New Testament is dealing with groups in the formation of churches. He gave almost no organizational rules. He is very pragmatic when talking of others. "When I wrote to you before, I told you not to associate with people who indulge in sexual sin. But I wasn't talking about unbelievers who indulge in sexual sin, or are greedy, or cheat people, or worship idols. You would have to leave this world to avoid people like that." 1 Corinthians 5:9-10 (New Living Translation). In his letter in the Book of Hebrews 13:16, he recommended pooling money in one church.

Protestants all think that they are in the right church or group, but it is a personal decision for each to make. They are advised not to judge the decisions of others. Jesus states in Matthew 7:1-3: "Judge not lest ye be judged. For with what judgment ye judge, ye shall be judged and with what measure ye mete, it shall be measured to ye again. And why beholdest thou the mote that is in thy brother's eye, but consider not the beam that is in thine own eye?" (King James Version) The Protestants became much more oriented to the individual as demonstrated by their willingness to splinter continually without significant conflict. Their splintering certainly eliminated the development of a large Protestant power base except in the common drive for individual rights.

Jesus did not produce an organizational or hierarchical group. He did say to his apostle Peter."…I tell you that you are Peter, and on this rock, I will build my church, and the gates of Hades will not overcome it" (Matthew 16:18). Peter is a derivative of the Greek word for "rock". Peter's letters in the Christian Bible do not give much organizational information. For the most part everyone was equal. In his letters in the New Testament, Saint Peter tolerated Roman type slavery, advised obeying the Roman authorities, and gave lesser positions to women. The Catholic Church and the Pope were the sole authority in Christianity from about 350 C.E. to the Reformation in the 16th century. They decided doctrine and enforced conformity.

Jesus treats almost everyone equally and individually. He is not explicit about structuring a group. Except for hypocrites, there are few people that are to be avoided. When Jesus is found speaking to a Samaritan woman at a well (John 4:6-30), his disciples were amazed.

At that time most Jews avoided the Samaritans as heretics. It was very unusual for a male Jew like Jesus to converse with a Samaritan woman. As mentioned previously, not only does he talk to her, but he tells her that he is the Messiah who was prophesized in the Book of Isaiah and that he will save the world. Also, Jesus dines with sinners and tax collectors (Mark 2:15-17). He has charged his followers to spread the "good word", not to vanquish others. Consequently, of necessity his converts mingle with all sorts of people.

Muhammad is very much involved in the preservation of his religious group or tribe. Organizational Rules were scattered about in the texts. To preserve the group, Muslim men can marry non-Muslims, but Muslim women are forbidden to marry non-Muslim men. In several places in the Qur'an, Muslims are advised to avoid contact with other groups. Qur'an 3:28 says, "Those who believe should not take unbelievers as their friends." Qur'an 3:118 says, "Believers do not make friends with any but your own people. They will spare no pains to corrupt you." One verse in the Qur'an 48:29 says, "Muhammad is the Prophet of God; those who are with him are severe with infidels but compassionate among themselves." Contextualization to a time of great danger to the tribe is important. Islam is in no danger of extinction.

Muhammad was clearly dealing with tribal survival when the Qur'an 2:190 says, "Fight for the sake of God those that fight against you, but do not attack them first. God does not love the aggressors. Slay them wherever you find them. Drive them out of the places from which they drove you." This competes with some Qur'anic passages that are more compassionate concerning "others" such as 23:95 which says "Requite evil with good." The verses advising an active and vigorous defense will have to be contextualized to a time when Islam was young and vulnerable. This is no longer the case.

Islam grew rapidly from the seventh through the tenth centuries. It appears that many conquered peoples adopted Islam rather easily. There were taxes on non-Muslims called "*jizya*" which were justified as payment for protection and services. One could avoid that tax by converting to Islam or joining the military.

The Moral Rules and Organizational Rules provided by Sharia were often an improvement over the empires that Islam encountered. The Religious Rules under Sharia promoted a group approach and did cause some problems for believers of other religions. A list of the restrictions on Christians is available in Endnote #[40]. Forced conversion was not usually demanded by Muhammad. Some Islamic Sharia law schools say that an infidel cannot testify against a Muslim. [41] Today Muslim women cannot marry non-Muslims under Sharia law in most Muslim majority areas. [42]

Moses, the Jewish prophets, the Catholic hierarchy, and Muhammad were trying to preserve their group or tribe. They defined loyalty to the group by adherence to the Moral Rules, Organizational Rules, and Religious Rules. The price of membership in the group was a pious conformity to their vision of God and their Religious Rules. If you did not outwardly conform, you were a heretic, infidel, or apostate. Death for apostate Jews who promote other gods was recommended in Tanakh, Deuteronomy 13:6-9 [43]. This has not been enforced by a Jewish organization since the Maccabees revolted and took power in Israel from the Seleucid Empire just before the time of Christ. The New Testament doesn't mention punishment for sacrilege or apostasy other than eternal damnation by God. Apostasy is not punished by death in the Qur'an but it is punishable by death in Hadith, Bukhari 9:83:17, "The blood of a Muslim who confesses that none has the right to be worshipped but Allah and that I am His Apostle, cannot be shed except in three cases: In *Qisas* (retribution) for murder, a married person who commits illegal sexual intercourse and the one who reverts from Islam (apostate) and leaves the Muslims." Death for apostasy is in the laws of numerous Muslim countries today. This clearly conflicts with the Qur'an (2:256) where it explicitly states that "There should be no compulsion in religion". Despite this, statements by every Sharia law school endorse compulsion and promote harsh punishment for apostasy and blasphemy.

Contextualizing to a time of existential threat can reconcile most of these conflicting passages.

As for central authority, Jews don't recognize any authority other than the Tanakh and Talmud. On religious matters Catholics recognize the central authority of the Catholic hierarchy or the Pope and trust them to interpret the scriptures. Protestant Christianity is not hierarchically organized. There is no overall authority except the Bible. Jesus' teachings could be recognized as a form of central authority for some, but he gives few rules. In Islam, Muslims follow the Qur'an, the Hadith, and various Caliphs, particularly the first four "Rightly Guided" Caliphs who were leaders for the first 30 years after Muhammad's death. Other Caliphs had varying degrees of political and religious authority for hundreds of years. Concerning the Right Guided Caliphs, the Sunni believe all four were divinely inspired. The Shia think that only one, Muhammad's cousin Ali, was divinely inspired. The Rightly Guided Caliphs' rulings are still studied in the various law schools.

The Jews were organized and charged by their God to be an example to the rest of the world, not to run it. (Isaiah 42:6). Christians are charged by Jesus to baptize and to spread the "good word" of forgiveness and love, not to be the government (Matthew 28:16-20). Islam's texts present a diverse picture. Muslims were not clearly charged to convert the world. The texts seem to recognize that the beauty and truth of Islam's message is pure and would eventually lead to world conversion. Terrorist groups like Al-Qaeda and ISIS talk of a militant world domination.

The word Islam means "submit". One submits to the word of God. The numerous Sharia law schools have different opinions about submission. The problem is submission to whose interpretation? How pious must one become? How much forgiveness is recommended? The Islamic texts do demand loyalty. Once one becomes a Muslim, in the conservative Muslim world, leaving is almost impossible without severe consequences.

Organizational Rules mentioned in all the monotheisms include very clear demands for justice and mercy. Justice generally implies that one gets what one deserves. Mercy implies that one is treated better than one deserves. The Jewish prophet Micah advises all to "act justly and to love mercy and to walk humbly with your God.". In the Tanakh in the Book of Leviticus, Jews are clearly advised to be just to the rich and the poor. In personal issues, Jesus emphasizes the very difficult task of interpersonal forgiveness or mercy rather than justice. Jesus' advice to Peter to forgive one's brother "seventy tines seven" is very difficult. Jesus does not explicitly address governmental justice. For Jesus it is Rome's job to justly punish those who lie, steal, murder, or break the organizational laws. The Qur'an is very clear that the poor and the rich should be treated justly. Additionally, all faiths are advised to give support for the poor through taxes or alms.

Rules in the Monotheisms: Individual Rights

The individual rights of speech, press, religion, habeas corpus, and the vote are relatively recent issues. Most of them are not specifically mentioned in the texts, but the texts all clearly recommend justice for everyone. True justice would involve individual rights. The Individual Rights are discussed here in sequence.

Freedom of Speech and Press

A principal use of freedom of speech is to control corruption and nepotism. Corruption and nepotism are the biggest problems in all political organizations, countries, economies, and societies. These problems can only be controlled if individual citizens feel free to report to an honest press, judiciary, and police. To report these problems a "watchdog" is needed in society, and an empowered and safe individual protected by individual human rights of freedom of speech and press would seem to be the only long-term answer. If a particular group's desires are more important than the individual's freedom of speech and press, unreported corruption will eventually destroy faith in the government.

Freedom of speech does not extend to lies, threats, and plots. Jews, Christians, and Muslims are all instructed to be truthful, honest, and to avoid false witness. The Ten Commandments state this succinctly for Jews and Christians. Jesus clearly supports these commandments. Muhammad's discussion of types of permissible lying has been addressed previously. White lies are permitted. Lying to avoid persecution for one's religion or to defend the religion is acceptable.

Where religion is concerned, freedom of speech or press can be limited by charges of blasphemy. This is generally defined as speech that defames or insults God, religious founders, or dogmas. Charges of blasphemy can be very serious in theocratic states. Jewish and Islamic texts tell their members to avoid blasphemy and have punishments recommended for those who do blaspheme. Jesus mentions blasphemy only once and says those who "blaspheme the holy spirit" will not be forgiven by God. He recommends no punishment on earth, but they will not go to heaven. 40% of the world's countries have laws against blasphemy in some form or another. These laws are only very rarely used, and when they are, most of those instances are in theocratic Islamic states, particularly Saudi Arabia, Pakistan, Iran, and Indonesia.

Freedom of Religion

Freedom of Religion in this book means one can worship as one wants. Theocratic states often have rules saying that one cannot leave the principal religion. Apostasy is forbidden. In Leviticus in the Jewish Tanakh, stoning is recommended for those who leave the faith. Jesus and Paul don't mention any punishments on earth, but apostates will probably be denied eternal life or access to heaven. The Qur'an and Hadith are ambivalent. Some verses say there is no compulsion in religion. Other statements in the Hadith propose punishing apostates with death. Again, contextualization to times of existential threat is needed.

Habeas Corpus

Habeas Corpus is not specifically mentioned, but justice is clearly recommended by all the texts.

The Vote

The religious texts give no clear organizational advice on how to select or change government, leadership, or policies. The individual right to participate with voting is not mentioned. Moses, Isaiah, Jesus, Paul, and Muhammad did not address it. Today most Jews and Christians allow the secular state to change government by holding elections. Many Islamic majority states have elections but have religious restriction on who can run for office. The Shia/Sunni schism was a disagreement over the means of choosing Islamic authority. Sunni thought that the religious rulers or Caliphs should be voted in by groups of elites. The Shia thought that the leader must be a descendant of Muhammad. The concept of Caliph is not used currently. The last Caliph was in Istanbul. When Kemal Ataturk took power in 1924, he abolished the Caliphate.

A friend recently said, "Democracy is overrated. The populace is so ignorant of current affairs, economics, and history in general, that it can make really bad voting decisions." This is like Churchill's statement, "The best argument against democracy, is a five-minute conversation with the average voter." I would agree that many citizens are poorly informed and sometimes make bad decisions, but if they do not think that they have a say in government, they will make many worse decisions. Cynicism about government leads to dishonesty, corruption and, ultimately, a lack of faith that destroys the institutions. To quote Churchill again, "The only government worse than democracy is all the others."

At times, people, including Thomas Jefferson, spoke about periodic small revolutions for the secular governments as if they were useful or necessary to maintain their vitality. However, revolutions are usually bloody and today involve much more than ousting a leader. When thinking about revolution in liberal democracies today, it is useful to remember that, if the revolution produces a very good government, the result will probably be another liberal democracy, hopefully more honest. Revolution in a functioning democracy is only necessary if the government is corrupt and interfering with the voting process. Steven Daisley says it well, "There is corruption in America, but America is not corrupt. There is poverty and injustice in America, but revolution provides no answers." The liberal democracy has had the elasticity to improve in all its problem areas with only a few destructive periods. The Civil War being the most destructive. The democratic debates about solutions are vigorous and open. Two big problems in capitalist democracy in this electronic age are that the money concentrated in a rich elite can have too much influence in the elections and that irresponsible conspiracy theories are too easily spread. If an unbiased supreme court does not void obvious gerrymandering, ruthless majorities can gain control of state government permanently. Corruption of the voting process is currently charged but unproven. Insoluble issues like agreement on abortion access and the proper amounts of taxes and reparations will plague all democracies.

Like the Pope in the Catholic Church, Islam had central leadership such as a Caliph for most of its history. There were Popes in Rome and Byzantium. The Caliph began in Arabia, moved to Damascus, peaked in Baghdad, moved to Egypt, and finally to Istanbul. The Caliphs were political and religious leaders and were generally chosen by elites. Sultan was a title of political power like a king. It arose in the 10th century. Historically, mosque and state were never separated until the fall of the Ottoman Empire at the end of WWI. After WWI Kemal Ataturk organized the Turkish army and was able to defeat Western attempts to colonize Turkey. In 1923 Ataturk became president of Turkey. He wanted to modernize and secularize the government, education, and the courts. He proceeded to disband the Caliphate and eliminate Sharia courts. He took the Muslim clerics out of education and popularized secular clothes and democratic government.

Much of the rest of the Islamic world was colonized after WWI and was not independent until after WWII. In the 1950's as various nations threw off colonialism there were numerous secular movements in the Muslim majority nations. Many of the states formed from the Ottoman empire tried forms of secular organization including democracy, Pan Arab nationalism, semi-socialist Baathism, and socialism. Due to corruption, nepotism, and religious turmoil, most of these nations failed to produce economic success. Most of the economic success that they have known has been due to the oil found in the area. Today most Muslim majority states hold elections, but in the more orthodox areas, the candidates must be approved by religious bodies and/or the laws must agree with someone's definition of Sharia. Iran, Saudi Arabia, and Pakistan are essentially theocracies. The clerics must approve those who run for office and their policies. Indonesia is becoming more theocratic under the influence of thousands of the Wahabi *madrassas.*

Current Individual Rights.

Currently many governments list the individual rights in their organizing documents. However, some are unable to secure the benefits because the population, the judiciary, and the police are corrupt and nepotistic. As US President and founder John Adams said about the US Organizational Rules, "Our constitution was made only for a moral and religious (Christian) people. It will not function with any other". It hasn't always been fair to women, labor organizations, and minorities, but it has allowed for improvement. Good government needs good rules and cooperating citizens. The citizens are much more likely to be compliant and law abiding if the laws protect their individual rights and their safety. If the citizens feel that corruption and nepotism are robbing them of their opportunities or freedom of expression, they will subvert the system whenever possible.

People today say that the government should not take away their individual "freedom of action". However, if misuse of "freedom of action" disrupts the community by being irresponsible, it can and should be

84

curtailed. Freedom demands responsible action. It does not extend to lies and physical threats. In speaking about individual rights, John S. Mill and others say one should not be allowed to be a public "nuisance". "Nuisance" like "freedom" is always up for definition and redefinition in the discussion of rights. Individuals' rights give us freedom of action, but not a license to undermine our essential institutions or continually irritate each other.

Justice and Social Justice in the Organizational Rules

Justice is always an area of concern in the texts. Classically justice refers to assurance of a fair outcome in a dispute or a fair trial if one is accused. For the purposes of this book, social justice demands that everyone should have an equal chance to succeed economically. This usually involves a decent education, a safe neighborhood, a job, and a fair and speedy resolution of disputes and accusations (habeas corpus).

Alms, charity, and social justice for the poor and disabled are completely rational and have been concerns since the beginning of human history. In all the ancient Mediterranean and Middle Eastern cultures, charity was encouraged. In ancient Egypt, "It was written that Egyptian deities expected any person seeking immortality to swear that they had never denied food to the starving, drink to the thirsty, or clothing to the ragged".[44] Historically, individual giving was usually publicized to bring honor and recognition to the giver. Also, philanthropic societies have organized in every significant civilization to take care of the poor. Organizationally the Roman emperor Augustus gave corn to those citizens who could not pay for it. The Song Dynasty (960-1279) in China provided retirement homes and public clinics. Giving to the poor and disabled is required by all the great religions and their prophets.

Many of the recurring debates in the capitalist democracies revolve around how much to tax and how much welfare for the poor and unemployed to provide. Adequate welfare would seem to be a moral imperative for those who are unable to find work or who cannot work. It is felt that if welfare benefits are too great, they will discourage initiative and diminish the work ethic in the citizens. That is being tested in the United States now. Generally, welfare and social assistance programs have increased over time as the West has become more prosperous and more concerned. It would probably be much more helpful to the poor to provide universal healthcare, childcare, free education, jobs for all, and/or universal basic income. Universal healthcare in the is available in almost all the liberal democracies except the US. Problematically, it is proving to be more difficult to fund and deliver as medical technology increases.

As mentioned above all the texts promote "justice" repeatedly. In the Tanakh, Micah 6:6-8, it says, "And what does the Lord require of you? To act justly and to love mercy and to walk humbly with your God." Leviticus 19:15 "You shall do no injustice in court. You shall not be partial to the poor or defer to the great, but in righteousness shall you judge your neighbor." Also, in the Tanakh, Isaiah the prophet says, "Here is my Servant whom I have chosen, the One I love, in whom I delight; I will put my Spirit on Him, and He will proclaim justice to the nations." That statement by Isaiah is taken by Christians and Jesus himself to refer to Jesus as this savior (messiah) who would bring justice (Matthew 12:18). Justice would certainly include individual human rights.

Jesus uses the specific word "justice" only once. In Luke 11:42 Jesus says, "Woe to you Pharisees, because you give God a tenth of your mint, rue, and all other kinds of garden herbs, but you neglect justice and the love of God." In Matthew 7:12, Jesus doesn't use the word "justice", but his emphasis on the General Admonition "Do to others what you would have them do to you" seems to cover justice clearly.

The Qur'an, 4:135, says, "Oh, you who have believed, be persistently standing firm in justice, witnesses for Allah, even if it be against yourselves or parents and relatives. Whether one is rich or poor, Allah is more worthy of both." Also, the Qur'an says that everyone with money must give alms to the poor. This is called *zakat,* and it is one of the Five Pillars of Islam. No system is outlined.

Socialism and Capitalism

The monotheistic texts don't give much advice on the capitalist and socialist economic systems. The texts appear to assume that the state is capitalist because private property is endorsed in all the texts. Socialism did not even exist as an option until the 19th century. There is a lot of scripture in all the texts advising that we give money or goods to the poor. This sounds more like philanthropy and welfare, but it could be describing a socialist approach. Justice in land use would seem to favor a more socialist approach. In Jesus' teachings, the parable of the talents endorses capitalist commerce and investment (Matthew 25:14-30) [35]. In one instance Paul does tell his parishioners to pool their goods and money (Hebrews 13:16). However, he doesn't go into detail about the procedure and only mentions it in one instance concerning one church. In addressing the consequences of excessive concentration of wealth in individuals Jesus says, "Again I tell you; it is easier for a camel to go through the eye of a needle than for someone who is rich to enter the kingdom of God" Matthew 19:24. The Qur'an in verse 2:177 says, "Righteousness is not that you turn your faces toward the east or the west, but [true] righteousness is [in] one who believes in Allah , the Last Day, the angels, the Book, and the prophets and gives wealth, in spite of love for it, to relatives, orphans, the needy, the traveler, those who ask [for help], and for freeing slaves; [and who] establishes prayer and gives zakah; [those who] fulfill their promise when they promise; and [those who] are patient in poverty and hardship and during battle. Those are the ones who have been true, and it is those who are the righteous."

Capitalism and socialism are the two principal organizational arrangements that governments can employ to run the economy. The benefits and problems associated with each are addressed in countless articles, books, and theses. They would fill a large library. Some religious people think that socialism's equal sharing of goods represents the proper way for a truly concerned society to approach economics. They feel that socialism is "on the side of the angels". Below is a brief exploration of these two options as they are addressed in the holy texts.

Capitalism is an economic system based on the private ownership of the means of production and their operation for profit. Most capitalist systems have some elements which are owned or operated by the state such as the roads, rivers, the military, fire departments, regulatory bodies, etc. A capitalist state must be highly regulated to avoid monopolies that limit competition or exploit the workers. Capitalists say that socialists have noble goals, but that socialist means are totalitarian, and socialist programs don't work to produce wealth and innovation. They think that capitalism within a meritocracy consisting of good taxation of the rich and adequate welfare for the poor is a much better option. Adequate taxation and welfare are contentious issues.

Capitalism allows creativity and creativity does create inequalities of outcome. Any system that allows individual creativity will create inequalities.

Socialism is a political and economic theory of social organization which advocates that the means of production, distribution, and exchange should be owned or regulated by the community. "Private property is theft" as put forth by P.J. Proudhon (1840). The elected government of a socialist community would carry out this distribution. The state would own everything. Socialists have noble goals of equity and righteous concerns for the lower classes and the poor. I generally think of socialism as a straightforward expression of concern for one's disadvantaged fellow humans. It has helped some populations to come out of abject poverty and illiteracy. "From each according to his ability. To each according to his need" is a wonderful ideal. Karl Marx popularized this slogan but did not originate it. The problems with socialism include the brutality required for its installation and maintenance, the stifling effects of its bureaucracy, and the inefficiencies of its economics. Capitalism's problems include insufficient welfare, big business's poor treatment of its workers, and vast inequities in wealth that can influence politics and the allocation of resources.

The capitalist approach to equity is termed the "welfare state". It was first used to describe England in the 1940's. The welfare state in the US was begun by Franklin D. Roosevelt's New Deal in the 1930's, and reached its current form with Lyndon Johnson's Great Society in the 1960's. The important parts of this legislation have included a minimum wage (25 cents per hour at first), retirement plans, Social Security pensions, Medicare, home loans, farm loans, labor regulations, the GI bill, disability insurance, Civil Rights legislation, and, ultimately, Affirmative Action programs as reparations for past racist transgressions. These benefits were not initially or fully available to African Americans until the Civil Rights legislation of the 1960's.

Both capitalism and socialism claim to be meritocracies, where one does not have to become brutal or corrupt to advance and flourish. Exams and education play a definitive role in determining one's options in both systems. To be fair and just a meritocracy based on education must provide equal educational opportunities for all people. Diligent work is the other way to improve one's status. Of course, luck concerning one's parents also plays a huge role in all these systems and their results.

In the larger sense most of the West is a meritocracy based in education and hard work. Equality of education depends on many factors. Healthcare, childcare, livable income, and family support play a large role in educational opportunity. The US is behind the other Western style democracies in that it doesn't provide healthcare and childcare. Lots of money and many different programs have been tried in efforts to improve minority education. They are part of an effort to help but have not been greatly effective. The breakdown of the African Americans family has been a serious problem. The fact that over 70% of African American children in the US are born out of wedlock has had a significant effect on family support and educational success [46]. Analisa Merelli's article "The US has a lot of money, but it does not look like a developed country," in *Quartz* on March 10, 2017, outlines its problems [45a].

Some of the family dissolution is due to the federal welfare program AFDC, Aide to Families with Dependent Children. It gave financial aide to women having children but paid them less if a male was in the household. This effectively subsidized children and discouraged marriage. Glenn Loury a African American economist, academic, and author, points out that lack of "social capital", similar to what is called "connections", is a serious problem for African Americans. They may get an education but know very few people who can get them a job. Today the hypersensitivity and touchiness in current interracial relations makes some interactions difficult.

Racism's legacy of poor schools, poverty-stricken neighborhoods, and a youth culture including gangs and drugs means that many poor minorities will not have an equal chance to move up in the capitalist meritocracy. A complete lack of handgun control means that it will also be very dangerous [46a]. Possibly the educational piece of the problem could be partially addressed by much smaller classes in ghetto schools, perhaps six students in a class for at least the first six grades.[47] Under that scenario, the school would serve almost as a family which could closely monitor the child's welfare. Classes of 24 or more students in problem areas makes education very difficult. It would only involve about 10-15% of the schools, and it may be cheaper than the subsequent welfare, law enforcement, and prisoner expenses.

Usually, a socialist meritocracy tries to educate all equally up to the early teen years when examinations are used to direct the students into different fields. Socialism has certainly improved literacy in poor countries.

There are several forms of socialism ranging from today's democratic socialism to strict Marxist communism. Democratic socialism ideally permits change through the electoral process. Theoretically it can allow varying amounts of personal property in a mixture of capitalism and socialism. The Scandinavian countries are frequently mentioned as example of "democratic socialism", but in truth they are capitalist economies with large welfare and social security benefits.

Socialism arose shortly after the democratic revolutions began in the Western monarchies in the late 1700s and 1800s. It accompanied the Industrial Revolution. Working conditions in the early Industrial Revolution were terrible. Slavery and serfdom were still present in many areas. For 100 years there were numerous uprisings all over Europe. In 1848 there were democratic and socialist-like revolts in virtually all the monarchies that dominated Europe. Engels and Marx's form of socialism called Communism appeared with the publication of the Communist Manifesto in 1848.

In the 1880's, Germany, under Chancellor Bismarck, passed reforms called "state socialism". The reforms were enacted mainly to control the increasing number of socialists in the German parliament. Bismarck's reforms included health insurance, disability insurance, and an old age pension at age 70. He banned work on Sunday and lowered the workday to 11 hours for women. The life expectancy in Germany then was 45 years. The reforms worked, and Germany did not become socialist.

Corruption is a major problem, if not "the" problem, that prevents the upward evolution of the large number of nations in the "developing world". One critic called these countries "the never to be developed world" because of their inability to control corruption. Perhaps socialism's best attribute is that its totalitarian nature can get corruption and inequalities under better control in very corrupt and crime ridden countries. The results are mixed. Totalitarian Communism in Russia, China, and Cuba got rid of hereditary elites, controlled gangster-like corruption, and nationalized all the land. They made the people safer, educated them, fed them, and gave them medical care. Unfortunately, socialism brought in its own form of corruption in the form of communist party nepotism and oppression of speech and activity. Russians had to have internal passports to travel in Russia and 80% of the peasants were denied these passports until 1974. They were basically serfs to the communist regime. All these changes came at an enormous cost in human lives. Some estimates approach 80 million. When the deaths of millions under communism are brought up, some dedicated communists say that "The real communists knew that we would have to sacrifice a generation." This brutality was dismissed by Stalin when he said, "One death is a tragedy. A million deaths are a statistic."

Once the people were fed, housed, given health care, educated, and land redistribution carried out, the governments began to use market type economics to improve their wealth and productivity. Russia ended up as a corrupt capitalist oligarchy. China has adopted autocratic capitalism (a form of totalitarian mercantilism) which is currently improving China's economy. Hopefully, the growth in wealth may create a larger middle class that demands more individual human rights and blunts imperial aggression against other nations. Cuba has had much success in getting rid of poverty, controlling corruption, and educating its people. Its economy is not improving, and one of its largest trading partners, China, recommends that it increase the size of its market economy. Venezuela's socialist revolution is not doing well. It is unable to control gang activity and is rated the most crime ridden country in the world at present. After controlling corruption, a socialist government could morph to a more market based economy to encourage innovation and production like China has done.

In the third world the questions around colonialism and exploitation are real and very present. How much of a country's land and resources should be owned by foreign corporations? How much should be privately "owned" in any way is a related question. How essential is land reform? Capitalist government could tend to break up excessively large holdings over time with adequate taxation of hereditary landed elites.

Francis Fukuyama's *End of history and the Last Man* is an argument for capitalism. Fukuyama says that socialism does not give an acceptable outlet for the organizational and entrepreneurial energy of gifted individuals. Capitalist democracy gives those with exceptional energy and charisma an outlet in that they can make money, innovate, and contribute creatively to society's improvement. They don't have to become corrupt, use force, or begin revolutions to become effective or prosperous. They must highly regulated and taxed to avoid using monopolies and privilege to unjustly amass wealth and power at the expense of others.

Economic discussions bring up the question, "Should the US or the West interfere in nations involved in socialist solutions?" Does the US government have any right or obligation to intervene in other nations to protect capitalist business interests? The US usually becomes involved for several reasons.

1. First the socialists take land from the hereditary elites and redistribute it. They also nationalize varying amounts of heavy industry, some of which are held by capitalist corporations. All this change involves force or brutality of some sort.

2. Secondly, socialists are totalitarian, and they eliminate freedom of speech and press.

3. Thirdly, it seems that no true socialist will be happy until every country is socialized. Socialism always wants to spread to other nations. To the socialist, socialism seems so right that it must be imposed everywhere that inequality exists, and inequality is everywhere.

Socialism's combination of nationalization of industry, forceful reallocation of land ownership, lack of freedom of speech, and the potential to foment revolution in neighboring states seems to spur the West to actively oppose socialist revolutions. Different administrations deal with it in different ways. Should the US help communist Cuba? Socialists in Haiti? Are the Cuban people better off as a whole? Yes. Should the Cuban government now allow some areas of capitalist practice? It might be a good economic idea.

Some philosophers and organizers have noted that "haste" might be the biggest problem in capitalist democracies. It is wise to bring the people to understand the desired changes rather than cramming very "progressive" cultural ideas down the throat of an unready populous. Radicals and progressives are always unhappy with the rate and extent of change. If, however, radical progressive minorities gain power and move too far ahead of the people, the more traditional masses may be willing to get rid of the entire democratic system by supporting some demagogue who seems powerful enough to oppose the radical progressives.

Individual Culture and Civilization

The word "Culture" describes how people approach each other and their values. Another definition of culture is "the customs, arts, social institutions, religious affiliations, achievements, and values of a particular society". Everyone is involved in some sort of culture. Usually, the type of culture determines how one reasons politically and religiously. As mentioned above, "group" culture reasons that individual rights will destabilize or weaken their identity and cohesion. "Individual" cultures reason that protecting the rights and the prerogatives of the individual will produce the best government for the most people. Ultimately the "values" of a culture are most important and will be discussed further on.

"Culture" and "civilization" are sometimes used interchangeably. Generally, the term "civilization" is used to describe a culture that has a lasting positive organizational and philosophic effect on a large number of people. Some philosophers, historians, and archeologists think that the capitalist liberal democracies that had their origins in the Protestant Reformation and Western Enlightenment are the best types of civilization.

Western influence and values have been spread over the world by commerce, missionaries, colonization, and humanitarian efforts. Many people think that Western type liberal democracy with highly regulated capitalism is the gold standard for government. A 1969 BBC 13-part TV series titled *Civilisation [sic}, A Personal View by Kenneth Clarke* presented Western civilization as the highest form of culture, politics, and organization. At that time, it was the most expensive series that the BBC had ever produced.

For Clarke, the best examples of civilization rose in Europe out of the Middle Ages. The Middle Ages were the 1000 year period of decentralization and insecurity that followed the sack of Rome in 450 C.E. Clarke's *Civilisation* [sic] series began by mentioning the Greek democracies and the Roman Republic. He then traced the origins of Western Civilization in Europe from the late Middle Ages. In Clarke's presentation, Christian based cultures played the dominant role in creating Western civilization with its liberal democracy, scientific miracles, artistic masterpieces, vast literature, human rights, and economic successes. For Clarke, Western civilization far out shown any other competitors. He didn't deeply investigate the economic history of colonialism that helped create wealth for the West.

It is obvious that European culture between 15th and the 20th century produced the most technologically and militarily superior civilization that the world had known until then. It resulted in a wave of exploration and exploitation of native peoples and their resources. Clarke gave full attention to the horrors of slavery from an English perspective. He pointed out that Western nations were the major slave traders on the west coast of Africa. The brutality and catastrophic effects of slavery were detailed. He also pointed out that after years of supporting the horror of slavery Western nations were the first nations in the world to ban slavery. The series did not extensively explore in detail the economic and cultural problems of colonization and exploitation.

For Clarke, the Western emphasis on the freedom of individual action produced opportunity, politics, literature, philosophy, art, government, technology, and sciences that seemed to define the best parts civilization. The rest of the world was going to have to catch up. For Clarke there was one great civilizing idea, and it depended on the empowerment of compassionate reason and the assurance of individual human rights. With the Reformation and the Enlightenment, Jesus' advice was finally realized when the church was removed from political power.

With the collapse of the Roman Empire, European government decentralized and fragmented into many monarchies or aristocracies. During the Middle Ages and on into the Reformation and the Western Enlightenment every nation was grabbing what it could from every other nation. Wealth and power were essentially based on land ownership and agriculture. Cottage industries provided the tools. In the West the ownership of land was invested in various monarchies who parceled out areas for various princes and favorites. The European monarchies fought each other constantly and raced all over the globe trying to build empires. The technical and scientific achievements coming out of the Reformation and Enlightenment ranging from ship building, to improved farming practices, to steam, to metallurgy, and weapons gave the West superior power that resulted in the age of "discovery", colonization, and exploitation. They brought varying amounts of racism, brutality, and devastating diseases. The colonizers eventually brought improvements in healthcare, agriculture, world market access, technology, and the ideals of democratic government. The oppression by Western colonization, the medical advances, the evils of slavery, the democratic ideals, the devastating diseases, and the technological miracles are now being weighed in scales of justice concerning Western civilization's legacy. World history had been the story of series of empires being born and decaying, however, the Western Enlightenment ushered in a new approach to science, government, and rights. International organizations were formed in efforts to decrease conflict and exploitation. Colonization and exploitation were halted by aroused native populations and enlightened Western ideas about one's obligations to "others".

As a contemporary follow up in 2018, BBC again did a nine part TV series called, *Civilizations*. Archaeologists, philosophers, artists, historians, and moderators visited sites all over the world and highlighted the architectural, artistic, and engineering marvels that were created by various cultures other than the West. Although they created exquisite art forms, beautiful spiritual traditions, innovative engineering, and architectural work, these cultures did not create great democratizing political philosophies, wide ranging and deep literary and musical traditions, or dynamic ongoing advances in technology and science.

How did the West get so far ahead and produce so much literature, art, and science in so many areas? There are many theories. Jared Diamond, in his book *Guns, Germs and Steel,* essentially ascribes it to geographic luck. Max Weber proposes the "Protestant work ethic". Rodney Stark promotes Christianity. Ian Morris ascribes it to capitalism, and Nial Ferguson to "six killer apps". These "apps" included competition, science, property owning democracy, modern medicine, the consumer society, and the Protestant work ethic.

In the late 1800's and the first half of the 1900's Max Weber's "Protestant Work Ethic" was the prominent theory. Today, Diamond's geographical thesis is accepted by many. He pointed out that the geography of western Europe and the US with their navigable rivers and temperate climate allowed more easily for trade, safety, and food production. Varying, heavily forested terrain broken by mountains and rivers allowed for more effective defense against nomadic hoards. They had periodic severe plagues, but because of their latitude, they avoided a lot of endemic tropical diseases like malaria and schistosomiasis.

In the Western Hemisphere the indigenous people created several very highly developed civilizations, but they were devoid of draft animals such as oxen and horses. This severely limited cultivation, engineering, and movement. In Africa geography, climate, and diseases made organization difficult and limited draft animal effectiveness. Also, there were very few navigable rivers.

Because of the geographical advantages and the intellectual exploration supported by the Christian universities, Europeans were able to develop their technical skills, industries, science, and political philosophies. For Diamond, the technologically powerful and philosophically democratic European cultures, who happened to be white, were not inherently superior. They were just geographically lucky.

It seems that they were equally fortunate to have a religious founder who separated church and state. Beginning in Islam in the 13th century, conservative clerical interference in education had slowed technological, scientific, and democratic advances in the Muslim empire. On the other hand, clerical and theological power decreased greatly in the West due to the Reformation and Enlightenment. This allowed for an easier approach to innovation in all areas.

Besides geographic luck, Western culture was singularly fortunate in that its religious thought was ultimately centered in Jesus' methods. As mentioned above, Jesus often taught in parables which encouraged reasoning. He separated church and state. There were no inherent obstacles dividing faith and reason. There were no serious religious constraints on education, experimentation, philosophizing, or the exploration of nature and its laws. After the Reformation and Enlightenment scientific findings did not have to be approved by a theocracy. No one theological group had enough power to stifle innovation.

Before the Protestant Reformation the monolithic Catholic Church certainly had lots of Religious Rules and punishments that eliminated freedom of religion, inquiry, and speech. The persecutions of the Cathars, Jan Hus, Galileo, and the Inquisitions were clear reminders. It is estimated that between 1478 and 1823 the Spanish Inquisition executed between 3,000 to 30,000 people as heretics. Freed from Catholic Church oversight, the Protestant religious scholars began to explore all the options in the Biblical texts. Like their Catholic forbearers, the early Protestants tortured heretics, fought over doctrine, and hunted witches for a period. Somewhere around 15,000 witches were executed in Europe during and after the Protestant Reformation. Fortunately, they did not find in Jesus a leader promoting Religious Rules and punishments. If he had given a lot of Religious Rules or joined church and state, all speculation and scientific discovery would have been subject to theological meddling, including charges of blasphemy and heresy. This would have been especially prominent if a politically powerful clergy had felt threatened by new democratic ideals.

The teachings of Jesus endorsed separation of church and state and supported no punishments. The punishments concerning heresy, sacrilege and apostasy were ended. Religious Rules had no punitive power in the Western liberal democracies. Ultimately, sacrilege was protected by freedom of speech and heresy was reduced to dinner conversation.

After the Reformation, it took several hundred years for the Western liberal democracies to fully codify Jesus' example of emphasis on the importance of every individual. This codification occurred almost 250 years ago, and the US is still working to create the full equality of opportunity that the Bill of Rights outlined.

Individual Rights a brief history

Ultimately, the type of culture determines how one reasons. Group culture reasons that individual rights will destabilize or destroy the group's identity, cohesion, and security. On the other hand, individual cultures reason that protecting the rights and the prerogatives of the individual will produce the best, freest, and most stable government for the most people. As discussed earlier, it was not until the US government revolted against British rule and adopted the Constitution and the Bill of Rights (1791), that individual human rights of freedom of speech, press, religion, assembly, the vote, and *habeas corpus* were finally codified in a governing document. These freedoms applied to white men only. Slavery existed and women were denied the vote until the 20th century. It was recognized that individual sacrifices must be made for the organization at times. On occasion, armies must be raised, and efforts must be directed to group support during times of stress such as pandemics and weather emergencies.

Hammurabi's Code in 1752 B.C.E. contained some habeas corpus rights concerning personal safety from arbitrary imprisonment or excessive punishment. All significant government before Greece's democracy and Rome's Republic were monarchical or tribal with few individual rights. Organizational Rules concerning individual human rights were first installed by the philosophers and statesmen who created the Greek democracies and the Roman Republic. They promoted some freedom of speech and voting, but only by free males. Some rules for a fair trial, reasonable punishments, and habeas corpus were adopted.

In first century C.E. the Roman Republic fell, and Augustus became emperor. Rome lasted as an empire for about 500 years. During the Empire period much of the public democratic discussion ended. During the following Middle Ages, the Greek and Roman literature and texts about government and philosophy were lost or left out of circulation in the West until refugees from the dying Byzantine Empire arrived in the later Middle Ages. In the eleventh and twelfth centuries Aristotle and the Greeks were revisited by the great Muslim polymaths, Averroes in Spain and Avicenna in Persia. During that time, they, and the Jewish scholar Maimonides, were attempting to reconcile Greek and Roman philosophy with their respective religions. Averroes' commentaries helped spread Aristotle to European Catholic universities run by the Scholastics. These universities had evolved from the medieval Catholic cathedral and monastic schools. Also, the Irish monks and scribes had preserved some old manuscripts and helped reintroduce Greek and Roman literature to the universities in the later Middle Ages. [49]

The Christian universities run by the Scholastics highly valued dialectical reasoning and debate. For the purposes of this book, the definition of "dialectic reasoning" involves the coming together of two or more points of view who want to find the best solution to their differences and may be willing to compromise. On the other hand, participants in a "debate" usually want their position to vanquish the other side. Scholasticism was a mixture of dialectic and debate. The Catholic Church was powerful, omnipresent, and oppressive, but the discussions of the Scholastics ranged over all sorts of issues. Someone said that when Aristotle was discovered by the early Jewish and Muslim philosophers that they embraced him, and when Aristotle was approached by the Scholastics, they dissected him.

In 1517 Luther began the Protestant Reformation when he put his 95 theses on the door of his church. The Reformation began to move the Catholic church out of political power. After the Protestant Reformation, the Western Renaissance and Western Enlightenment produced philosophers who, like the Greeks, employed reason, dialectic, and debate to explore government and individual rights. Kant, Hobbes, Locke, Adam Smith, and Rousseau were predecessors to the American revolution. Hegel, John S. Mill, Marx, Engels, and others were prominent shortly afterward.

Ironically, the threats from the Islamic Ottoman empire in the 1500's probably prevented the Catholic Holy Roman Empire from concentrating its forces against the Protestants and crushing them. At that time the Muslim Ottomans were menacing the Holy Roman Empire and were defeated at the Siege of Vienna in 1529 and again at the Battle of Vienna in 1683.

Coming out of the Middle Ages the Catholic Church played a large role in government. These governments were dominated by group cultures, mostly in the form of monarchies. The monarchies were providing safety from invasion and some internal stability for commerce. After the Reformation in the 1600's each country had a dominant religion, and with a few notable exceptions, Europe was generally Catholic in the south with Protestant nations in the north. The Catholic Church and its rulings limited individual actions to varying degrees.

After the Protestant Reformation, the Christian world was experiencing an explosion of different Protestant sects. Every Protestant was alone before God, and the scriptures were the only authority, *sola scriptura*. This essentially removed the Catholic Church from authority and made every Protestant responsible for their fate. Martin Luther had little trust in the uneducated masses and would probably roll over in his grave at this insinuation that he was making every peasant a theologian. Protestants disagreed so much that no one sect became large enough to dominate any government. After attacking each other initially, the sects were being forced to live together by compromise. Internal dissent was constant within the different Protestant sects. Eventually, instead of destroying a particular sect, dissenters just left and formed another. The splintering and diversity limited the power of the Protestant clergy. Today estimates of the number of Protestant sects vary from 2,000 upward to 10,000 depending on definitions.

On the other hand, the power structure of the clergy in many predominantly Catholic, Islamic, and Eastern Orthodox nations remained unified and strong until the nineteenth century. The religious hierarchies in these nations continued to be very powerful influences in the monarchies. Powerful clerical organizations have recently taken over in several Muslim nations including Pakistan, Saudi Arabia, and Iran.

Before the liberal democracies began to emerge in the late 1700's, authoritarian government was the norm for governments. Only rare exceptions like Prussia's Frederick the Great (1712-1786) were interested in granting any degree of freedom of speech, press, religion, and assembly to their citizens. He also reformed the judiciary, allowing non-gentry to become judges and lawyers, and he eliminated judicial torture. He did not change the social order or allow a voting democracy. Frederick was a unique ruler, a benevolent monarch, and his freedoms were quickly eroded by his successor.

In the 1700's, predominantly Protestant immigrants were populating and creating a new nation in North America, most of it at the expense of indigenous peoples. At that time every nation or kingdom was attacking every weaker neighbor. When the US was colonized, the world standard for action was one of conquest. If a group or country was stronger than another, it usually took it over, by force. Initially Spain and Portugal took over much of the Western hemisphere. The US took North American land from native Indians, Spain, France, England, and Mexico. Until the League of Nations and the United Nations were formed, invasion and domination of weaker neighbors had been standard action for essentially every tribe, monarchy, and republic in history. It is still happening today to a much smaller extent.

Western civilization was the first cultural enterprise that used a reasoned dialectic process to articulate and codify some individual human rights. Most of the creation of the US Constitution occurred when the various representatives were locked in a "smoke filled room" in Philadelphia and forced to compromise. Their application was very imperfect, and, because of slavery and racism, it took a bloody Civil War and almost 200 years of political activism to pass the Civil Rights Laws that finally granted equal rights to all citizens. The US is still dealing with the residual effects of its racist history, particularly concerning economic and educational equity.

The US had no neighbors that were serious existential threats. It had no dominant organized conservative religious structure. It had a religious infrastructure that was completely fragmented because Protestantism was such an individual religion. Any overall religious structure was out of the question. In a world where every country was fighting its neighbors and religion orthodoxy was contested in all the European monarchies, North America was the perfect site to create a nation dedicated to the protection and empowerment of the individual. In essence, to get thirteen mostly Protestant Christian colonies to stay together, all the important players had to have equal individual rights. Fortunately, the principal leaders were educated and interested in reasoning. Many had read the Greeks, Locke, Kant, Hobbes, Rousseau, Hume, Adam Smith, and other political philosophers. Some knew of Fredrick the Great's innovations. They were essentially locked in and forced to compromise in order to make difficult decisions and create a new dialectic based on individual rights. The questions of slavery and women's equality were 'bridges too far'. These question's time would come in a liberal democracy that allowed reasoned debate and empowered citizens. Jesus was the principal religious figure. Besides separating church and state, he centralized the General Admonitions and preached respect for the Moral Rules and the

Organizational Rules. That was very helpful. Also, Jesus gave almost no Religious Rules that would confuse and divide the citizens over questions of public piety.

The French Revolution and the *French Declaration of the Rights of Man and the Citizen* followed the Bill of Rights in 1789. This document also empowered the individual. Because of the pressure of adjacent monarchies and a very powerful monolithic conservative state religion, the road was much rockier for France. Napoleon's rise promised more rights, but he succumbed to imperial dreams and diluted the republican possibilities. Later, when in exile on St. Helena, he is quoted as saying, "They wanted me to be Washington, but I couldn't do it" [49a]. However, the "democratic cat was out of the bag", and Europe and the world went off on a 150 year period of revolution and reformation of the ideas of government and rights.

After 1791, the Bill of Rights was considered the gold standard for good government. Many of the nations were overthrowing monarchies in the 1800 and 1900's and adopting these individual rights in some form or another. The 1948 United Nations Declaration of Human Rights signed by most countries included the individual Human Rights. The communist countries, apartheid South Africa, and Saudi Arabia did not sign. Most Middle Eastern and Northern African Muslim countries were colonized by Europeans to some degree at this time and consequentially consented. At that time there were almost no states involved in Sharia law. Despite endorsing and codifying the individual rights, many nations were unable to enjoy these rights due to corrupt justice systems.

There have been changes since 1948. The Organization of Islamic Cooperation (OIC) is the largest organization of Muslim states. It was founded in 1969 by the heads of state of 24 predominantly Islamic nations and is today run by the foreign ministers of over 50 Muslim nations. In 1990, the OIC unanimously adopted the Cairo Declaration of Human Rights in Islam. The declaration omitted freedom of speech, press and religion as Western constructs. They felt that these rights were inimical to Sharia supported law. Also, in 1993, in Vienna, at the UN World Congress on Human Rights, freedom of speech, press, and religion were intentionally left out of the final document because of pressure by socialist, Islamic, and dictatorial states. Democratic hopefuls will have to learn to deal with these restrictions on individual freedom.

After the Civil War, President Abraham Lincoln's assassination deprived the nation of a visionary leader for union and progress. Reconstruction was ended too soon and too completely. The freed slaves were given no land and poor education. This ensured that they would remain poor and powerless. Later lynching made African American activism extremely dangerous and was used to suppress reform. Then the Jim Crow laws created by Southern politicians deprived the African American community of access to federal loans for housing, education, farms, and GI bill for education. "Red lining" of African American poor areas made it difficult to get home loans and mortgages. Contemporary policies of drug enforcement laws have created a disproportionately large African American prison population. In short, some parts of US history have been brutal and oppressive. The US has more to do.

In 1964 and 1965 with the Civil Rights Acts, the US finally equalized rights in the US. In 1966 the UN International Covenant on Economic, Social and Cultural Rights (UNICESCR) recommended the following as additional Human Rights: food, housing, education, job, vacations, health care, and good pay. Others wanted to add childcare and guaranteed income. The US did not ratify these rights. The US said that these were "goals" to be achieved, not rights to be granted. Declaring them as "rights" would confuse the courts and turn judges into legislators. All Western nations who are highly developed are working to assure these benefits to their citizens to some extent.

The US founders risked their fortunes and their lives to begin a state charged to empower the individual and separate church and state. On signing the Declaration of Independence Ben Franklin famously said, "We must all hang together, or, most assuredly, we shall all hang separately." It is a compelling narrative of risk, enlightenment, progress, and rational creation. This narrative has been the principal story of the US for many years.

Today a more recent narrative of US history with a different emphasis is promoted by progressives. "Progressive" is a label given today to the more radical leftists and activists. This narrative correctly points out that the individual rights in the Bill of Rights were not given to all citizens immediately, slavery still existed, and only land-owning white men had the vote. Also, indigenous peoples and labor movements were oppressed and occasionally brutally attacked by government and capitalist forces. After emancipation in 1865, African Americans had to live through the racist era of lynching and Jim Crow laws for 100 years before the Civil Rights Act of 1964 and the Voting Rights Act of 1965 gave them equal rights.

This recent progressive narrative has been described as "Woke" (as in "awakened"). The "Woke" narrative is centered on slavery and racism. It points out the hypocrisy in large parts of the founding story. Also, *The 1619 Project* by the New York Times says that slavery has been the center of our national enterprise and the original source of our wealth. *The 1619 Project*, "Woke" sensibilities, and *A Peoples History of the United States*, by Howard Zinn, present the US story from the point of the native peoples, the slaves, and the minorities. It is a compelling narrative. Besides pointing out the oppressive and hypocritical areas in the US founding, this narrative highlights the remaining racial inequities in the US economic, educational, and judicial systems. The judicial racism has been almost eliminated. The narrative also addresses the injustices inherent in colonization and the exploitation of weaker societies. These critics of Western civilization point to the shortcomings in its claims to greatness.

Today, almost everyone recognizes that despite their great progress relative to the rest of the world, the African Americans population in the US was put at a disadvantage economically and educationally. To rectify these, there are many programs of affirmative action requiring quotas to produce a more equitable place in society for African Americans and minorities. The right says that some are excessive, unfair to whites today, and create an unpleasant confrontational atmosphere in African American- white relations. The progressives say that they do not go far enough.

The Woke narrative points out the remaining differences in education and wealth. To spread knowledge of these issues, a program of reeducation about diversity has been implemented in many schools and in the diversity workshops (DEI, Diversity, Equity, Inclusion) in the workplace. This program has been called the installation of Critical Race Theory (CRT). Most parents don't mind if teachers instruct the children about the brutalities and oppression in the history of the US. In a recent Pew Research pol 77% of Republicans and 96% of Democrats alike agreed that "we should acknowledge the terrible things that have happened in ouzr nation's history regarding race so students can learn from them and make the future better." There are very different ideas about how this is to be done, and how old the children must be before they explore these serious issues. An agreeable balance has not been met.

CRT began in the 1970's as an exploration of the remaining racist statutes left over in our laws, public policy, and public discourse. It has broadened to include a discussion of LGBTQ rights and identity issues. It has become a program to instruct children and workers on how to recognize and overcome the remaining racism and gender insensitivity in our speech and interactions. Issues such as "white supremacy", "anti-racism", "white privilege", "whiteness", and gender fluidity are discussed. This has become an issue in the culture wars in the US because many parents do not want their children in the first three or four grades to be introduced to racist, sexual and gender questions. They feel that these are too confusing for children that young. [50] Others point out that this constant hyper emphasis on race makes African American/white interactions stilted and uncomfortable. People talk of reaching a "Woke breaking point". They support programs such as affirmative action and yet are dismayed by the extremes that result in non-prosecution of shop lifting, tolerance of vandalism, and the spread of dangerous tent cities.

"Woke" sensitivity demands that one constantly evaluate and aggressively criticize all discourse for racist possibilities. The consequences can depend on whether the subject or author is allowed to repent or change their opinions. Is change, forgiveness, and acceptance possible? Real? Is an apology for something said or done years ago acceptable? A charitable approach may work best. Constant harping on language and definition makes discourse and community very difficult and uncomfortable. Overt racism is now unacceptable by almost all parties.

It seems that now overt racism is thoroughly condemned by the society and government. We are dealing with the residuals of racism and have proposed numerous educational and social programs to produce a more equitable society. As always, we disagree about how much we can afford to tax and spend.

Some African American activists think that the US is still very racist and that only radical approaches to our vocabulary and laws are of any use. Black Lives Matter has used the "Woke" meme to point out the remaining inequalities. Woke has also come to be associated with gender identity politics.

According to the African American Woke activist and author, Ibram X Kendi (*How To Be An Anti-Racist*) enforced quotas will be essential to achieving racial equity. Until all percentages and economic measurements are racially equal, society will be racist. In his view, one is either a racist or an active anti-racist. There is no middle ground. Saying "I am not a racist" means that one is unaware of the true nature of racism. For Kendi all inequalities between whites and African Americans are the result of racism. All activities directed toward equality must be carefully evaluated, statistics kept, and transgressors must be "called out" or cancelled. Unfortunately, true to this logic, Kendi recommends appointment of a Department of Antiracism (DAR). The DAR would not be accountable to voters or legislators and would have the power to suppress "racist ideas". It could unilaterally veto or nullify any program or law at any level of government that the DAR decided was not actively 'antiracist'. His recommendations involve a lot of quotas to be set and targets to be hit. Kendi goes on to essentially say that capitalism is racist and to truly be anti-racist, you also have to be truly anti-capitalist.

The US founder's narrative has some clear areas of hypocrisy but was ground-breaking in its attempts to empower the individual. Including and providing charitable readings of both historical narratives is a way to maintain civil discourse. Using the ideals of the founding narrative while correcting the inequities identified in the slavery centered narrative would seem to preserve and improve the US.

The culture wars in the US have intensified in the educational system. In the US, some progressives, socialists, and cultural radicals have reached positions of power in the educational system. They have used innovations in education to promote their visions of the good, moral, "Woke" life, which parallels some parts of the socialist agenda. They think that the government must be heavily involved in economic and cultural issues to produce a just nation and that reasonable equity is a primary goal.

German Marxist student activist in the 1960s, Rudi Dutschke, outlined a long term approach to promote a socialist type of social engineering and education. He called it "the long march through the institutions", particularly the educational institutions. Some conservative thought believes this socialist "March" began in the 1960's, and it is today being brought forward under CRT and Woke activism in the educational system. The conservatives seem to feel that this is a very real threat to Western culture, morals, freedom of speech, and capitalist opportunity. Liberals think that progress is occurring too slowly.

Because I paint an optimistic picture of liberal democracy, one of my teachers labeled me a "Western exceptionalist". A Western exceptionalist is someone who adopts an uncritical narrative praising Western culture. I like to think that I do not ignore the very serious problems within US culture and with US foreign policy. It does appear that liberal democracy is the best form of government, but it requires a relatively honest population. The West certainly has committed its share of atrocities. Besides chattel slavery, the US has been involved in numerous disasters including war on native Americans, ruthless strike breaking, military brutalities in the Philippines and Viet Nam, and political intervention and destabilization in numerous Central American countries. Viet Nam was a very controversial and divisive war. The US and the UN had just finished rescuing South Korea from a totalitarian nightmare and thought they could do the same in Viet Nam. They were wrong. Despite all their sins, the US and the Western democracies have defeated some very bad dictators. They have also been the origin of large peaceful and progressive movements that have seen the world become less and less violent and oppressive. The science created in the West has provided lifesaving vaccines, antibiotics, and GMO foods that have fed millions. Also, the world has become less violent in general. Steven Pinker's work such as *Enlightenment Now* points this out in detail. Minorities in the US are generally richer and safer than they are elsewhere. On the other hand, Howard Zinn thinks the US has done more harm than good. That might be expected from sincere socialist who thinks that the only just world is a socialized world. On the other hand, a prominent African American educator said that he was going to be sure and impress on his children that there is vast opportunity for African Americans in the US and that hard work will be rewarded. The educator said he couldn't run for congress on that platform, but that is how he would raise his family. Certainly, African Americans should be aware of the disparities and their origins and work to correct them. However, progress has been made, diligent work will be rewarded, and one can live a fulfilling life in the US without becoming bitter, corrupt, or brutal. [50a]

Concerning "US exceptionalism", I think Richard Rorty expressed it well when he said, "National pride is to countries what self-respect is to individuals: a necessary condition for self-improvement…. just as too little self-respect makes it difficult for a person to display moral courage, so insufficient national pride makes energetic and effective debate about national policy unlikely." One can believe that the West wants to do the right thing and seriously criticize its methods. The fact that the West allows for open serious criticism, puts it in an exceptional category of nations.

The fact that the US is the most powerful nation in the world allows it to act everywhere. The results of its actions and the side effects of its power have caused many problems at home and abroad. Its suppression of socialist movements worldwide is controversial. It has also spread scientific progress, health care, and democratic ideas over large areas. The West has set a governmental standard that much of the world would love to emulate. Recent examples of unrestricted immigration and lack of the will and moral confidence to enforce the laws concerning such things as shop lifting and vandalism are self-destructive strategies. [51] It is clarifying to note that the US/Mexican border is the only significant national border between a third world country and a first world country. Seventy-one countries have walls on their borders.

Because of its unique geographic and philosophical situation, the US became the first liberal democracy. A deeply flawed liberal democracy, but one that proved to be capable of progress. It needed radical and humanitarian people like Abraham Lincoln, Frederick Douglas, Sojourner Truth, Harriet Tubman, Susan B. Anthony, and Dr. Martin Luther King to point the way and fill in the gaps in the Constitution[52]. I must admit that King's, Lincoln's, and Douglas's idea of everyone progressing together rather than separately is dear to my heart. Perhaps separateness is, or was, a necessary emotional phase in the struggle to defeat racism. I hope that now we can begin to move on through unity. In the West, the laws necessary for legal equality have been passed. It will take a major national effort to bring more equity to education, family income, and family structure. I think that Dr. M. L. King recognized that it would not happen quickly when he said, "The arc of the moral universe is long, but it bends toward justice."

Artifacts and Values in Group and Individual Culture

As discussed above, cultures come in the two "Types", group or individual. Both cultural "types" have Cultural <u>Artifacts</u> and Cultural <u>Values</u>. Cultural Artifacts are interesting but, like Religious Rules, not essential. On the other hand, good Cultural Values are essential to the economic and political success of a society.

Artifacts of culture: These are the dress, music, art, language, grooming, Religious Rules, rituals, ceremonies, and food preferences of a group of people. The artifacts have no intrinsic meaning. The only meaning they have is that given by the group. They do serve to link people together for support, and they remind us of our good times and memories. Human nature is such that every culture thinks that it is as good or better than every other culture. All cultures justify any deviations from rational democracy as the results of special problems due to political hardships, Religious Rules, geography, or historical oppression.

The artifacts serve to maintain and support the better parts of the culture or its identity. Assigning existential value to these artifacts can cause distress when others do not take them as serious issues. If someone adopts the dress, food, art, or music of another culture some call this "cultural appropriation". This adoption can be viewed as a complement or an insult depending on the circumstances. Now groups want to control their image and profit from it as artists have done for years. When people are relaxed and feel secure humorous jibes concerning unusual artifacts can be viewed as acceptable even when they are close to insulting. The powerful cultures like the US are diverse and secure. For the most part, they do not mind being criticized or mocked. Religious Rules are a type of artifact and can create very sensitive issues in weaker cultures where religion has been something that has allowed them to withstand very difficult periods of deprivation or oppression.

Values of a culture: Values ultimately determine the economic and civic success of a country or culture. Cultural Values are, to a large extent, determined by the type of culture: group or individual. Middle class individual values are dominant in materially successful Western cultures. Various other value sets include Bohemian, religious fundamentalist, revolutionary, tribal, utopian, absurdist, contrarian, and "other class" values.

Individual culture's values include many Middle-Class values:

1. Honesty.
2. Hard work.
3. Individual Rights.
4. Respect for women.
5. Ambition.
6. Respect for legitimate authority.
7. Thrift.
8. Appreciation of education.
9. Optimism.
10. Strong families.
11. Also, most educated individual citizens value equality before the law because they themselves will be judged by the legal institutions.

The principal weaknesses of Middle-Class values have included various amounts of:

1. Selfishness and greediness. (Bourgeois values)
2. Racism.
3. Homophobia.
4. Xenophobia.
5. Smugness.
6. Sexism.

In group cultures the values can be more complicated. The list of group values can, and usually does, include many of those desirable qualities listed above. However, most group cultures add various mixtures of some of the following values that can contribute to corruption:

1. Tribal or group thinking. A concern for a particular segment of the population to the detriment of others. This can be religious, tribal, racial, class, or otherwise,

2. Nepotism. (Preferential promotion of group members)

3. Loyalty to the group or figure at the expense of the individual.

4. Valorization of strength and petty violence.

5. Toleration of low-level criminality and corruption by group members.

6. Unequal or oppressive treatment for women.

Honesty and its public form, obeying the law, are among the most important cultural values governmentally. Without a generally honest populace, reasonably unbiased judges, and the empowered individual "watchdog", liberal democracy and capitalism can not control corruption.

Perhaps the internet may someday be able to take over the role of "watchdog" on corruption. Now, the internet dialog is distorted by so many lies and the spread of false conspiracy theories that it is hampered in its ability to clearly focus concerns on illegal or immoral actions. Although the internet's accuracy is questionable, it is a form of free speech and clearly does expose some hypocrisy and government excess. Its anonymity presents some problems concerning harassment. Probably the worst aspect of the internet is that it has facilitated communication and organization among disturbed and fanatical people. It has allowed people to act out anonymously and threaten others. Previously, people with oppressive or violent views had difficulty finding others with similar disturbing ideas. It is said that ISIS was made possible through the internet.

The Moral Rules, General Admonitions, and some types of Organizational Rules are included by necessity in the laws of almost every group or nation. Every functional social and governmental arrangement is concerned with them. If the people and the government do not support them, corruption is inevitable. Western civilization has proven to be relatively low on corruption. Below is the World Corruption Index map, 2017, compiled by Transparency International. The darker the country the worse the corruption. Protestant Western type democracies are generally the most honest. [54]

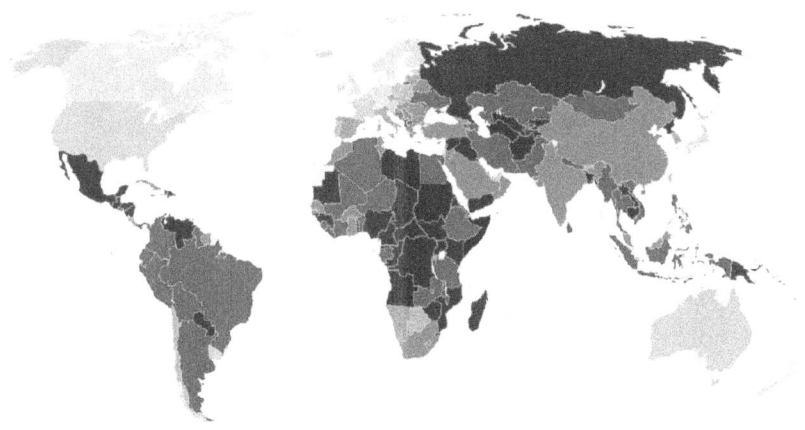

How does one judge the amount of corruption? Do you have to pay bribes to do business? Is theft a serious daily problem? Is extortion common? Do you have to be in a certain group to be promoted? Do people pay their taxes? Do monopolies dominate business? Do you feel safe?

Transparency International has two tools that it uses to measure corruption, the Corruption Perceptions Index and the Global Corruption Barometer. The Corruptions Perceptions Index reflects the opinions of experts and businesspeople. The Global Corruption Barometer represents ordinary citizens. One of Transparency International's principal questions on its Global Corruption Barometer asks individuals, "Have you had to pay a bribe to get a government service?" This is a question that Transparency International asked of thousands of people worldwide. Bribery of this sort is not common in the West. Individuals can and will report it to a relatively uncorrupted constabulary. Crony capitalism involving the use of government powers to benefit various businesses is present in much the same corruption distribution pattern. A detailed definition of corruption can be extensive and is available in Endnote *(55).

Some of my acquaintances say that corruption is widespread in the US. I asked them, "Have you ever had to pay a bribe for a government service or contract?". They all answered "no". Their assertions of corruption are based on the fact that politicians become very rich today. The money often comes from ridiculously large honoraria for speaking, large amounts of money to write their memoirs, and directing charities that they organize and manage. These activities are all above board and reported. The sources of their wealth are known and taxed. The voters and businesses know where the candidates stand. It is much better than bags of money under the table. One continuing concern about corruption is the gerrymandering of voting districts. In the US it can only be controlled by an impartial judiciary supporting individual rights.

Because of the Trump presidency and the associated explosion of conspiracy theories concerning the electoral system and the government, the US citizen may now feel that government is more unstable and possibly corrupt despite the lack of any proof of corruption. The tolerance of extremist groups at the highest levels on the right seems to have encouraged extremism from the left.

Additionally, in group-oriented countries, nepotism is ubiquitous. It is a way for those in charge to consolidate power and wealth. It is also a way for poor people to support each other. Without the support of an extended family in corrupt and dysfunctional countries, life is very difficult. Extortion and thuggery are the lowest forms of corruption. This is rare in the Western democracies.

An anecdotal story, *What I Learned in the Peace Corps in Africa*, from Karen McQuillan, a Peace Corps volunteer in Senegal, illustrates some of the differences in values. She is a political conservative and was in Africa in 1971. This is an excerpt from a paper that she wrote in 2018. She states:

"This country was not a hellhole. Very poor people can lead happy, meaningful lives in their own cultures' terms. But they are not our terms. Sex, I was told, did not include kissing. Love and friendship in marriage were Western ideas. Fidelity was not a thing. …The Ten Commandments were not disobeyed – they were unknown. The value system was the exact opposite. You were supposed to steal everything you can to give to your own relatives. There are some Westernized Africans who try to rebel against the system. They fail.

In Senegal, corruption ruled, from top to bottom. Go to the post office, and the clerk would name an outrageous price for a stamp.

Private business was not illegal, just impossible, given the nightmare of a third-world bureaucratic kleptocracy. All the little stores in Senegal were owned by Mauritanians. If a Senegalese wanted to run a little store, he'd go to another country. The reason? Your friends and relatives would ask you for stuff for free, and you would have to say yes. End of your business. You are not allowed to be a selfish individual and say no to relatives. The result: Everyone has nothing.

The more I worked there and visited government officials doing absolutely nothing, the more I realized that no one in Senegal had the idea that a job means work. A job is something given to you by a relative. It provides the place where you appropriate everything to give back to your family."

Today, many poorly functional democracies have the individual human rights in their organizing documents. According to Pew Research in 2017, 97 nations out of the 167 in the UN defined themselves as democracies. 21 were autocracies and 46 were mixed. Unfortunately, the rights are unevenly observed in some democracies. In some of the newer democracies, the citizens do not yet fully trust the government. Corruption, family obligations, tribalism, and bribery make personal economic progress very difficult and, sometimes, impossible. This results in various forms of economic and judicial disfunction in taxation, allocation of resources, and enforcement of the laws. Land reform is incredibly difficult and is an important issue in many emerging democracies.

There is a brief poignant video of an elderly Pakistani man standing in line to get a green card to go to the US. All around him are people demonstrating against some aspect of US policy. He is asked, "Why do you want to go to the US?" He responds, "Because they obey the law."

To summarize the type of Culture's relationship to Organizational Rules:

Individual culture —

1. Individual Human Rights are primary.

2. Liberal democracy has generally led to progress in all areas. Trust in honest elections will be essential.

3. Capitalism is valued and frequently creates economic inequality. Allowing creativity will always produce inequality. There is nothing wrong with it, but there are reasonable limits, and people will have different ideas.

4. Middle class values provide a great basis for capitalist economic function and success. Family values in the middle classes are essential

5. The empowered and safe individual can serve as watchdog on corruption.

6. Equity, a fair chance, is a goal for all people. Education is probably the only long-term solution, and it requires an equal starting point which is expensive if it is to be fair. The welfare state programs can fulfill our obligations to the poor.

7. The overall goal is to create the possibility of happiness.

Group culture —

1. Since the dawn of humanity, the primary way to assure some security has been group organization. Groups are highly valued because of

their stability in dangerous places.

2. Preservation of the group is very important. Family is valued.
3. Internal corruption and nepotism are often present and overlooked.
4. "Others" are created.
5. Apostasy is punished.
6. Promotion usually depends on conformity and loyalty.
7. Racism is a form of group culture.
8. Some groups promote and enforce a particular religion.
9. A benevolent dictatorship or socialism can be a stage on the difficult road to control corruption.

Slavery and Rights

Slavery is mentioned in all the texts. There are several forms of slavery including serfdom, chattel slavery, forced marriage, and indentured servitude. In many societies slaves had some rights. In some cases, the owner could do with the chattel slave as he wished, even kill. There were all sorts of variations in different cultures and religions concerning the ability of owners to mistreat slaves. The monotheisms condemned the mistreatment of slaves. The Qur'an said it was acceptable for men to have sex with one's female slaves, Qur'an 23:5. Context is important. Serfdom means that one is tied to the land. Serfs could not be bought or sold, and had rights over their own bodies, but they could not leave the estate that they were born on.

Slavery existed in the monotheisms from their inceptions. Jewish slavery consisted of chattel slavery and indentured slavery. There were Jewish laws prohibiting the abuse and killing of slaves. Jews usually only became slaves if they were prisoners of war, unable to support themselves, or had unpayable debts. Many became slaves to other Jews. A Jew could be held as a slave for only six years, then he must be let go with some money and food. If the Jews obtained a non-Jew slave, they were supposed to offer the slave conversion. Non-Jew slaves who converted were to be freed after some period. If a Jew was the slave of a non-Jew, there was an obligation on the Jewish community to buy his/her freedom.

Christianity arose under the Roman Empire which had millions of slaves. Most of them were prisoners of war or slaves bought from other countries. Jesus, Paul, and Peter did not question the institution of slavery, but clearly recommended that we be kind to everyone. Mistreating of others was to be avoided.

In early Medieval Europe, the sale of Christian slaves to non-Christian lands was forbidden by Christian doctrine. By 1200 almost all chattel slavery in Northern Europe had been transformed into serfdom. The Black Plague devastated the work force in about 1400. It also empowered some workers and serfs because of competition for labor. Serfdom was not completely ended in England until the Tenures Abolition Act in 1660.

One biproduct of all the colonizing and empire building by the Europeans was a great increase in the international slave market. From the 16th to 19th centuries, about 17 million were involved in the Middle Eastern, Slavic, and North African slave trade, and approximately 11 million slaves arrived in the Western Hemisphere, about 388,000 in the US. [56]

In 1435 at the beginning of the Age of Discovery, the Catholic Pope Eugene IV, became concerned about the enslavement of native Christian converts in the Canary Islanders by the Portuguese. He issued a Papal Bull or decree condemning this action of enslaving Christians. The decree specifically said that native Christian converts should not be enslaved. This was generally ignored. In 1452 Pope Nicholas V issued a decree entitled Dum Diversus saying that Muslims and people who were not Christians could be enslaved.

When the abolitionists in Western nations began attacking the institution of slavery in the Christian countries in the 1700s and 1800s, they stated clearly that enslaving of others, particularly Christians, by other Christians was not in accordance with Jesus' teachings. In response the advocates of slavery introduced the idea that African Americans were an inherently inferior race that was not equal to the rest of humanity. Even if they were Christians, they were not equal to white Christians. The concept of racial differences was born. The slavers virtually invented racism.

There was a cruel sophistry concerning the difference between the "slave trade" and "slavery". In 1792 Denmark became the first country to ban the "slave trade" but did not liberate their slaves. Slaves in the Danish colonies were not liberated until 1848, 15 years after the British had liberated the slaves in their colonies. When abolitionist pressure began to be prominent in the US, several Bishops in the Catholic Church in the US argued that the "trading of slaves" was against Christian doctrine, but that Christian doctrine did not demand the liberation of the slaves already in servitude. It took a very bloody Civil War to decide the question.

The Marquette University Faculty Blog summarized the liberation of slaves in various US states thusly. "In 1780, Pennsylvania became the first state to abolish slavery when it adopted a statute that provided for the freedom of every slave born after its enactment (once that individual reached the age of majority). Massachusetts was the first to abolish slavery outright, doing so by judicial decree in 1783. The remaining New England states–New Hampshire, Connecticut, and Rhode Island–adopted gradual emancipation schemes modeled on Pennsylvania's statute in the mid-1780s, and the United States Congress abolished slavery in future states north of the Ohio River in the Northwest Ordinance of 1787. Gradual emancipation came to New Jersey in 1804 and to New York in 1817, albeit with an operational date of July 4, 1827. In 1828, New York abolished slavery outright, as did Pennsylvania in 1847 (an act that liberated the state's fewer than 100 remaining slaves). Somewhat unusually, New Hampshire appears to have formally abolished slavery in 1857 (apparently more than a decade after the death or manumission of the last New Hampshire slave)." The US abolished slavery in 1865 with the 13th Amendment to the Constitution.

Slavery was abolished in Russia in 1723, but the slaves became serfs, tied to the land. Russia ended serfdom in 1861. In 1807 England and the US ended the "slave trade" among nations but did not emancipate those already slaves. The English sent warships to interrupt the trade. England did not formally liberate the slaves in all its colonies until 1833.

Islam too began in an era of slavery. Like early Christianity, it did not explicitly ban slavery. There are extensive rules from the Qur'an and Hadith promoting the welfare and good treatment of slaves in the Islamic texts. Muhammad said that one of the things that makes God very happy is to free slaves [56a]. In general slavery was permissible for prisoners of holy war and the children of slaves. A freeborn Muslim could not be enslaved unless it was for a criminal offense and was only for a limited time. Slaves could convert, and this would improve their chances of freedom, but did not grant it. Slaves could also marry. The owner could have sex with his women slaves (Qur'an 23:5). Because of the restrictions on enslaving Muslims, the later Islamic slave trade did much of its business in the Christian areas of Eastern Europe and Western Asia.

In the 16th through the early 18th century, the Barbary Pirates in Ottoman areas of north Africa were attacking European and American trading ships. They were also capturing numbers of Europeans for ransom and in many cases for sale into slavery. The European nations were paying protection money to keep their commercial ships from being attacked. In the late 18th century, the Barbary Pirates were demanding more payoffs from the US and other European nations. The US Navy was ultimately charged with organizing a multinational force and subduing these states. They did so in two successive wars ending in 1815.

In the 1700s and 1800s the options for holy war against infidels wherein slaves could be taken by Muslims were almost over. Arabic slave traders began capturing sub-Saharan Africans and selling them to the Atlantic slave trade. Some of them were Muslims which was clearly against Islamic law. This led to abolitionist movements within the Muslim world. The slave holding powers were powerful and numerous, and it wasn't until 1846 that the Bey (ruler) of Tunisia made Tunisia the first Muslim nation to ban slavery. Some slave trading continued in the Ottoman Empire into the early 1900's. After WWI the Ottoman Empire was broken up and the various colonized states formed from the empire eventually banned all slavery by the 1940's.

Slavery is condemned everywhere in the world today by all the monotheisms. However, in the world in general it is estimated that 28 million people are in forced labor and 22 million are in forced marriages.[57]

4. Religious Rules

The Religious Rules are all revealed to prophets by God. They are concerned with the creation of purity and piety or holiness. The Moral Rules, General Admonitions, and Organizational Rules can all be arrived at by reasoning. The Religious Rules would not necessarily occur to someone using reason. Stoics and atheists follow numerous Religious Rule type pieties or processes for self-improvement or self-actualization, but they are not trying to please a God.

Following the Religious Rules as an individual is not problematic. It brings a lot of happiness and fulfillment to many people. In group-oriented societies, one can be labeled a heretic, a blasphemer, an infidel, or an apostate if one does not observe the culturally accepted Religious Rules. As mentioned, these labels can be very dangerous in nations where Religious Rules are enforced by the state or fundamentalist mobs.

If you want to be enlightened, receive "grace", go to paradise, or be "saved", some believe that you must prepare yourself to receive these gifts. As the hippies used to say, "If you want an airplane to land, you have to build an airport". When combined with the Moral Rules and the General Admonitions, many feel that the purity outlined in the Religious Rules is necessary to build a "holy airport". Others think the Religious Rules are nice but inessential pieties.

As mentioned above, one of the biggest problems with Religious Rules is that they recur with each new generation. Once a prophet has given a Religious Rule, it is written down, and it never goes away. One generation may deal with a Rule constructively, but the next generation may, under economic or political stress, have elements or fanatics that bring up that Rule in a coercive context. Every generation must deal with all the Rules. Some generations do it oppressively. Iran, Pakistan, ISIS, Indonesia, and Turkey have recently become more severe with dissidents.

Religious Rules also make common things serious. Common actions can carry tinges of heresy. What you wear is serious, what you eat is serious, what you say is serious, how you relate to the other sex is serious, how you pray is serious, your music and dance become serious, art can be serious, satire, criticism, discussion, etc. Religious Rules can make almost everything unnecessarily serious and tense. This is not to say that these things are unimportant. It is simply to state that there are many opinions. To single one out as exclusive is fine for personal satisfaction, but don't expect everyone to have the same response. When viewed from a neutral position, some Religious Rules seem so unimportant that one wonders how they became problems. Most democratic citizens feel that God will take care of questions of sacrilege, heresy, and apostasy. We don't need to get involved.

Most Religious Rules indicate no clear punishments for non-observance. They should not be an issue. However, important problems occur when those who do not comply are labeled heretics or apostates because of their lack of observance. Is one a heretic, blasphemer or apostate if they do not observe the ritualistic Religious Rules?

Religious Rules are not essential to the daily welfare of the community as far as safety, nutrition, shelter, organization, and rational justice are concerned. Religious Rules address dietary choices, clothing, rituals, belief, apostasy, sacrilege, women's roles, and some aspects of sexuality. The Religious Rules are there to maintain or achieve some form of group purity or piety approved by God. The types of Religious Rules are listed below. After that listing, the problems of interpretation, judgment, enforcement, and punishment will be addressed. Lastly, there will be a section reviewing the historical effects of Religious Rules in the various religious.

Chapter 5
Religious Rules: A List

Religious Rules fall into several categories:

a. Daily activities. Do's and don'ts. Don't drink alcohol, don't shake hands, don't cut your hair, don't shave, pray regularly, don't sing, don't dance, don't listen to music, don't use machines, no transfusions, don't swear, don't gamble, don't eat pork, prepare food in certain ways, do or don't wear certain types of hats, scarves, underwear, etc. Also, there are rules about how to perform ablutions and how to kill animals respectfully and with as little brutality as possible. Food prepared according to Jewish rules is called *kosher*. That prepared to Muslim standards is called *halal*. These Religious Rules are viewed as necessary to follow the will of God, maintain a holy atmosphere, and be kind to animals. A few might have originated out of health concerns in pre-scientific societies. Today, in a post-scientific world, they can serve as personal suggestions or reminders of God, but fundamentalists take them as absolute and essential group actions that are needed to create sufficient piety. Music is not specifically forbidden in the Qur'an, but a very few conservative Protestants and much of Islam forbid it generally because it may cause lascivious thoughts and temptations. Many rules concerning funny hats, beards and hairdos appear just strange or silly to outsiders. The orthodox see them as essential reminders of the presence and power of God.

b. Rituals. Rituals are ceremonies consisting of a series of actions performed in a prescribed way. They are usually accompanied by the reading of texts or performing prayers. Sometimes there is singing or dancing. Ablutions can be part of the rituals. The repetition of the General Admonitions during the rituals or in sermons, prayers or songs can remind us to be compassionate. Group rituals such as communion, baptism, daily prayers, and pilgrimage can be some of the most satisfying of human events. They can get us together to calm our fears or to stir our better emotions. Hopefully, they will be carried out in the sense of the General Admonitions so that the rituals will remind us to be less judgmental and kinder.

Gathering the extended family for these rituals is the source of much happiness and many warm memories. They are some of the most enjoyable parts of life for many people. They lend an importance to religion that is truly unique. The common ceremonies include regular worship, marriage, baptism, fasting, prayer, confession of sins, holidays, funeral ceremonies, mourning, pilgrimages, confirmation, communion, etc. Many seem to be designed to make sure that the important moments in life are clearly recognized and done to the satisfaction of the community and God. Religious Rules often tell us how they are to be performed. These rules can include who does what during the service, who can be included, how the ritual is to be performed, what the surroundings should be like, what music, if any, is to be allowed, what positions one should take, which way to face, how to dress, how to move one's arms, etc.

Women are generally not allowed to serve or preside in many rituals in orthodox Judaism, Catholicism, Islam, and some conservative Protestant sects.

The ritual of public marriage ceremonies can help to limit the exploitation of women. Rational society and religion both have imposed various rules to avoid the sexual exploitation of the young and vulnerable. By compelling the males to go through the public rituals of marriage, the community can control and avoid the exploitation of women and the young. Marriage and divorce obligations can also benefit women by ensuring some degree of financial security.

Jews usually congregate to celebrate Passover, Yom Kippur, Rosh Hashanah, Shabbat, Hanukkah, and various important days. Head coverings, certain clothes, kosher foods, and some hair styles are recommended by the more orthodox. Men and women are often separated. Scripture readings remind the faithful of their history and obligations. Haredi and other very orthodox Jews observe many of the Religious Rules in the Hebrew Bible. Reform Jews seem outwardly more concerned with good acts rather than Jewish Religious Rules. "Deeds rather than creeds."

There are two rituals or sacraments in most of Christianity: communion and baptism. These are Religious Rules. Jesus said it would be good to remember him by celebrating his Last Supper with his apostles. (Matthew 14:22-25) This is called Communion or Mass and is a celebrated act in all Christian sects. They all do it differently. No punishments are recommended if you don't. Jesus also recommended baptism. It consists of immersion or sprinkling with water as a sign of being cleansed and, in a way, reborn spiritually. Again, no punishments on earth if you are not baptized. Baptism and communion are Religious Rules and the two most prominent sacraments of most Christian sects. The celebrations around Christmas (Jesus' birth), and Easter (Jesus' resurrection from the dead), engender group gatherings and celebrations. They are a source of warm memories. In the past, if one did not participate in baptism, communion, and celebrations, one was open to charges of heresy.

Catholics have seven sacraments: Baptism, Confirmation or Chrismation, Eucharist, Penance, Anointing of the Sick, Holy Orders, and Matrimony. Several are concerned with clerics and celibacy. Jesus does not mention celibacy. Paul obliquely recommends it. His first letter to the church at Corinth says "To the unmarried and the widows, I say that it is well for them to remain unmarried as I am" (1 Corinthians 7:8). Catholic priests and nuns were not required to be celibate until the 12th century. Many Buddhist priests are expected to be celibate. Most of Protestantism and all of Islam think that celibacy is unnecessary and not helpful.

Muslims generally adhere to the Five Pillars of Islam and the Six Articles of Faith. Hadith of Jibril (Gabriel), Bukhari Hadith, and Muslim Hadith all contain these important lists. The Qur'an does not give a specific list like the Ten Commandments. Shortly after the fasting month of Ramadan, Eid al-Adha is celebrated. It is the holiest festival on the Islamic calendar and celebrates Abraham's willingness to sacrifice his son, Ishmael, to God. God intervenes and a sheep is sacrificed. Ishmael went on to become a great leader, and his people eventually became the Muslims. The children of his half-brother, Isaac, went on to become the Jewish nation. Judaism thinks that Isaac was the one to be sacrificed by Abraham.

Islam forbids monasticism and does not endorse celibacy. Apparently, Muhammad felt that the leaders should live lives like the communities that they serve. Muslims also have the Six Articles of Faith or Belief. They are: there is one God, the Qur'an is the word of God, Muhammad is God's last prophet, there will be a judgment day, angels exist, and everything is predestined by God. Predestination and judgment by God would seem to be antithetical. Why would God judge a person for doing something God knew that the person would do? I don't have an answer. Predestination is for Calvinists, Catholics, and Islamic theologians to wrestle with. [58]

For many people, the monotheistic God is thought to be unusually concerned about being praised and making sure that no other God gets the credit for creation or any of its benefits. The first four of the Ten Commandments listed here seem to express this.

1. I am the Lord thy God. Thou shall have no other gods before me.
2. Thou shall not make unto thee any graven image.
3. Thou shall not take the name of the Lord thy God in vain.
4. Remember the sabbath day, to keep it holy.

Many rituals are designed to focus the community and give sufficient praise to the creator God. If we do not comply, will we displease God? One of my editors, expressed the nature of praise differently. She wrote,

"It is healing to us to remain in an attitude of praise and adoration toward God." Prayer and worship aren't necessarily designed to appease a God. They are more to remind us of the main precepts, the wonder of creation, and the General Admonitions.

c. Beliefs. Religious Rules concerning beliefs are present in every religion. A list of one's beliefs is called a "creed". Wrong beliefs can be defined as "heresies". This doesn't have to be a problem since no one can truly know what another believes. People can be forced to publicly profess a creed. In general, the great monotheisms agree that one must believe that there is one all-powerful God. This God knows all and judges us, hopefully mercifully. Importantly, if one does not comply with the Religious Rules, some assume that he/she is a heretic and should be shunned or punished. Conservative clerics usually feel that heretics can create problems in society and must be identified and controlled in some way.

Most religious prophets, teachers, or organizations set up a series of things for the member to "do" that prove to others or to God that one believes. These things to "do" include reciting various creeds.

Jews are supposed to believe that there is one God and that the Old Testament Biblical Prophets are his messengers. Jews are also to believe that they were chosen by God to be a moral example to the rest of the world and should act as such. Much of the Jewish law is found in the Torah, the first five books of the Tanakh. Moses is particularly prominent, and many think he is responsible for the first five books of the Tanakh. The Talmud is a scholarly critique and codification of Jewish law. The law written in the Talmud had originally been an oral tradition carried on by the rabbis. It was first written down as the *Mishna* in about 200 C.E. The *Gemara* was further commentary on the law and the *Mishna*. It was written down over the next 300 years.

Protestants and Catholics believe that the Bible is inspired by God. There is no prescribed punishment on earth for lack of belief, but most Christians think that orthodox belief is necessary for salvation or eternal life. The only Religious Rule that Jesus gives regarding belief is that we are to believe that he is the Son of God, John 3:16-18. "For God so loved the world, as to give his only begotten Son; that whosoever believeth in him, may not perish, but may have life everlasting". Once Jesus is very specific in stating that belief is essential when he says in John 14:6 "I am the way and the truth and the life. No one comes to the Father except through me". In two other passages a holy voice from above calls Jesus the Son of God, Matthew 3:17 and Luke 3:22. This belief, honesty, and kindness to others might get one to heaven. This succinct demand for belief concerning Jesus' divinity occurs in only one of the four Gospels of Jesus, so that its importance is not completely clear. It also does not occur in the only prayer that Jesus teaches.

The Lord's prayer (King James Version):

Our Father who art in heaven,

Hallowed be your name.

Your kingdom come,

your will be done,

on earth, as it is in heaven.

Give us this day our daily bread,

and forgive us our debts,

as we also have forgiven our debtors.

And lead us not into temptation,

And deliver us from evil,

For thine is the kingdom and the power and the glory forever.

Amen

This one Religious Rule concerning belief in the divinity of Jesus caused almost all the issues in Christianity. Various church bodies developed creeds that must be recited and rituals that must be performed. If one was negligent, one was often punished or shunned. Christians at worship frequently recite the creeds which are lists of their beliefs. There are many creeds. The Apostle's Creed and the Nicaean Creed are among the most prominent.

Apostle's Creed:

"I believe in God, the Father Almighty, Creator of Heaven and earth;

and in Jesus Christ, His only Son, Our Lord,

Who was conceived by the Holy Spirit, born of the Virgin Mary, suffered under Pontius Pilate, was crucified, died, and was buried.

He descended into Hell; the third day He rose again from the dead;

He ascended into Heaven, and sitteth at the right hand of God, the Father almighty; from thence He shall come to judge the living and the dead.

I believe in the Holy Spirit, the holy catholic Church, the communion of saints, the forgiveness of sins, the resurrection of the body and life everlasting."

As quoted previously the Qur'an states that if one does not believe the whole Qur'an that "grievous punishment" can await them in the afterlife (Qur'an 2:85-86). Schismatics who want to pick and choose among the Qur'an's verses can be punished in the afterlife. They could also be recognized as heretics here on earth. Compassionate contextualizing and charitable close reading solve many of these issues. These types of verses can be assigned to different aspects of Muhammad's roles on earth. It is reasonable to think that during the earliest days of existential threats to Islam that those of questionable faith might not be given roles of influence. Perhaps today we can emphasize the compassionate approach recommended more frequently as in the verse "There shall be no compulsion in religion" Qur'an 2:256.

In Islam, the worst of sins is belief that there is more than one God (*shirk*) (Qur'an 4:48). No direct punishment on earth is recommended. The biggest problem is that one might be labeled a heretic or apostate if one hinted at polytheism. One could then be punished for apostasy. This sort of cascade of accusations beginning with heresy and progressing to sacrilege, to blasphemy, to apostasy can cause punishments for acts that originally had no recommended punishments. Punishment for blasphemy is not mentioned in the Qur'an, but blasphemy is forbidden by law in many predominantly Islamic states and punishable with death in some [59]. These laws are rarely enforced by the state, but they are intimidating. Fundamentalists mobs occasionally kill blasphemers [60]. Some of Islam sees the Christian doctrine of the Trinity as a polytheistic heresy and blasphemy. Many Christians see the Trinity as just the three ways they encounter God. It is a complex and sometimes confusing theological issue.

The Ten Commandments specifically mention that one should worship only the one God and should not worship idols or graven images. Jesus doesn't include the commandment on idolatry in this list of important issues. Paul says to, "flee from idolatry". No punishments on earth are mentioned by Jesus or Paul. Can one use statues, paintings, or other representations to focus one's attention without "worshiping idols"? Roman Catholics have no problem with images. The Eastern Orthodox church had several periods in the 8th and 9th centuries when no images were allowed in the churches. Only crosses were permitted. After the Reformation some Protestant Christian mobs destroyed many of the images and statues in French Catholic churches and monasteries. The Protestants felt that all the statuary were the prohibited graven images mentioned in the Ten Commandments. Some Protestant fundamentalists and Reformed Calvinist churches are very concerned with images. They have no pictures or statues in their churches. Judgment of others on the issue of idolatry would seem to be arbitrary since it is impossible to know what is in another's soul.

As far as idolatry, most Islamic law schools and scholarship prohibit depicting Muhammad in pictures or sculpture, and some Muslim scholars prohibit pictures of humans of any kind. They seem to feel that images might lead to a form of polytheistic *shirk*. Hadith Bukhari 7:62:110 states, "The Hadith also reports that the Prophet said that the angels would not enter a house where there are pictures". Recently fundamentalists destroyed two large world-famous Buddhist statues in Afghanistan in 2001. In 2006 over 200 people worldwide died in riots protesting unflattering pictures of Muhammad by a Danish newspaper.

e. Apostasy This concerns giving up one's religion. The Book of Deuteronomy 13:6-11 in the Tanakh (The Christian Old Testament) recommends killing apostates who advocate other religions. No Jews or Christians recommend this today. Jesus implies that nonbelievers will not go to heaven but recommends no punishment here on earth. The Qur'an doesn't recommend the death penalty for apostasy and states that "There should be no compulsion in religion." (Qur'an 2:256). In places the Hadith recommend death for those who disrupt Islamic society with disbelief. Hadith Bukhari 9:84:57 says, "It is acceptable to kill anyone who leaves the faith. I would have killed them according to the statement of Allah's Apostle, 'Whoever changed his Islamic religion, then kill him'". Another prominent Hadith. Bukhari 9:83:17 states, "Allah's Messenger said, "The blood of a Muslim who confesses that none has the right to be worshipped but Allah and that I am His Apostle, cannot be shed except in three cases: In *Qisas* (retribution) for murder, a married person who commits illegal sexual intercourse, and the one who reverts from Islam (apostate) and leaves the Muslims." The Hadith are more concerned about this than the Qur'an.

Contextualizing and placing the death penalty for apostasy in the time of Muhammad's tribal wars, can explain the different approaches. Wael Hallaq, a noted Islamic scholar, states that "[in] a culture whose lynchpin is religion, religious principles, and religious morality, apostasy is in some way equivalent to high treason in the modern nation-state". Many conservative Muslims think that Islam is under threat. At a minimum, apostate Muslims are frequently shunned by their family and community. In the US, openly apostate Muslims have formed a nonprofit organization named Ex-Muslims of North America (EXMNA) to protect and support those leaving the religion. It is a 501c organization with a website.

Some Islamic scholars feel that any utterance that implies disbelief is apostasy. Therefore, heresy becomes apostasy. Twelve Muslim majority states have the death penalty for apostasy, and in thirteen others apostasy is illegal. Punishments range from disenfranchisement, to taking away one's children, to physical punishment, to execution [61]. It is extremely rare that a Muslim majority state carries these out. However, religious mobs and vigilantes can and do threaten or kill those charged with these issues [60]. In this internet age of easily formed religious mobs, accusations can be very dangerous. Some Islamic nations don't punish apostates, but they do not control or punish the fundamentalist vigilantes that carry out violence on apostates. It is probable, that in most predominantly Islamic states today, one can sit in a café and discuss apostasy, blasphemy, and sacrilege without much trouble. Doing it to a larger audience is another more complex and dangerous issue.

Shunning for apostasy is frequent in all the monotheisms. No family of any religion wants apostate members. Apostasy can be a particular personal danger in Islam when it involves the legal system of a state operating under conservative Sharia.

At this point in time, the Islamic law schools seem to have many conservative members who want to punish apostates. Their influence concerning apostasy is great as can be seen by the map below. It highlights the countries with draconian punishments for apostasy. The following statement covers opinions on apostasy from one school of Sharia law. Others are about this severe.

"Once a person becomes a Muslim, he cannot recant. If he does, he will be warned first, then he will be given three days to reconsider and repent. If he persists in his apostasy, his wife is required to divorce him, his property is confiscated, and his children are taken away from him. He is not allowed to remarry. Instead, he should be taken to court and sentenced to death. If he repents, he may return to his wife and children or remarry. An apostate female is not allowed to get married. She must spend time in meditation in order to return to Islam. If she does not repent or recant, she will not be sentenced to death, but she is to be persecuted, beaten, and jailed until she dies."

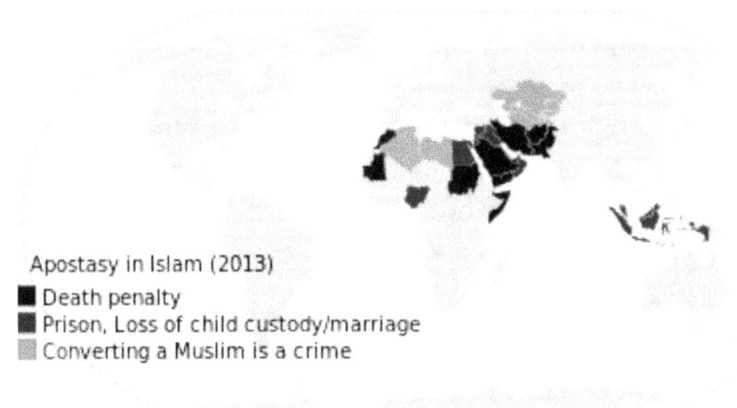

Apostasy in Islam (2013)
■ Death penalty
■ Prison, Loss of child custody/marriage
▓ Converting a Muslim is a crime

Today a Pew Research finding concerning death for apostasy in Islam reports that opinions vary greatly across the Islamic majority nations. 78% of people in Afghanistan support the death penalty. In Kazakhstan only 1% do.

Today almost no one is executed by the state for apostasy, but charges of apostasy can be very dangerous. Politicians can be removed from office. Occasionally, fundamentalist Muslim vigilantes kill those accused of apostasy or blasphemy. Just yesterday, March 4, 2022, two Sunni Salafist suicide bombers killed 63 and wounded over 200 Shia who were praying at a mosque in Pakistan. Fundamentalist Sunni generally think Shia are apostates.

f. Women. There is a variety of vaguely Religious Rules concerning women and their roles in the society and the religion. Women have lesser positions in the Hebrew Scriptures. When women are mentioned by Paul and Muhammad, they are usually separated and given lesser value. [62] Jesus treats them as equals. Before the protections of functional liberal democracy and technology, women frequently needed sheltering.

In various tribal or aristocratic tyrannies, women who were outside the home were exposed to confiscation or exploitation by more powerful men. A religion that protected the families and promoted domestic male dominance was very desirable, particularly to the less powerful males.

There are Religious Rules controlling women's appearance from all the Prophets except Jesus. Some level of modesty is recommended or demanded so that men will not be tempted or so that rituals like prayer are properly carried out. There are numerous websites where information concerning dress and grooming are discussed. A website Al Islam.org expresses the opinion of many Islamic websites when it states that temptation is such a powerful driver that women's appearance should be controlled to avoid problems. Also, makeup and nail polish are discouraged during prayer. They are felt to block the water used in cleansing from reaching the skin or nails.

Before modern conveniences, women's labor was essential in preparing the food, caring for the children, and maintaining the home. That occupied most of their time. Educating them was a luxury. Today, with modern conveniences and relatively safe societies, separation and education are not the issues that they once were. Most families no longer need to place restraints on women. The spread of organized law and order and the invention of guns made women more capable of protecting themselves. Ultimately, these events seem to have helped eliminate the need to control and shelter women. They have resulted in the empowerment of women in many societies.

Today, in many of the Protestant churches in the West, women's roles are generally equal to men's roles in the ceremonial, theological, and administrative aspects of religions. Paul assigned them lesser roles in some of his writings (First Timothy 2:11-12). Catholics don't allow women to perform many parts of the services and rituals. Jesus treated them equally but engaged in no rituals other than baptism and communion. In most Christian sects any believer can perform baptism in an emergency. Everyone is generally equal in those performances.

In 7th century Arabia, Sharia law was a step forward for women. Muhammad eliminated the killing of girl children in times of famine. He encouraged the polygamous marriage of men to women who had lost their husbands. In several verses, women were assigned some lesser legal status and less inheritance (Qur'an 2:228), but the fact that they had legal status was new and important. In a controversial verse, the Qur'an (4:34) says "Men have authority over women because God has made one superior to the other, and because they spend their wealth to maintain them. Good women are obedient. They guard their unseen parts because God has guarded them. As for those from whom you fear disobedience, admonish them, and send them to beds apart and hit them. Then if they obey you, take no further action against them."

g. Proselytizing. Jews are not missionary. They do not seek to convert others actively. The more orthodox emphasize the Jewish community's continued mission as an example to the world. They do accept converts.

Christians are clearly told by Jesus to spread the word of God. Matthew 28: 19-20. They send missionaries everywhere and have opened many thousands of schools and universities that teach literature, science, philosophy, history, etc. as well as Christian doctrine. Christian majority countries allow proselytizing of all sorts.

Most Islamic majority countries forbid attempts to convert Muslims. (U.S. Department of State's 2016 International Religious Freedom Report.) This is probably because of the prohibitions on apostasy. Apostasy is so dreaded by the Islamic community and family that condemnation of apostates is clearly recommended. "Their reward will be the curse of God, the angels and all men: under it they shall abide forever."(Qur'an 3:88-90) There are no exact written prohibitions concerning Christian proselytizing in the Qur'an. The Qur'an does repeatedly advise Muslims to avoid social contact with non-Muslims. (Qur'an 3:28, 3:90, 3:118) There are various rules limiting the building of churches. Many Christian communities in Muslim states have difficulties with militant fundamentalist Muslims including occasional murder in Egypt, Pakistan, and various dysfunctional communities [63].

h. Sexuality and Marriage. Sexuality is discussed here under two headings: adultery and fornication. Adultery is sex between someone who is married with someone who is not their spouse. Fornication is sex between non-married people.

All the Moral and Religious Rules concerning sexuality were written before science explained, and was able to control, reproductive biology. Menstruation used to be such a mystery, pregnancy such a difficulty, jealousy so dangerous, heredity so important, and sexually transmitted disease such a problem that control of the whole process was very important. It occupied a lot of thought, and many rules regarding sexuality were designed to avoid conflict and exploitation in the community. With safe birth control, antibiotics, knowledge of physiology, and medically controlled delivery, sexual activity is a lot less physically dangerous today. The deeply emotional issues of intimacy, inheritance, desire, lust, dominance, possessiveness, exploitation, and, particularly jealousy, remain.

Many Jews, Christians and Muslims consider their prophet's rules around sexuality to be Moral Rules. In them adultery and fornication are dealt with as almost the same thing. These sexually based rules do not concern the day to day running of the government or the general safety of the community like Moral Rules do, so I have placed fornication in the category of Organizational Rules. Adultery remains a Moral Rule for most religious people. The emotional and financial issues around sexuality and marriage have important effects on our communities daily, but they are not directly concerned with community safety, criminality, or business issues.

Arranged marriages are not required in the monotheisms, but in these very paternalistic societies, they are common in some areas of Islam and Hinduism. The lesser power assigned to women and the historical controlling paternalism of their societies seem to promote it. Forced marriages are illegal in many cultures. Forced marriage is forbidden in Islam. (Hadith Bukhari 6968). The United Kingdom's Forced Marriage Unit says that it gets reports of about 400 per year, almost all are Islamic. 85% women, 15% men (*Muslim Women's Network*, UK, June 2011).

Women must have consent of legal guardian for marriage in Islam. Guardians can be fathers, brothers, uncles, or other males. If the guardian will not consent, she can appeal to religious authorities. The future spouse must be a Muslim in good standing to be approved by the authorities.

Adultery is the subject of a lot of religious writing in all the monotheisms. It is specifically mentioned in the Ten Commandments. Adultery disrupts the harmony of the family and society, and for many people, it has Moral and Religious Rule components. Adultery's emotional damages to family and relationships are real and powerful. All the major religious texts clearly condemn adultery. They are less clear about fornication. Many religious scholars think that adultery and fornication should be treated as the same thing.

In the Jewish Torah (The first five books of the Tanakh and the Law of God as revealed to Moses), it is clearly stated that the prescribed penalty for adultery is death. (Leviticus 20:10). The Jewish Tanakh recommends stoning a prospective bride if she is found not to be a virgin in Deuteronomy 22:20-22. Jews have long since given up using the Religious Rules to punish adultery or anything else.

Jesus says that adultery is a sin but recommends no punishment here on earth. Jesus in the New Testament is asked to judge a woman caught in adultery. The local religious authorities are trying to trap him. If he says stone her, he will be complying with the Jewish law, but he will be acting contrary to his compassionate message. If he says let her go, he will be going against Jewish law. After drawing in the sand for a moment, he looks up and says, "He among you who is without sin can cast the first stone." The accusers are dismayed, and they disband. Then Jesus forgives her, and she receives no punishment. (John 8:1-11)

The Qur'an recommends flogging for adultery (Qur'an 24:2) or confinement until death (Qur'an 4:15). Some of the Hadith clearly recommend stoning to death (Bukhari 6:60:79, Muslim 17:4192). The Qur'an does not recommend stoning. Conviction requires that four males must testify, and some experts say the accusers must witness penetration. This is so extreme that conviction would be very difficult. Also, it is a very serious sin for a witness to lie in the case of adultery. False accusations about adultery can be punished by flogging or death. Today most Islamic law schools recommend that convicted adulterers are to be lashed or stoned to death (Oxford Encyclopedia of the Islamic World). Sex with one's slaves is, clearly permitted. (Qur'an 23:5)

Fornication is a different matter now that sex is safer and birth control is available. Fornication is not discussed as such in the Tanakh, but as mentioned above in Leviticus, a betrothed Jewish woman who is not a virgin is to be stoned. Paul says fornicators will not enter the kingdom of heaven. "Do you not know that wrongdoers will not inherit the kingdom of God? Do not be deceived! Fornicators, idolaters, adulterers, male prostitutes, sodomites, thieves, the greedy, drunkards, revilers, robbers—none of these will inherit the kingdom of God." (New Revised Standard Version. 1 Corinthians 6:9–10). Jesus implies fornication is a sin but proposes no punishments. "For from within, out of the heart of men, proceed evil thoughts, adulteries, fornications, murders" (Mark 7:21). In Matthew 5:27, Jesus says that if you lust a woman in your heart, you have already committed adultery. A difficult standard. Concerning punishments in general, Jesus in one verse recommends that one should punish oneself rather than having others do it. In one of the Gospels, Jesus' recommended self-punishments are rather drastic. "Tear out your eye...cut off your hand, if they offend you." (Matthew 18:7-9) These recommendations are not enforced by the religious community or the government. They are generally considered to be metaphorical.

The caste system still has very strong and dangerous remnants in Indian society. [64] Hinduism formerly had several punishments for adultery, particularly across caste lines. These punishments were enforced when the caste system was in effect. In the past, those in the upper castes convicted of adultery could get away with some sort of relatively minor punishment. Those lower down were killed. In India since 1950, many rulings and affirmative action laws have been enacted to eliminate the caste system, but it remains in effect within the culture. Particularly, women in rural areas have a difficult time.

Buddhist monks are defrocked for fornication, but Buddhists are not punished by the religious authorities in any way for anything. There are five fundamental precepts of Buddhist morality: Buddhists must refrain from taking life, committing theft, indulging in sexual misconduct, giving false speech, and using intoxicants.

Confucius opposed excessive licentiousness as a practical matter due to the accompanying problems. He recommends against licentiousness in a framework of ethical self-cultivation. Confucius, unlike Aristotle, thought that punishment did not work well to control people [65].

> "If you try to guide the common people with coercive regulations and keep them in line with punishments, the common people will become evasive and will have no sense of shame. If, however, you guide them with virtue, and keep them in line by means of ritual, the people will have a sense of shame and will rectify themselves."- Confucius.

Cultures are sometimes defined by how they maintain control and keep order. Guilt cultures rely on the citizen's sense of personal failure to maintain a moral standard. Shame or honor cultures rely on fear of being degraded in the opinion of others and losing status. Fear cultures rely on fear of punishment. Individual religious cultures can rely on all three, but guilt is felt to be the most prominent. Group cultures can also rely on all three but have a particularly strong shame component.

Separating the sexes before marriage obviously limits the promiscuity problems, and covering the women is thought to decrease excess sexual thoughts and temptations. The statistics on Internet pornography indicate that pornography is common in repressive societies. Today with birth control and safer sex, many feel the religious controls around sexuality are excessive and neurotic. They feel that some of these rules create more problems than they solve. In a culture that prioritizes the individual, like the West, social mingling is felt to be more important and emotionally healthier than separation. To avoid exploitation, most of the nations in the world have established age limits to consent in the late teens.

Religious Rules about covering, mixing, dating, dishonoring the family, and adultery are sincere group efforts to make society more pious, pure, and secure. They create problems if enforced by the state or by threats from religious vigilantes. In many cases guilt and shame work well to control disruptive activities without creating tragedies.

"Honor killings" are particularly awful results in Pakistan, Iran, and parts of India. The following quote is from Brandeis University, *The Feminist Sexual Ethics Project. Honor Killings, Illicit Sex, and Islamic Law.*

"These killings, which occur with shocking regularity in certain parts of the Middle East and South Asia, target women whose actions—actual or suspected—violate the honor of their families, an honor that is thought to depend on the sexual purity of its female members. Anything from speaking with an unrelated man, to rumored pre-marital loss of virginity, to an extra-marital affair can be cause for an attack, often carried out by a father or brother. In some especially tragic instances, even women and girls who have been raped are slain to remove the stain from the family honor. As with other forms of intimate violence against women, perpetrators are seldom punished."

There are about 5000 a year worldwide, with about 1000 in Pakistan. 80-90 percent are women. There is no mention of honor killing in the Qur'an or Hadith, and Muslim scholars are almost unanimous in condemning the practice. The secondary status of women, the strict piety, the shaming of group consciousness, and the paternalism that still exists in certain middle eastern and south Asian societies seem to have allowed honor killing to continue.

Some apologists compare honor killings to "crimes of passion" in the West. In reality honor killings are brutal events intentionally and premeditatedly carried out by family males and supported by the female elders in an attempt to control their daughters. On the other hand, Western "crimes of passion" are actions fueled by jealousy or anger between two mates, one of whom has broken very serious vows or relationships. Many crimes of passion are spontaneous, and some are instantaneous. Crimes of passion are for personal revenge. Honor killings are about control and bizarre concepts of "honor". As mentioned above, in some instances, females who were raped are considered to have dishonored the family and are the victims of honor killing. Western crimes of passion are completely unrelated to honor killings. Equating the two is a blatant sophistry.

"Dowry deaths" where the wife is killed because she did not provide enough dowry occur principally in Iran, Pakistan, India, and Bangladesh. From 8,000 to 12,000 per year are reported. The lower status of women and the power of the patriarchy seem to set the stage for these atrocities. Dowry deaths exist only in group cultures including Hindus, Sikhs, and Muslims. They are not mentioned in any religious texts.

Female genital mutilation (FGM) is very controversial. It exists primarily in Sunni Islam in the Middle East, Africa, and Indonesia. It consists of some form of cutting the external genitalia of women to decrease their sexual desires. A few Coptic Christians in Africa perform it. FGM is not mentioned in the Qur'an, however one Hadith supports it. The four principal Islamic schools of jurisprudence support it to some degree or another. The Hanafi and Hanbali schools say that it is "noble" for women. The Maliki say it is recommended. The Shafi' say it is obligatory. The principal Islamic figure in Iran, Ali al Sistani, a Shia, says it should not be done. Ali Gomaa, a Sufi and former Grand Mufti of Egypt, stated: "It's prohibited, prohibited, prohibited."

FGM originated before Islam but was grafted on. A stern patriarchal ideology concerned about public piety, control, shaming, the secondary status of women, and the need to force female obedience probably promoted FGM. It is also practiced by animist groups in Liberia. Some Coptic Christians in Ethiopia and Egypt participate. No Jewish, Catholic or Protestant organizations support it. Despite some clear legal support for FGM by the main Islamic jurisprudence law schools, the Organization of Islamic Cooperation condemns it. The Muslim Brotherhood recommends it.

Some apologists suggest that female genital cutting, or mutilation should be compared to circumcision. This comparison is completely erroneous. Female genital cutting has to do with control of women and their sexuality by force. Also, certain types of it can cause serious problems with infection, intercourse, and childbirth. Male circumcision, on the other hand, is done for ritual membership or health. It doesn't affect sexual performance or pleasure. Circumcised males have less phimosis, smegma infection, and penile cancer. The female partners of circumcised males have less cervical cancer. This juxtaposition of FGM and male circumcision is a completely misleading sophistry.

Map of FGM prevalence worldwide.

The questions around sexual temptation, covering and purity could be put under several headings in this book. In all the monotheisms women are advised to avoid tempting men to think sexual thoughts with lascivious attire. Modest dress and various degrees of covering are advised for women. How much? That is a difficult question to answer. Enforcing arbitrary standards by the state or vigilantes goes against Western assurances of individual freedom. Shouldn't the men have more control of their impulses? Western democracies have dress standards generally based on mutual consent of the citizens, but they are extremely lax. In orthodox Islam wearing nail polish, lipstick, and other makeup at prayer or in front of men who are not her family is frequently forbidden. A typical quote from one of the Internet sites giving advice on Islamic issues says to avoid makeup and to cover as much as possible. Questionable clothes, makeup, and nail polish should not be worn during prayer "…because purity of clothes and body are essential for the prayer to be valid".

Prostitution is legal in about half the nations in the world, limited in about 15%, and forbidden in about 35 percent. In almost all Muslim countries it is illegal. Generally Islamic nation's laws permit flogging or prison as punishment. Other nations recommend fines or prison. Confucianism allowed for concubines.

i. Homosexuality. Somewhere in each of the texts of all the great monotheistic religions, homosexuality is mentioned as a practice to be avoided. The Hebrew Scriptures or Old Testament recommends killing homosexuals (Leviticus 20:13). Jews don't pay much attention to any of the punishments prescribed in the Old Testament. There are no laws against homosexuals in Israel. Israeli law does not allow for same sex marriage but recognizes same sex marriage done elsewhere.

Paul in the New Testament recommends against homosexuality but describes no penalty on earth (1 Corinthians 6:10; 9:11). Jesus never mentions it. Some Western Christians object to same sex marriage but recommend no punishments for homosexuals. Sixty-nine countries have laws criminalizing same sex relations. Almost all of them are in Africa and the Middle East. (Human Rights Watch)

In Islam, the Qur'an (4:16) says to "punish" homosexuals. It doesn't say exactly how. They may then be forgiven by God if they repent. Some of Muhammad's sayings in his Hadith recommend "turning them out" (Hadith, Bukhari 7:72:774). Others recommend stoning them to death (Hadith, Dawud 38:4448). Thirteen Islamic majority countries have the death penalty for homosexuality [66]. These are infrequently enforced by the state, but they do create dangerous possibilities. Extremists in ISIS and vigilantes in Iran and Pakistan have killed gays recently. As recently as 2019, Saudi Arabia beheaded five men for homosexuality. Although ISIS rose from distressed Islamic peoples, and claims Islamic sanction, the only Muslims supporting ISIS are the Wahabi in Saudi Arabia and Qatar. Recently a shooter, named Omar Mateen claiming allegiance to ISIS, killed 49 people in a mass shooting at Pulse, a gay nightclub in Orlando, Florida.

Confucius didn't condemn homosexuality. However, Confucianism's emphasis on family harmony has tended to make Chinese generally disapprove of homosexuality. The principal texts of Hinduism and Buddhism are mildly ambivalent and have no significant problems with homosexuality.

The tolerance and diversity championed by today's Western societies would categorize condemnations of homosexuality as bigotry. Today, in the West, it is recognized that a small percent of the community is homosexual. Sexual activity among consenting homosexual adults is legal and marriage is accepted in 29 countries (*Human Rights Campaign: Marriage Equity around the World, 2019*). There is a fine line between tolerance and promotion that disturbs some in an open society. Overt pressure to participate in homosexual experimentation in adolescence would seem to be a poor idea. Adolescence is confusing enough. As a rule, in the West, individual decision is the norm. Youthful medical and surgical issues concerning gender fluidity issues are very controversial.

i. Polygyny. (Multiple wives) Religious Rules authorizing polygyny seem to be designed to benefit males and the desires of the powerful. In poor dysfunctional countries polygyny could theoretically be a desirable alternative for widows and poor women. In societies without good welfare systems, it can offer financial assistance and security for widows or women. It was possibly first promulgated in Islam to deal with 7th century Arabian widows created by tribal feuding. Polygyny gave them needed protection.

Some studies show the severe emotional price that polygyny exacts in modern western nations. [67] The lack of intimacy, impossibility of equality, and inevitable jealousy combine to make polygyny a poor choice for most women. Emotional bullying of the insecure would still be possible. Groups of wives could result in disturbing pressures on young women. Is polygynous union better than no union in a society with adequate welfare? Can a person become deeply emotionally intimate if s/he has more than one sexual partner?

The Jews in the Old Testament had numerous examples of polygyny. Since about 1100 C.E., Judaism has discouraged it. In Genesis, 2:24 it states, "Therefore a man shall leave his father and his mother and hold fast to his wife, and they shall become one flesh". Generally, Christianity and Judaism have taken this to mean that a man should only have one wife. Jesus was unmarried and repeats this verse when speaking of marriage. The ancient Greeks and Romans were monogamous but frequently had concubines and mistresses. Polygyny was socially improper.

Polygyny is legal in 80 countries, but is slowly diminishing in all parts of the world today. Muhammad was polygynous and had nine wives. Life was hard, and, in early Arab society, widows were frequently taken as extra wives for their protection. Widows derived many benefits from polygyny. Muhammad married Aisha, his third wife, at about age nine according to the Hadith. (Hadith: Bukhari 5:58:234, Muslim 8:3311) Some say that it is not clearly known how old she was, and all think that the marriage was not consummated until she was sexually mature. She was devoted to Mohammed and outlived him by forty-four years.

The Qur'an has two statements on multiple wives. Sura 4:3 says, "If you fear that you shall not be able to deal justly with the orphans, marry women of your choice, two or three, or four; but if you fear that you shall not be able to deal justly (with them) then only one." Qur'an Sura 4:129 says: "You are never able to be fair and just between women even if that were your ardent desire."

India outlawed polygyny in 1956 for Hindus. Indian Muslims may have four wives under certain difficult conditions. It is not clearly forbidden in Hinduism or Buddhism but is frowned upon whenever it is mentioned. The 1948 UN Declaration on Human Rights condemns polygyny. Many Muslim countries allow up to four wives.

k. Children and sex. Sex with children before puberty is condemned today in the world. It is not mentioned directly in the Jewish or Christian texts. Most Christian and Muslim nations now have an age of consent in the mid to high teens. In the Book of Matthew, Jesus says you would be better off to have a millstone tied to your neck and thrown into the sea than to injure a child on purpose. Muhammad's 3rd wife was very young, but most scholars think that the marriage was not consummated until puberty. (Hadith, Bukhari 7:62:64)

Chapter 6

Religious Rules: Interpretation, Judgment and Enforcement

Some religious rules can have multiple meanings and can be challenging to interpret. Here are some examples

A. Interpretation problems. What do these the Religious Rule intend or mean? Interpretation can be challenging.

1. <u>No work on the Sabbath.</u> Do home improvements or helping a neighbor involve forbidden work? Can I do charity work? Can I practice medicine? Modern utilities require constant attention.

2. <u>Don't drink alcohol.</u> Don't drink to excess? Don't ever drink? Forbid drink to others?

3. <u>Don't worship false idols.</u> No drawings? No statues? No holy sites? Destroy the images of other sects?

4. <u>Be modest and don't flaunt your sexual allure.</u> Nail polish? Facial makeup? Completely cover? Force women to cover? Wear a hijab (head scarf)? [68]

5. <u>Don't murder.</u> Does this mean only premeditated murder? In self-defense? Animals? Abortion? War?

6. <u>Is fornication ever allowed?</u> Is consensual premarital sex OK?

7. <u>No mingling of the sexes.</u> No dating? No parties? No dancing?

8. <u>Attitudes towards homosexuals.</u> Punish them? Kill them?

9. <u>Polygyny.</u> Allowed? Encouraged?

10. <u>Arranged marriage.</u> Forced marriage? All the monotheisms condemn forced marriage, but it still plays a role in the Middle East and India.

11. <u>Punish apostasy.</u> Shun apostates? Kill apostates? (69)

12. <u>Spread the word.</u> Become a missionary? Forced conversions?

13. <u>Don't eat pork.</u> It is frequently mentioned that some of the Religious Rules, particularly those concerning food, seem to address health concerns in a prescientific era. For example, in the past avoiding pork avoided trichinosis. This may well be true, but we are no longer "prescientific". These food rules are adhered to for traditional or ritual value, and members of a group can be judged on their adherence.

14. <u>Don't divorce except for adultery.</u> None of the prophets like divorce, but it is allowed in all the religions except Catholicism which considers it a sin. Jesus recommends divorce only for adultery (Matthew 5:31-32). Orthodox Judaism requires that the male must consent. The Qur'an says that God dislikes divorce very much. Islam makes divorce easier for the male, but he must restore any dowry.

B. Judgment problems. Who is to decide if a Religious Rule is broken?

1. The state courts?

2. Religious courts? Composed of ministers? Scholars? Clerics? Self-appointed vigilantes?

3. Each person?

4. Are you supposed to tell on others? Does one sin by not telling?

5. Is a punishment to be meted out? How much of a punishment?

6. Is leniency or forgiveness to be allowed?

7. What is minor, and what is major?

8. Is this rule being brought up for political purposes or harassment?

9. Is a particular difference of belief considered heresy and blasphemy, or is it honest criticism? Can people disagree without dangerous consequences?

C. Enforcement problems.

1. Who is to enforce and punish? Which rules are to be enforced?

2. Can you give a harsh punishment for a minor infraction? Should one be merciful?

3. Only officers of the nation state?

4. Church officials, religious clerics, or mosque appointed authorities?

5. Can one inflict punishment on people who are not in the church or religious community?

6. Should everyone be involved in enforcement? Should I punish others for Religious Rule infractions?

7. Should we punish or kill adulterers? Homosexuals? Apostates? Heretics? Blasphemers?

Currently Jews generally use reasoned analysis of the Tanakh and the Talmud to decide how to answer these questions. Catholics recommend that one come to the Catholic Church for guidance. Protestant churches and ministers frequently give opinions to the members, some much more extensive than others. There are hundreds of Christian websites, but a moderate search reveals that almost none deal with Religious Rules other than belief. Punishments are not recommended. Islamic religious sources, particularly the Sharia law schools give very detailed legal advice on all these Religious Rules. Islamic web sites give this advice also. Some recommend many punishments. A brief search of the internet revealed several dozen Islamic sites in English.

Enforcing the Religious Rules has caused serious problems: inquisitions, holy wars, schisms, physical mutilations, misogyny, homophobia, punishment for victimless crimes, and family arguments of all sorts.

Religious Rule Consequences

In general, one must obey the Moral Rules and follow the General Admonitions to be saved or go to heaven. All the General Admonitions recommend that we should "be kind and honest with each other". The Religious Rules add an additional set of requirements. It seems obvious that adherence to the Moral Rules and General Admonitions offers benefits to society. Following the Religious Rules can make one feel comfortable, pious, or holy but, they do not usually offer benefits to others or the community. If imposed by authority, Religious Rules eliminate the primary individual human rights.

Many individuals voluntarily adhere to Religious Rules as a means of remaining purely focused on God or eternal salvation. Many adhere because their lives are fuller and less chaotic when licentiousness and temptation are lessened. Most adhere because they are born into a particular religion, and they like the family, the rituals, the celebrations, and the safety of a warm community. Personal adherence to the Religious Rules is not the problem. However, wherever there are prominent Religious Rules, there is the possibility that someone in the community will want to create a "holy" environment based on Religious Rules. They may want to use the state or a mob to produce and enforce their idea of piety.

Judaism has survived as an international tribal entity far longer than any other prominent tribe or group. It appears this is due to a combination of a concise set of fundamental rules (i.e. The Ten Commandments) and the fact that they were not charged to convert others or dominate them. They did have over 600 rules, but they were only for the Jewish people. Very importantly, they were ordered not to marry outside of Judaism. The Talmud says that a marriage outside the faith is not recognized as a marriage. Other than the instructions to take the land of Canaan by force, they were only charged to be an example to others. In taking Canaan they were told by their God to kill all the inhabitants. (Joshua 6:21, 9:24).

The Religious Rules only applied to the Jewish people, and reform or moderate Jews ignore most of them.

As a side effect, Religious Rules also divide the world into groups or tribes of "others". There is the group that follows the Religious Rules, and the group that does not. Judaism was very tribal in its thinking. However, they had no interest in converting or coercing others. In Christianity, Paul's letters generally recommended avoiding drunkards, fornicators, and similar others. Jesus mixed frequently with nonbelievers and never ostracized people. As mentioned previously the Qur'an recommends in some places that Muslims avoid the company of infidels. Most of these Qur'anic recommendations for separation and avoidance can be contextualized to the times of open conflict.

In this milieu of Religious Rules, people can be judged by their actions. If they do not openly profess the right beliefs, follow the Religious Rules, wear the right clothes, pray at the right times, eat the right foods, avoid alcohol, avoid dance, etc., they are judged to be lesser and often can be treated as such. It is certainly not a good idea to associate with thieves, bullies, and liars, but avoiding and judging others based on adherence to Religious Rules can create unnecessary tension. When adherence is demanded by the community or state, the enforcement can easily create a very oppressive atmosphere.

Totalitarianism can be the result of insistence on following Religious Rules. Religious Rule "reasoning" which leads to political totalitarianism can go something like this. "If we are pure enough and please God, the state will surely be successful. It the state is not successful; it is because we are not pure enough. When the state is not doing well, it is because we are not pious enough, and we need to crack down on impurity. The state must enforce more piety. More piety is the answer." The totalitarian net tightens.

"Islam is the answer" is a common sentiment in some Muslim religious groups. Many feel that a stricter adherence to Islam's Religious Rules and Sharia law would have material as well as spiritual benefits.

"Islam is the answer" is also the motto of the Muslim Brotherhood. It is very conservative and lately has done a lot of charity work to enhance its image and gather followers. It gained power through election in Egypt but proved to be very oppressively orthodox. It recommends FGM [70]. It was removed from power by a military coup. Any totalitarian Islamic system might decrease corruption, but, like socialist solutions, it would certainly be at the price of loss of personal freedom. Ironically, some form of temporary totalitarian system may be the only way to gain control of the endemic corruption that eliminates progress in all sorts of poorly performing governments.

The Religious Rules can also be used as weapons against political foes. Charges of heresy and blasphemy can confuse or corrupt the electoral, political, and judicial process in any government or culture that recognizes sanctions based on Religious Rules.

To Summarize

Religious Rules:

1. Are revealed.
2. Concern holiness, purity, or piety. They are supposed to please God.
3. Create "others" by dividing people into groups.
4. Their origins are in the texts and must be dealt with repeatedly in each generation.
5. They invite the creation of religious courts, judges, and police. They can join church and state. They can eliminate individual human rights of speech and religion.
6. They can confuse the political process with charges of blasphemy, heresy, and apostasy.
7. They make many common actions and interactions serious. Everything can become serious.

Chapter 7

How much of a Pious Environment?

Groups or leaders may feel that the actions of people outside the group cause problems for the pursuit of the piety that is needed to attain heaven or paradise. A pious atmosphere is very important to many religious people. Jewish scripture encourages a lot of piety. Jesus says most pious acts should be private matters. When discussing piety, Muhammad says that "Men are equal like the teeth of a comb. The only difference between one or the other is the level of piety" Hadith *Shah Waliullah* 16:40. Other people may do things that are confusing, encourage temptation, offend the group, or outrage the sense of propriety. There are several possible courses of action.

1. One can **ignore** these confusing acts or tempting issues.
2. One can actively **punish** or confine those who disturb the pious environment.
3. One can view the perpetrators as just part of the process that one must deal with and **incorporate** them into one's practices or spiritual journey.
4. One can try to **change** the environment and the perpetrators through education, conversion, and/or evangelism instead of punishment.

#1. Ignore. As far as #1 is concerned, to some extent, everyone ignores religious differences and temptations. It is necessary for daily life.

#2. Punish. Some religious communities do lots of judging and punishing of heretics, blasphemers, and the noncompliant. When the religions enlist the state, it becomes totalitarian. When the religious followers become extralegal vigilantes and punish others, it is awful.

#3. Include. All Eastern religions and mystics endorse this inclusion aspect to some extent. Almost everything that is not patently dangerous or grossly immoral must be included and worked through. Forgiveness is the only path in many cases. Arriving at mutually agreed upon decisions through forgiveness and inclusion is usually a sign of maturity.

#4. Change. Christians generally are very interested in conversion and education. They have founded thousands of schools that teach and discuss everything. They send missionaries all over the world, to convert, not conquer. Saudi Arabian Wahabis support *madrassas* (religious schools teaching mainly the Qur'an) that promote a very fundamentalist Islam throughout the Middle East, Africa, and Indonesia. Many worry that these schools will create a new crop of fundamentalist vigilantes. They have already made Indonesia less tolerant and harsher.

Eternal life, enlightenment and happiness are great rewards for following the Religious Rules. The stakes are high. People get very serious about Religious Rule observation and acts of heresy or sacrilege. For Orthodox Judaism the laws and the Religious Rules must be followed. For Reform Jews, good deeds are more important than piety. For many Christians a moral life, kindness to others, service for the poor, and orthodox "belief" in the divinity of Jesus are the things necessary for salvation. More fundamental Christians, Muslims, and Jews must be moral and "do" the right action as described by the Religious Rules. All religions have aspects of both orthodoxy and orthopraxy. As far as specific Religious Rules go, Christianity is almost completely an orthodoxy; the specifics of one's beliefs are most important. Orthodox Judaism, conservative Christianity, and much of Islam can be very concerned with following the Religious Rules or orthopraxy. One's actions vis-a-vis the Religious Rules are often seriously important in a group-oriented society.

Buddhism and Hinduism are a mixture. Some orthopraxy and some orthodoxy. No punishments. Confucianism and Taoism are not about salvation. Confucius says that "Man cannot know such things."

Reason alone dictates that disturbances, and noxious intrusions on other's environment should be limited. In individualistic democratic societies, this is decided by mutual consent under the protection of individual rights. Religious communities frequently want to maintain a level of public piety that is much stricter than the general norm. Roger Scruton, in his book *The West and the Rest*, argues that the differences and problems between Islam and the rest of the world, particularly the West, are essentially the result of desiring different levels of piety.

The mass celebrations and rituals of the Hajj (pilgrimage to Mecca) are unique to Islam. Judaism and Christianity have nothing like them. They are particularly impressive and memorable to those who attend. In daily life the timed prayer rituals can be very reassuring and pleasing. They can give a deep sense of community. Rituals are particularly strong in conservative Judaism and observant Islam. Christians in the West are accustomed to a teacher, Jesus, who recommended that the pieties are private matters. One should pray, give money, fast, and forgive out of the public view (Matthew 6:1-20) [7].

As discussed earlier, Islam is ambivalent concerning the question: Is there one Islam or many? Externally politicians and clerics want Islam to be seen and treated as one community. However, internally there are serious differences about leadership, and recurrent severe violence between some sects and against other religious groups. Some influential Muslims seem to feel that outside action against any Muslim entity or nation is action against Islam as a whole. If Islam want to be seen as a whole, critics will point out that numerous groups claiming Islamic membership are brutal and oppressive.

They also seem to feel that their beloved Islam is being prejudicially judged in a generalized and inaccurate way. They feel that colonialism and exploitation have caused most of the problems in the Islamic world and that the religion is being unfairly blamed for problems produced by this Western interference.

Since 1990 Pakistan has had the death penalty for blasphemy. As mentioned above Pakistani Prime Minister Imran Khan recently defended these potentially lethal laws for those who offend the Prophet Muhammad by "imputation, insinuation or innuendo". Khan urged the Organization for Islamic Cooperation (OIC) to protect the Prophet from criticism. At the OIC's 14th Islamic Summit in Mecca Khan said, "It was up to us to explain to the Western people the amount of pain they cause us when they ridicule or mock our Holy Prophet," Also, "I would like to say from this platform that in the forums like the United Nations and the forums like the European Union, we must explain to them that they cannot hurt the sentiments of 1.3 billion people under the garb of freedom of expression." Other religions are less concerned about criticism.

Prime Minister Khan correctly notes that in France and Germany, in spite of freedom of speech laws, holocaust denial speech is against the law and can be punished. He and President Erdogan would like similar legal punishment for ridicule of Muhammad. It seems clear that it is reasonable to note that Holocaust denial is a lie about documented historical facts used only in racist anti-Semitic discourse and that it is threatening in nature. Threats are not protected speech. In the West ridicule of important figures is everywhere. The West is used to an environment where Judaism, Christianity, and Jesus have been and are subjected to all sorts of degrading depictions and insults. An artwork with a statue of Jesus on the cross in a glass of urine is one of the most famous examples[71]. Most reasonable people will not tread heavily on other's religious sensibilities. Those that do can be mean-spirited. Some critics should probably be shunned intellectually but punishing them for expressing their opinions is contrary to basic rights.

All religious people want respect for their prophets. Many secularists see little to respect. To the secularists, religion causes many problems, and all the monotheisms have many issues that need corrective criticism. In this climate, freedom of speech almost guarantees that prophets will be "disrespected". In the light of these facts, the current requests by President Erdogan in Turkey and President Khan in Pakistan for prohibitions on critical discussions of Islam and Muhammad are seen by Westerners as anti-democratic infringements on the freedom of speech and inquiry.

Today terrorists claim Islamic sanction for all sorts of atrocities from beheadings in ISIS Syria, to the slaughter of women in West Africa, to the murder of several hundred Sufis in Egypt. All these people say that Muhammad's message is their inspiration. These are all seriously wrong perversions of Muhammad's message, and they represent what fanatics of all sorts will do.

Christianity and Islam would like to see all people united in their particular dogmas and creeds. The Jews aren't interested in conversion. They are an example. Christians actively proselytize all the time. Christ charged them to bring a message of love, justice, and salvation to all peoples. Islam means "submission", submission to God and the instructions that Muhammad brought us. Some think that Islam will spread to all because it is the truth. They feel that the others will eventually see the truth. Other more fundamentalist worshipers want to force others to conform.

Chapter 8
Mysticism

Like "mysticism" itself, all talk about mysticism and mystics becomes diffuse and esoteric rather quickly. With that in mind, here is the definition of mysticism from Encyclopedia.com:

> _Mystic: A person who believes in the spiritual experience of absolute truths that are beyond the intellect. Many seek, by contemplation, ritual exercises and/or self-surrender, to obtain unity with or absorption into the Deity or this absolute._

Mysticism may not have a place in this discussion of Religious Rules. What I think of as mysticism relies on individual experience and is so personal that external group Religious Rules demanding particular pious actions have little to no relevance. True mysticism usually concerns an enlightening experience. It is a personal event, hardly ever a group event. People who have had these experiences do ban together for support and companionship. True mystics by my definition have little to no interest in miracles or the supernatural.

Most importantly, true mystics live lives of benevolence toward others. Truly enlightened mystics are kind and not doctrinaire. They also recognize that there are many ways of being a mystic and many paths to enlightenment.

Some people are lucky and have the incredibly peaceful experience that, in the end, all hopes and desires are completely fulfilled. The event is often accompanied by the experience of space and time as one thing. The experience is complete, does not last, and is truly ineffable. Some participate in spiritual rituals and ceremonies in the attempt to have the experience again. Some take drugs. Some people have intimations of this experience and become searchers or mystics in an attempt to have the complete experience. In one sense religious people are divided into three groups, those that have had the experience, those that have not, and those who want the experience.

Those who have had a religious or transformative experience know that they were lucky. They know that underneath consciousness there is no more fear. They know that time and space become one and, that, in the end, all is fulfilled. They are generally kind and optimistic.

Paul Tillich in the *Dynamics of Faith* says that we can be fulfilled only insofar as the thing we put our faith in is fulfilling. If we put our faith in money, we can be fulfilled only in so far as money is fulfilling. If we wish to be ultimately fulfilled, we must put our faith in something ultimate. True mystical or enlightened experience gives us a view of the ultimate, if only briefly.

Faith, understanding, and religious experience are the three types of religious knowledge. Having faith implies some doubt. It usually means one "believes" he/she is on the right track. A truly religious experience eliminates doubt, at least for a moment. One experiences fulfillment of all of life and desires. Unfortunately, it doesn't last long. One is left with a sense that all will turn out beautifully, but one cannot recapture the same state of absolute emotional positivity. One can "understand" that all turns out well, but, as Werner Earhart said, "Understanding is the booby prize". There is no substitute for the experience. Once you have had it, it fulfills all experiences of life and shows that time and space are the same thing. However, the pure emotional clarity that it brings doesn't last. Some people do all sorts of things to have the experience again. These are the mystical practices. Some just live in peace. There is an apocryphal story about an enlightened Buddhist monk who meets a child who is enlightened also. After only a few pleasantries the monk says, "How long have you known?" The 11-year-old child responds, "Since I was six."

The key word in mysticism is "experience", and the key experience is one that puts the individual in a state of "enlightenment". (Grace, moksha, satori, nirvana, Fana Fillah, etc.) A mystic can be said to focus on the direct experience of a God. Some Sufis say, "A contact with God". Some say, "A conversation with God." Some people have these experiences by random luck. Others meditate, fast, dance, study, pray, isolate themselves, flagellate themselves, take chemicals, etc. to repeat the experience or have it for the first time. The experience itself is ineffable. Poetry or song are among the best ways to approach it in words. Mirabai, Kabir, Rumi, Omar Khayyam, and Rainer Marie Rilke are well known mystic poets. In general, the images that they create inspire one to think more broadly and optimistically. The most profound experiences seem to move one beyond hope and fear.

By one way of thinking Hinduism and Buddhism are essentially groups of people or mystics organized in the search for this experience of enlightenment. The Hindus recognize that there are many ways to enlightenment or union with "God". They have names for the different paths to this union. The term "yoga" means "union". The various pathways to union include bhakti yoga (love or devotion), jnana yoga (knowledge or scholarship), hatha yoga (physical disciplines), kundalini yoga (sexual practices), raja yoga (meditation), and karma yoga (duty to one's family or place in life). In its principal, very abstract way of viewing life, Hinduism thinks that one can reach enlightenment by almost any path. The various forms of yoga include almost everything. Some paths are more treacherous and confusing than others. Generally, piety is thought to be a very good path, and sexuality a precarious path. *Fana fillah* is a term used by Sufi Muslims to describe their experiences when performing their religious rituals. It is said feel like a contact or conversation with God, if only briefly.

Grace is a Christian term for being lucky enough to be given a vision of the reality of existence and of Jesus' sacrifice and gift to the world. William James wrote a book, *Varieties of Religious Experience*, that gives a clear and extensive overview of the subject from a Western viewpoint.

Jesus summed up the individual nature of mysticism in two statements, "The kingdom of heaven is within." (Luke 17:21), and "You shall know the truth, and the truth shall set you free" (John 8:32). John of Patmos, the author of the last book in the Bible has Jesus saying "Behold, I am making all things new" Revelations 21:5. Also, we are told that Jesus spent "forty days in the wilderness" confronting his temptations before beginning his teaching (Matthew 4:1-10, Luke 4:1-13). That sort of discipline and practice is common to mystics, monks, and holy people of all sorts.

In early Christianity the Gnostics claimed to have special enlightened knowledge (*gnosis*) of God in the form of mystical or esoteric insight. They were not very interested in concepts of sin, but rather in enlightenment through correct knowledge. For them the lack of this correct knowledge creates sin. This knowledge is brought by various "messengers of light". Jesus was one of these messengers. The Gnostics were denounced as heretics in the second century and most of their texts were destroyed.

There are groups promoting practices which are designed by holy men/women to create a pious atmosphere or mood wherein one can feel holy or close to their God. The mood can be quiet, as in a monastery, or filled with music or chanting, or a scene of mass flagellation and wailing. Participants like to create these atmospheres where one feels close to God or has an experience of holiness or an insight into a truth.

In some way, acceptance is deeply involved in mysticism. True acceptance seems to involve some sort of profound internal peace in the face of death or injustice. This level of acceptance encourages one to act compassionately even though our situation appears ultimately hopeless. One is beyond hope and fear. Like Camus' Sisyphus, mystics can be ultimately condemned to failure but fulfilled in their efforts.

Mood making can be a byway on the path to enlightenment. My bias is that I think that the experiences of divinity or truth that happen during mood making are only valid if they increase one's compassion and kindness concerning others. Meditation, dance, chanting, flagellating, worshiping, etc. can be wonderful, but they must be optimistic, endorse brotherhood/sisterhood, and create a sense that we are all equal. If they create a sense of power or a mind frame that states "I know, and you don't", they are not truly mystical by this definition. There is an apocryphal story of the great holy man who lived on the mountain and became truly "enlightened" and at peace with the world. He came down from the mountain to the city. When he was walking on the street, someone bumped into him. His anger flared. Obviously, he was enlightened only while in a cave on the mountain. Mood making is fine, but don't substitute it for essential and difficult truth which is associated with benevolence, forgiveness, and kindness.

A short list of people, literature and groups interested in mysticism would include St. John of the Cross, St Theresa of Avilla, Jewish adherents to the Kabbalah, the Sufis, Hasan al Basra, Rumi, Mirabai, Kabir, Rilke, George Gurdjief, Madam Blavatsky, the Gnostics, Meher Baba, Rosicrucians, Masons, monks, nuns, fakirs, Hindus, Buddhists, Paramahansa Yogananda, Ram Das, Hari Das, Maharishi Mahesh Yogi, Shunryu Suzuki, numerous Zen masters, and many, many more.

I think that true mystics who have had a genuine religious or ecstatic revelation realize that there are many paths to enlightenment available all the time. The don't feel themselves to be better, just luckier. Meher Baba, a Hindu mystic, sums true mysticism when he says, "Don't worry. Be happy."

True mystic: my definition.

1. Most have "experienced" the "truth" of the universe, often by sheer luck.

2. They are usually optimistic, cheerful, compassionate, and they get along with mystics and compassionate people of all other types and religions.

3. They know that the "truth" of the universe is available to everyone all the time.

4. They know that there are many ways to experience enlightenment and that most involve luck. (Grace, moksha, etc.)

5. True Mysticism does not include magic or the supernatural. It is just the "knowledge or experience of transcendent truth".

6. Supernatural events such as magic and suspension of the laws of nature have almost no importance to them.

7. Many spiritual followers think that there are many enlightened individuals living among us, and often, "Those who say, don't know. Those who know, don't say."

8. They know that orthodoxy and orthopraxy are not essential, but often standards are needed to keep potential miscreants in line. Punishment for not observing Religious Rules is obscene.

9. As far as faith healing is concerned, I think that there are two issues. Some people are so stressed by life's events that they become ill or dysfunctional. A mystical experience can certainly help them. On rare occasions, the immunological or reparative systems of a few people seem to be mobilized to overcome diseases or deficiencies that normally are incurable. A mystical experience involving acceptance of the vagaries of life may facilitate these events.

Formal Mystics: (Monks, nuns, hermits, Rosicrucians, Gnostics, Hassid, Kabbala, Masons, Sufis, etc.) These people are sure that there is a truth "beyond the intellect." They may or may not have had an enlightening experience. They often organize in groups to assist each other.

1. Some practice pieties, join groups, perform rituals, do "spiritual" exercises, practice deprivations, meditate, study, or dance to experience this truth or enlightenment. Some can be rigid and impatient.

2. There are mystics that feel that theirs is the only path to follow to enlightenment, or that they and their followers have special knowledge unavailable to others. In the wrong hands this can lead to fanaticism or cult formation and exploitation of naïve individuals.

3. Some are interested in magic or supernatural events.

4. All the monotheisms have mystic adherents. Most are compassionate and tolerant. Mysticism in Islam is highly recognized and formalized as Sufism. Kabballah is formalized mysticism in Judaism. Most of the Christian mystics were absorbed into Catholic holy orders of one sort or another. Protestant mystics don't have any formal organization.

Sufis

Sufism is the most prominent form of Mysticism in Islam, and it is highly organized. There are many branches, and they all perform some form of *dhikr*. *Dhikr* is a meditation practice consisting of the repetition of phrases or prayers to produce remembrance of God. Some dance or whirl (They are the Whirling Dervishes of Islam) to reach states of consciousness where they develop this clearer remembrance of God. Almost all Sufi orders are against violence. Most of the calm, good humored, tolerant Muslim leaders that we see on Western TV, in discussion groups, or otherwise, are Sufis. Sufism is generally apolitical but historically has had militant elements during times of conflict. Some Muslim states support Sufism as a counterweight to fundamentalist Salafism. [73]

Some say Sufism was present in the original organizing elements of Islam. The Sufis became formalized into different orders about 300 years later. Some prominent formal Sufis, like Al Ghazali in the 11th century, promoted a sharply critical assessment of philosophy. They directed Islam away from reasoning and appreciation of Aristotelianism. Unfortunately, in giving almost exclusive importance to a rigid approach to theology in all education, they created a backlash against human reasoning that set back science in the Muslim world. More on this in Chapter 9.

Some fundamental Muslims, particularly Salafists, think that Sufis are heretics and apostates because they venerate predecessors and saints. Fundamentalist Muslims think this is a form of polytheism, *shirk*, the worst of Muslim sins. Below are excerpts from an article in the New York Times, "Who Are Sufi Muslims and Why Do Some Extremists

Hate Them?" The article by Megan Specia appeared after Islamic fundamentalists killed 305 Sufis at a mosque in Egypt in 2017.

"Its (Sufism's) modern-day adherents cherish tolerance and pluralism, qualities that in many religions unsettle extremists.... (This wasn't always true)

In modern times, the predominant view of Sufi Islam is one of "love, peace, tolerance," Mr. Knysh explained, leading to this style of worship becoming synonymous with peace-loving Islam...

While it (Sufism) is sometimes misunderstood as a sect of Islam, it a broader style of worship that transcends sects, directing followers' attention inward. Sufi practice focuses on the renunciation of worldly things, purification of the soul, and the mystical contemplation of God's nature. Followers try to get closer to God by seeking spiritual learning known as *tariqa*...

While some Muslims view Sufis as quirky, even eccentric, some fundamentalists and extremists see Sufism as a threat, and its adherents as heretics or apostates."

Cults and Messiahs

People join cults for a multitude of reasons. Often, they are looking for a family or a community. The leaders are usually very charismatic. Membership can engender a sensation of joy and brotherhood that is profoundly moving. Cults can be very interested in mysticism of some sort. When an intelligent charismatic figure leading one of these groups gives a new way of looking at the world that makes greater intellectual and emotional sense, one can be very impressed and want to know more.

L. Ron Hubbard introduced many Westerners to the better parts of Hindu/Buddhist thought under the guise of Scientology. The experience of Eastern wisdom and practice can be intellectually very seductive to people brought up in the West. Hubbard seemed to be wise beyond Western culture, and he was embraced by many as an answer to their anxieties and understandings. Unfortunately, he and his organization became very oppressive and paranoid. Others like Bhagwan Shree Rajneesh have included sexual "freedom" of some sort, which entices many apostles and acolytes into their cult-like groups.

The leader of the group can become viewed as integral to the experience and preservation of the community. The leader, the "message", and the new experience of community can create loyalty and a lack of clear judgment. This can lead to the formation of religions, brotherhoods, organizations of all sorts and, unfortunately, cults.

When the "messenger" is viewed as essential to the "message", the messenger's every action becomes important or divine. People who feel this will follow some ego driven "messengers" into other dangerous and depressing areas. There is an admonishment in benevolent mystic circles that advises one, "Don't confuse the messenger with the message." In other words, maintain faith in a message of tolerance and brotherhood, but don't ascribe special powers to any leader who strays from that message.

Frequently when one has the "message", everyone outside the group is an "other". This can create situations that are limiting and dangerous.

Jim Jones, a preacher and cult leader in San Francisco in the 1970's, gave his followers a feeling of brotherhood, love, acceptance, appreciation, and mutual support that they had never had before. It was very pleasant. He ultimately had them drinking cyanide in a South American jungle. Over 900 died. The power given to these leaders is occasionally used to exploit women sexually and to create communities that are very oppressive, demand obedience, and forbid apostasy. Several recent cults come to mind including Scientology, the Branch Davidians, and Bhagwan Shree Rajneesh.

Chapter 9

The History of Religious Rules

Historical Jewish Issues with Religious Rules

A very brief, mostly political, Jewish History:

17th century BCE Abraham, Isaac and Jacob settle in Israel.
Forced to move to Egypt due to famine.

13th century BCE Moses leads Exodus out of Egypt. The Jews wander
in desert for 40 years.
The Torah and Ten Commandments received at Mount Sinai.
They settle in Israel by defeating and killing the Canaanites.

1020 to 720 BCE First kingdom, Jerusalem the capitol.
First temple built in 1000 BCE.

720 BCE Crushed by Assyrians. 10 of the twelve tribes lost.

586 BCE Defeated by Babylonians and most Jews taken to Babylon.
First Temple destroyed.

515 BCE Return to Israel from Babylon and rebuild the temple.

332 BCE Alexander the Great captures Israel.

166–63 BCE Maccabean revolt. Jewish self rule for 100 years.

63 BCE Romans conquer Palestine and call the land Judea.

30–33 C.E. Jesus's ministry.

66–135 C.E. Jews revolt several times. Crushed by Romans. Temple destroyed for last time in 70.

Jews forced to spread over Roman empire.

135–1880 Jews spread over Mediterranean and Europe. Many to Poland and Russia under King Casimir of Poland. Many years later violent pogroms in Russia and Poland encourage immigration to Palestine.

1897 First Zionist conference begins the movement to create a Jewish state in Palestine..

1919 Ottoman empire collapses after WWI. Balfour Declaration pledges support for Jewish homeland in Israel.

1941–1945 Holocaust. Half of all Jews killed.

1948 State of Israel proclaimed.

1949 to now Jews fight off 2 major invasions 1948 and 1967. Jews gain control of all of Israel. Palestinians want to return to land that they lost in the wars.

The Jews have 613 rules or laws in the Hebrew Scriptures. They cover almost every act. A list is easily available on the Internet. Many are Religious Rules, and several of them concern punishment. Since the temple was last destroyed in 70 CE, Jews have had little political power to enforce Religious Rules until the formation of the modern state of Israel. Jews were charged by their god to be a good example to the rest of the world, not to convert it. Judaism is not missionary and makes almost no attempts to enlist others. It does accept honest conversion without great difficulty. The Jewish Religious Rules are speaking to Jews only. The strictly observant Judaism that enforces Religious Rules has been small and separatist. It does not concern others much. It is growing in influence in Israel.

Conservative and orthodox Jews adhere to the Religious Rules to one degree or another. There are several instances in the Jewish Bible of punishment being carried out by the religious community. One man was executed for picking up firewood on the Sabbath (Numbers, 15:32-36), and some fornicators and adulterers were stoned to death. Today the larger Jewish community is not interested in punishment concerning Religious Rules. They let God do that. They generally do not enlist the state in enforcement. The general statement concerning those who do not keep Religious Rules is that they "shall have no share in the world to come", from the Talmud, *Mishna,* Sanhedrin 10:3.

Historically worship in Judaism centered on the Temple in Jerusalem. The first temple was built around 10th century B.C.E. and destroyed by the Babylonians in about 586 B.C.E. Most of the Jews were taken to Babylon. Upon returning to Israel, they rebuilt the temple by about 515 B.C.E. It was destroyed by the Romans in 70 C.E. The Religious Rules involved diet, circumcision, rest on the Sabbath, pilgrimage, rituals, and animal sacrifice at the Temple. The Temple is supposed to be placed on the site where Abraham was going to sacrifice his son on God's demand. Also on the site is the Dome of the Rock, one of the holiest sites in Islam. It is said that Muhammad's Night Journey to see the prophets and God in heaven began on that site. Muhammad received the details of prayer at that time.

Since forming the Jewish state of Israel, the Jews have not enlisted the state in punishing people for breaking Jewish Religious Rules.

The Maccabees were one historically prominent Jewish group that used violence where Religious Rules were concerned. They were a very orthodox group of Jews who revolted when the Hellenistic Seleucid rulers suppressed the practice of Judaism. Using guerilla tactics, they captured much of Israel about 160 years before the time of Christ. Preserving the Jewish Religious Rules was an existential issue for them. In trying to protect and preserve Judaism as they saw it, and as a warning to the community, they occasionally killed Jews who were unobservant or who associated with the Seleucid government. They ruled Israel for about 100 years until conquered by the Romans. The Romans were continuously involved in suppressing various messiahs who were advocating revolution. After being thrown out of Palestine briefly, the Romans returned in force and obliterated the Jewish Temple about 70 C.E. Many Jews were forced to leave Palestine at that time.

Halakhah is the collective word for Jewish law and means "the way". One should follow "the way" or the "path" to be a proper Jew. There are no recent examples of punishment of non-observant Jews by the state or religious vigilantes. Ultimately reform and conservative Jews are characterized by their general willingness to employ reason and to discuss, debate, contextualize, and modify almost any rule. They generally do not punish each other over Religious Rules. Apostasy has no serious consequences for most reform Jews. Orthodox and fundamentalist Jews can shun those who leave, and it can be emotionally and financially devastating.

Haredi is an ultra-orthodox branch of Judaism which is very concerned with piety. They can be aggressive in trying to control the piety of their neighborhoods. However, they are very small in number, though growing rapidly because of very large families. They think that they must repopulate the Jewish community that was so devastated by the Holocaust.

Judea was taken over by the Romans in 63 B.C.E. To keep peace, the Romans had a history of tolerating the gods of conquered people if they would sacrifice to the Roman gods also. The Jews would not sacrifice to Roman gods, but the Romans tolerated this since the Jews had been militarily helpful to Julius Caesar. In 66 C.E. when Nero was Emperor, the Roman governor took some funds from the Jewish temple. A group of Jews called *zealots* revolted and took over Jerusalem and most of the province of Judea killing many Roman soldiers. Nero sent three legions to Judea, retook Jerusalem, and bloodily suppressed the rebellion. The Temple was destroyed in 70 C.E. Many Jews were scattered, and some sent into slavery. There were two more revolutions. The last in 135 C.E. was called the Bar Kochba Revolution, named after Simon Bar Kochba. He claimed to be the Jewish Messiah that was predicted in the Tanakh.

Many Jews who had recently accepted Jesus as Messiah would not join the revolt, and a number of these new Christians were killed by Kochba's revolutionaries. Some historians think that this revolt clearly separated the Christians out as a different sect for the first time. This revolt was crushed by Rome with great difficulty, and Judaism was suppressed. The name of the province was changed from Judea to Palestine. Afterwards Jews were not allowed in Jerusalem, and many were sent into exile as slaves. Judaism was still a legal religion in the empire.

The Jew's short-lived revolt was really the only "successful" one in Roman history. Jews were not persecuted per se in the Roman Empire. They were a recognized religion. When Christianity became the state religion, some restrictions were put on Jews, but Antisemitism as we know it generally began in the Middle Ages. Due to their religious practices Jews were readily recognizable and different.

In the early Roman Empire Christianity was not a recognized religion, and Christians were heavily persecuted and martyred. Tiberius tried to make Christianity an official religion and accept Jesus as a Roman god, but the senate refused. Christians were severely persecuted until Roman Emperor Constantine recognized them as an official Roman religion in 313 C.E. Before a major battle Constantine had had a dream that he would have a victory if he fought under the sign of the cross. He painted crosses on his soldier's shields and won the battle. It quickly became the dominant religion. In 395 C.E, emperor Theodosius made Christianity the official religion of the Empire. Like many religious leaders in history who were given political power, Catholic Christianity's leaders began suppressing other religions.

After being dispersed following the destruction of the Temple many Jews ended up in Christian Europe where they usually lived in separate groups or areas in the towns. They were forbidden by their religion from eating with others and could not marry outside the faith. They were not allowed to bow down to the local gods and their holy days were different. It is postulated that this made them appear arrogant. Some became wealthy because they could lend money, and, most Christians could not until after the Reformation in the 16th century. During the early Middle Ages, there were occasional attacks on Jewish communities spurred on by charges that they were the killers of Christ. It was also convenient that the Jewish money lenders were killed so debts did not have to be repaid.

The two major plagues in the 500's and 1400's were, in many places, blamed on the Jews. They were killed and their property taken. The Crusades in the 12th and 13th centuries often began with horrific massacres of Jewish communities. The Crusades were seen by many as attacks on non-believers, and some "Crusaders" felt that attacking the local Jews was easier and more profitable that going to Jerusalem to attack Muslims.

Because of the persecutions in the 13th century, King Casimir III of Poland, offered protection and sanction to Jews. It is estimated by some that half of Europe's Jewish population moved to Poland and the Ukraine. The Jewish population was successful but occasional attacks on the Jewish community occurred for the next four to five centuries. Unfortunately, that part of Poland was taken over in 1790 by the Russia Romanovs. The Eastern Orthodox church has historically been anti-Semitic which has been reflected in its liturgy [74]. Jews were always considered foreigners in Russia. Beginning in the late 1800s there was a long period of attacks on the Russian and Polish Jewish communities called *pogroms*. These lasted to some extent until the Communists took over in 1917. The Communists were against all religions, and anti-Semitism varied in intensity throughout the life of the Communist state.

In the 1500's in Germany, the Protestant Reformation was beginning, and Martin Luther wrote some very anti-Semitic papers. These were later emphasized by Hitler in his anti-Semitic programs of annihilation.

The differences and the jealousy of success in hard times made Jews easy targets. They were the targets of religious and economic antisemitism. They were pushed into money lending and pedaling of goods. They were not allowed to own land in many places. In commercial circles they became successful, and others were jealous. At times they were blamed for the ills of capitalism.

In the 19th century they became the targets of racial antisemitism. They were felt to have genetic and racial characteristics that were inimical to other races. They were felt to be inherently a threat to the values and safety of a society. It was easy to do since they were identifiable, and people were jealous of their success. This reached an apogee in Hitler's holocaust. They were accused of causing all of Germany's problems around WWI. They supposedly caused the war to make money, then they caused Germany's defeat by economic manipulations. Germany had lost the war even though they never been invaded lost a battle on their land. Hitler lied that Germany was betrayed by the Jews. Hitler used this lie to justify the Holocaust and kill six million Jews. They were starving after the war, and the Nazis said this was the fault of Jewish market manipulations.

Despite all this, the Jews have survived and now flourish in Israel. They are just about the only peoples who have kept their tribal cultural identity through any significant period. Perhaps the clarity and brevity of the Ten Commandments are the reason that the Jews have remained a functionable and recognizable tribe through such a long period of time. Don't lie, murder or steal are good rules on which to base a government. Being nice to your parents, and avoiding adultery makes for group harmony. The fact that they were not charged to convert others may have helped. Military defeat, forced diaspora, and persecution seem to have eliminated the need to enforce internal punishments for heresy and apostasy. The Jews had a clear and concise moral identity.

Their history of Talmudic study and debate probably made them value education. Their commitment to debate and study through the Talmudic tradition seems to have allowed them to take advantage of the commercial, scientific, and technological advances opened by Western civilization.

The Ten Commandments. There are several groupings.

1. I am the Lord thy God; thou shall not have any strange gods or idols before Me.

2. Thou shalt not take the name of the Lord thy God in vain

3. Remember to keep holy the Sabbath day

4. Honor thy father and mother

5. Thou shalt not murder

6. Thou shalt not commit adultery

7. Thou shalt not steal

8. Thou shalt not bear false witness

9. Thou shalt not covet thy neighbor's wife

10. Thou shalt not covet thy neighbor's goods.

The Ten Commandments support the principal morals needed for good rational government. They work well. The first 3 commandments are Religious Rules. The first two are negatives, requiring no actions. The third, "Remembering the Sabbath to keep it holy", is a Religious Rule observed by Conservative and Orthodox Judaism. Fundamentalist Jewish communities are stricter and more intrusive in this observance. As mentioned before, one passage in the Jewish scriptures (Numbers 15:32-36) says that a man was caught picking up firewood on the Sabbath and was executed for it. Fortunately, this was not adopted as a regular practice. The Commandment "to keep the Sabbath holy" is vague enough to allow different approaches. Working on the Sabbath could certainly be construed to violate the commandment by more conservative elements. It could be labeled sacrilege or a sign of apostasy. The enforcement of rules such as this has varied over time.

The Seven Laws of Noah are in the Jewish Talmud. [75] They are very similar to the Ten Commandments. They forbid stealing, murder, blasphemy, idolatry, eating flesh taken from a live animal, and adultery, but say nothing specific about being truthful. The Laws of Noah advise humanity to establish secular courts to administer justice.

The violent issues today around the state of Israel are not the direct result of Religious Rules. They are political issues and stem from a long history of anti-Semitism, the search for a safe space, and Israel's forceful dislocation of the local Palestinian inhabitants. The injustices and attacks done to the Palestinians on the one hand, [76] and the random rockets and suicidal bombing of Israelis by the Palestinians on the other hand seem to have resulted in stalemate. It appears that any solution will have to involve forgiveness and compromise. They don't seem likely at present. The territorial issues concerning Israel have essentially no connection to Religious Rules.

Historical Christian Issues with Religious Rules

A very brief, mostly political Christian History:

Year 1 to 33 C.E. Jesus is born. At about age 30 he spends 40 days in the wilderness, is baptized by John the Baptist and begins his ministry. He heals the sick and preaches his message of tolerance, faith, and compassion from 30-33 CE. He is crucified in 33 CE and rises from the dead 3 days later. Shortly afterwar he ascends to heaven.

33–68 C.E. Peter, Paul, and other Apostles spread the faith and build congregations.

68–313 C.E. Christians persecuted and frequently martyred.

313 C.E. Emperor Constantine makes Christianity a protected religion and ends persecution.

330 C.E. Constantine divides Roman Empire into Roman and Byzantine halves.

385 C.E. Edict of Thessalonica makes Christianity the official religion of the Roman Empire. The Catholic Church becomes the head of Christianity.

1054 C.E. Christian Church divided into Catholics in western Empire and Eastern Orthodox in east. Seljuk Turks threaten Constantinople.

1091–1291 C.E. The eight Crusades to gain access to Jerusalem and to assist the Byzantine Empire.

1184 C.E. Crusade to eliminate the Cathars and the installation of the first Inquisition.

1517 C.E. Martin Luther attaches the 95 Theses to the church and begins the Protestant Reformation.

1534 C.E. Henry the Eight of England establishes Anglican Church eliminating Catholic domination of England.

1648 C.E. Treaty of Westphalia ends 30 Years War and separates countries in middle Europe into Protestant and Catholic.

1791 C.E. During the period called the Western Enlightenment, the Bill of Rights in the US Constitution codifies the separation of church and state. Other democratic countries and international organizations follow suit over the next 160 years.

1823 C.E. The last inquisition in Spain is shut down.

Christianity's problems with Religious Rules depend on which parts of the Bible that one thinks are most important. Some Christians give equal importance to the whole Bible which includes all the Religious Rules in the Old Testament. Some give more importance to the New Testament. Some, including myself, think that the teachings of Jesus in the four Gospels are most important and should be considered Christianity's definitive teachings and answers. After all, the Old Testament is contradictory and confusing, Paul needs some contextualizing, and the religion is founded in the validity of Jesus' teachings and sacrifice.

Most Christians today adhere to Jesus' admonitions and avoid punishing others over religious matters. Jesus recommends no punishments here on earth. In one passage he does recognize that his teachings will cause divisions in families, and that some people will fight and kill each other over his teachings and message (Matthew 10:33-37) [77]. The mysteries of healings, resurrection, walking on water, and salvation remain mysteries.

Those who include the whole Bible must deal with lots of conflicting Rules. The Old Testament includes the Moral and Religious Rules that the Jews deal with. The New Testament contains the biographies and teachings of Jesus, letters from Paul and a few letters from other disciples. Paul's letters are concerned with forming a church, and they have some beautiful inspirational passages. They also have passages that give problematic opinions and instructions about women, slaves, fornication, and homosexuality that are not included in Jesus' teachings. The last book, *Revelations,* consists of a series of mystical revelations recorded by a man named John the Elder.

It might be that a great part of Jesus' genius was to recognize that, if he gave many Governmental Rules and Religious Rules, humans would really mess them up. Jesus' other strokes of organizational genius were to recommend against judging others, to put forgiveness central, to separate church/state, and to avoid proposing punishment for religious issues here on earth.

Friedrich Nietzsche, the German philosopher, dismissively considered Christianity to be a religion of slaves. He seemed to want a more robust Messiah who would fill the heroic role of organizer and conqueror. It seems that Jesus was so clear about human foibles that he knew to stay focused on interpersonal kindness rather than giving legal and organizational instructions that, over time, could be misconstrued by humans. This was an approach too passive and patient for Nietzsche's taste.

As mentioned previously the principal Religious Rule concerning eternal life or salvation is in the Gospel of John. In John 3:16 Jesus says, "For God so loved the world, as to give his only begotten Son; that whosoever believeth in him, may not perish, but may have life everlasting". The Gospel of John also quotes Jesus as saying, "I am the way and the truth and the life. No one comes to the Father except through me" (John 14:6). Also, "I am the resurrection and the life, he who believes in me, though he die, yet shall he live" (John 11:25). If one does not believe this, many Chris tians think that one is a heretic. If one does not believe and profess this, they will not go to heaven. As discussed above, this is clearly explicit in the Gospel of John out of the four gospels that chronicle Jesus' life and teachings. Also, this belief is not expressed in the one prayer that Jesus recommended, the Lord's Prayer. [78] Jesus says that if you do not believe this, you will not get to heaven. You will also miss a life-giving relationship with Jesus and the recognition of God's forgiveness. That is enough punishment. Jesus does call God his father. In his role as the Christ, Jesus often refers to himself as the "son of man" who will die to atone for humanity's sins.

There is another statement that can be seen as a rule or guideline. This is Jesus' statement that he will build his church on "this rock" referring to his disciple Peter, whose name means "rock" in Greek. The Catholic Church recognized Peter as its founder. Peter's letters in the New Testament give controversial advice about slaves and women, but they do not give extensive Organizational Rules. Incidentally, this is the only time Jesus mentioned any organization of a "church". The mission of any church would seem to be the maintenance and spread Jesus' teachings. Jesus clearly ordered his followers to spread his message of good will and salvation. Catholicism assumed that mantle and the role of expert, proponent, interpreter of the Bible, and maintainer of the faith. Generally, the Catholic Church encourages the faithful to come to the church for the proper interpretation of Jesus teachings. Catholicism did not promote individual reading of the Bible or literacy until the Protestant Reformation put enormous pressure on it.

If one does take Peter as the founder of the church, what would one do differently? His two known letters contain two short references concerning slavery and woman's duty to be obedient. In I Peter 2:18-19 he says, "Slaves, accept the authority of your masters with all deference, not only those who are kind and gentle but also those who are harsh. For it is a credit to you if, being aware of God, you endure pain while suffering unjustly." Peter also advises the people to obey Caesar. "Show proper respect to everyone, love the family of believers, fear God, honor the emperor" (I Peter, 2:17). He also tells wives to obey their husbands (I Peter 3:1). He issues no specific Religious Rules, punishments, or other Organizational Rules.

To properly interpret, preserve and observe the teachings, Catholicism has created seven sacraments, ordained legions of priests and nuns, developed an extensive hierarchy, begun countless schools, and told its members what to do concerning all sorts of issues. It has also promoted celibacy. Paul's First Letter to the Corinthians 7:8 mentions celibacy thusly, "I'm telling those who are single and widows that it's good for them to stay single like me." In the 6th century St. Augustine also promoted celibacy after being unsatisfied with a life of debauchery. Jesus didn't mention it. Catholic priests and nuns did not have to be celibate until the 12th century.

In other Gospels, Jesus is specifically asked what one must do to have eternal life or "be saved". In Luke 10:27 he says, "Love the Lord your God with all your heart and with all your soul and with all your strength and with all your mind and love your neighbor as yourself." These are Admonitions without specific content. He emphasizes no Religious Rule or punishment. In the Gospel of Matthew (Matthew 19:16-19), Jesus says we must also follow the commandments. A young man had asked, "Which ones?" There are a lot of them. Jesus replied, "You shall not murder, you shall not commit adultery, you shall not steal, you shall not give false testimony, honor your father and mother, and love your neighbor as yourself." None of these are Religious Rules. They are Moral Rules and General Admonitions.

So, we return to "belief" in the divinity of Jesus as the principal Christian Religious Rule from Jesus. This one Religious Rule has caused almost all the problems in Christianity. It moved the question of Christ's divinity to center stage. The Catholic Church was monolithic and had definite ideas about what to believe. If one did not conform to the official standard, one was a heretic and could be punished.

A Trinity was developed to describe three ways in which a Christian might encounter God, as God the Father, God the Son, and God the Holy Spirit.. The Trinity's various permutations cause arguments to this day. The early Catholic Christian Church said that it knew what was best for the people. The Church said that everyone must come to the Catholic Church for all answers and follow the teachings of its leaders, priests, and educators. The Catholic Church also offered forgiveness with confession and contrition. Punishment was felt to be a Catholic Church prerogative even though Jesus recommends none. Brutal inquisitions were carried out. Crusades were organized. Heretics and "witches" were occasionally burned on the orders of various Catholic clerics and later, for a brief time, on the orders of Protestant groups.

To make sure that everyone "believed" the right thing, the early Church demanded that one openly profess definite creeds. Besides the belief in one God and that Jesus was the Son of God, they included belief in Jesus' resurrection from the dead and belief that there will be a judgment day when God judges everyone according to his/her adherence to the commandments. Again, no Religious Rules other than belief.

Blasphemy, another Religious Rule, is mentioned once by Jesus. "Truly I say to you, all sins shall be forgiven the sons of men, and whatever blasphemies they utter; but whoever blasphemes against the Holy Spirit never has forgiveness but is guilty of an eternal sin" (Mark 3:28-29). It is not clear exactly what that means. It would seem to be an intentional act of cursing God. Again, no punishment is mentioned. If Christianity joined church and state and had law schools and courts, this verse would be construed to mean almost anything. It could cause all sorts of trouble.

Besides giving almost no Religious Rules, Jesus got rid of almost all the Religious Rules from the Old Testament. There were many rules about food and sacrifice. When asked what to eat, Jesus said "Don't worry about what goes in your mouth, worry about what comes out of it" (Matthew 15:11) (John 12:7). Animal sacrifice was very important and central to Jewish worship at that time. When at the Jewish Temple in Jerusalem Jesus pointedly said, "I desire mercy not sacrifice" (Matthew 9:13). When asked what to wear, he said don't worry about it (Matthew 6:28). When asked how to pray, he gives the "Lord's Prayer" which essentially says that one should thank God for your life and tells one that they will be forgiven insofar as they forgive others (Matthew 6:14-15). There is no mention of any Religious Rules or Jesus himself. Someone mentioned that unscripted Christian prayer comes in three categories: "Please, I'm sorry, and thank you".

Jesus recommends praying, fasting, and alms giving in private (Matthew 6:1-18). This is very different from organized ritual fasting and public prayer. Baptism, marriage, and communion are group events.

In his Sermon on the Mount in the book of Matthew, Jesus gives The Beatitudes. [79] They are descriptions of the blessings bestowed by God on the poor, the disadvantaged, and those trying to do the right thing. They are not stated as Religious Rules that one must act in one way or the other. It seems obvious that to "love God" one would act according to the descriptions in the Beatitudes, but, as usual, Jesus avoids direct orders and gives no punishments. He concludes the sermon by saying that the people who do not act in accordance with the Beatitudes will have a lesser place in heaven. Still in heaven.

Hypocrisy is dealt with in Matthew and Luke. The "woes" described by Jesus in Matthew 23:1-39 and Luke 11:37-54 are all about hypocrisy, particularly priestly hypocrisy. "Woe unto the hypocrites", the very pious who profess one thing and do another. "Then Jesus said to the crowds and to his disciples: 'The teachers of the law and the Pharisees sit in Moses' seat. So you must be careful to do everything they tell you.

But do not do what they do, for they do not practice what they preach. They tie up heavy, cumbersome loads and put them on other people's shoulders, but they themselves are not willing to lift a finger to move them"- Matthew 23:1-4.

Jesus does ask that we celebrate the Lord's Supper or Mass in remembrance of his sacrifice. There are no extensive directions, and no punishments are mentioned for failing to do so. Almost all Christian sects do this and perform baptism in one way or another.

Concerning alcohol, when the host at a wedding ran out of wine, Jesus "changed the water into wine." John 2:1-11[80]. At his last supper with his apostles, they drink wine. There is no mention of a prohibition on alcohol. In 1 Corinthians 6:9-10, Paul goes on to say," Or do you not know that wrongdoers will not inherit the kingdom of God? Do not be deceived: Neither the sexually immoral, nor idolaters, nor adulterers, nor men who have sex with men, nor thieves, nor the greedy, nor drunkards, nor slanderers, nor swindlers will inherit the kingdom of God."

Paul also writes in a letter to Timothy who was building a congregation, "In like manner also, that women adorn themselves in modest apparel, with shamefacedness and sobriety; not with braided hair, or gold, or pearls, or costly array; but, which becometh women professing godliness, with good works. Let the woman learn in silence with all subjection. But I suffer not a woman to teach, nor to usurp authority over the man, but to be in silence" (First Timothy 2:9-15). Some sects have turned these into Religious Rules. Paul was definitely a man of his time. Jesus makes no such statements.

As previously mentioned, when asked to stand in judgment of a woman caught in adultery, Jesus said "Let he among you who is without sin cast the first stone." He essentially advocated forgiveness rather than punishment. The accusers were in disarray and left. The text in John 7 then goes on to say, "Jesus straightened up and said to her, 'Woman, where are they? Has no one condemned you?' She said, 'No one, sir.' And Jesus said, 'Neither do I condemn you. Go your way, and from now on do not sin again.' As mentioned before, that would imply that she has the "free will" to sin or not sin.

Jesus speaks a lot about transgressions and fiery punishment in the afterlife, particularly in the Gospel of Matthew, but he doesn't advise us to do it here. God will take care of it later. In several places, Jesus says that people will disagree with each other and fight over his message (Matthew 10:33-39).. He does not encourage his believers to do so. He does say that a true follower will love him, Jesus, more than his mother, father, or other family member. At times, he seems to include everyone in heaven, just different levels. In Matthew 5:19 just after he states the Beatitudes, he says, "Therefore, whoever breaks one of the least of these commandments, and teaches others to do the same, will be called least in the kingdom of heaven; but whoever does them and teaches them will be called great in the kingdom of heaven."

The Catholic Church holds that the scripture is authoritative but doesn't trust the average parishioner to interpret it correctly. The leaders recommend coming to the church for guidance. There is much merit to this position. It can dampen extremism. In the past in the hands of rigorously pious clergy, the Church's instructions have made the situation worse, resulting in inquisitions and persecutions. Excommunication is now the only punishment in this life.

Doctrine concerning correct belief is central to the Christian church. It was debated early in the Christian history, and charges of heresy (wrong belief) became Christianity's principal issue. For over 300 years, the Roman state suppressed Christianity. The church had little power to prosecute minority positions within the church, so, at first, heretical issues were exercises in internal debate. In 313 C.E. Constantine made Christianity a protected religion within the Roman Empire. Shortly thereafter, a council was convened at Nicaea to clarify the correct belief about the Trinity and Jesus' relationship to God. The Bible that Christians have today was organized around this time, but it was not officially canonized at these councils or any councils for that matter. It came into being over the next few hundred years by general usage. The Edict of Thessalonica in 380 C.E. made Christianity the state religion. This edict ordered people to believe the official Catholic Church doctrine. The Roman Empire got involved in enforcement, and the first heretic, Priscillian, was executed by the Roman state in 385 C.E. He was a Spanish bishop who was charged with sorcery. There were a few random executions for heresy until the Inquisitions. The first Inquisition to "expose heretics" began about 1100 with the Cathars and Waldensians in southern France. [81] The Cathars were obliterated in a church led Crusade. Some Waldensians survived and later joined with the Calvinists after the Reformation. Some form of Inquisition existed until the Spanish Inquisition was officially stopped in 1834. The Inquisitions had long before lost their credibility. When, in 1823 the Spanish Inquisition executed its last heretic, the rest of Europe was horrified. The victim, a teacher named Cayetano Ripoll, became a deist hero.

Around 1070 the Seljuk Turks took most of modern Turkey, Syria, and Jerusalem. They almost took Constantinople. Jerusalem had been ruled by Fatimid Muslims in Egypt. The Fatimids were relatively tolerant and had allowed Christian pilgrims to visit Jerusalem. Catholics had been able to expunge their sins by pilgrimage to Jerusalem. The Seljuks closed the road to Jerusalem and stopped allowing Christian pilgrims from Europe to visit Jerusalem. The Crusades to Jerusalem were organized to open passage to Jerusalem for Christian pilgrims and to support the Eastern Orthodox Christian Church in Constantinople against the Seljuk Turks. Subsequently Jerusalem was taken back by the Fatimids shortly before the Crusaders reached Jerusalem. The Crusades were a product of several impulses:

1. Open the road to Jerusalem for Christian pilgrims and penitents.

2. Assist the Eastern Roman Empire in its battles with the Seljuk Turks.

3. A response to 300 years of land grabs in Europe by Muslim warriors.

4. A few went to make their fortune.

The Pope in Rome also said that those who participated would be forgiven their sins.

Some note that the Crusades were a way to get the younger sons of rulers out of the country so they would stop plotting and killing each other. However, many very prominent kings and rulers also went, including Saint Louis IX of France, Richard II of England, and Frederick II Barbarossa of Germany. A few of the Crusades began with devastating Jewish pogroms in Europe.

Churches were opened in the Crusader states but forced conversion of the captured areas during the Crusades was not much of an issue. For the most part the Crusaders went to open the way to Jerusalem for pilgrims and get atonement for their sins. After they captured Jerusalem and perpetrated a horrific massacre of Jews and Muslims, almost all the Crusaders wanted to go home. Conquest of further lands or conversions were not planned. The Crusaders created monkish warrior orders, Knights Templar an\d Knights Hospitaller, to stay and keep the pilgrimage road open. The Crusades were religious only in the sense that Christian pilgrims wanted access to Jerusalem for religious reasons. There were eight major Crusades. The Crusades ended after 200 years in about 1291 with the fall of the city of Acre. The Crusades made no money and ended because the European rulers stopped paying the church to support them.

If you are trying to have a rational discussion about religion, someone will bring up the Crusades as an example of Christian Holy War. The Crusades are an example of arrogant piety but have no basis in the teachings of Jesus. He never advocates pilgrimage or violence. He does recognize that some conflict will occur because of his teachings. He doesn't endorse holy sites or Crusades.

After the Crusades, wars between Christians and Muslims continued in the west until the Spanish drove the Muslims out of Spain in 1492 and, in the east, until the Ottomans were halted at the Siege of Vienna in 1683. By the end of the 1800's France and England colonized all of

Muslim North Africa from Morocco to Egypt. When the Ottomans were defeated in WWI, the empire was broken up, and the Middle East (Iraq, Syria, Palestine, and Lebanon) was colonized by England and France. Kemal Ataturk organized the Turkish army remnants and repulsed the British and French attempts to colonize Turkey. After becoming president, Ataturk began organizing the country along secular lines. Turkey became a local power and the most prosperous Muslim Middle Eastern state. Turkey's government is currently becoming more religious and regressing democratically and economically. The colonization in the Middle East lasted until the 1940's and 50's when all the Muslim nations regained their independence. More on this below.

Beginning in the fourth century, the Catholic Church became a player in politics and worldly power, and the Church was the authority on all things religious. The Church enforced this view until Martin Luther's Protestant Reformation (1517) said that the Bible was the only recognized authority, "*sola scriptura*" ("only scripture"). The opinions of the Catholic Church were no longer supreme. Everyone had to go to scripture for the answers. Protestantism put every man and woman directly before God and responsible for his/her own salvation. Every Protestant was responsible for his/her own interpretation of the Bible. Most felt that this meant that everyone had to read the Bible. This put a tremendous push behind universal literacy in all Protestant sects. To promote literacy and the Bible, the Protestants have started innumerable schools, colleges, and universities. They explored the Bible and became adept at debate and dealing with disagreement. These two characteristics might have helped them to become effective democratic citizens and comfortable with compromise. It also promoted honesty because every individual was clearly going to be judged by God on one's honesty. Fortunately, the Protestants eventually learned to solve issues by forming another sect rather than having to destroy an existing one. They have formed thousands. My interest in using Jesus' teachings in the Gospels as the highest authority is an ongoing issue only in small parts of Christianity, if any.

Beginning in the 1500 and 1600's many wars were fought between Protestant and Catholic rulers. To gather support and troops, these leaders frequently labeled their opponents as heretics, but the conflicts were mostly concerned with land, power, and politics. After the Reformation, the 30 Years War between Catholics and Lutherans destroyed most of Germany by 1648. The Treaty of Westphalia ended the war and allowed each ruler to choose the state's religion. Incidentally, this treaty was the first attempt to draw national boundaries. It also said that people should be allowed to practice their particular faith in most areas without interference. The French Catholics massacred Protestant French Huguenots intermittently for 100 years up until 1685 when Louis XIV outlawed Protestantism. In 1572 In the St. Bartholomew's Day Massacre between 5,000 to 30,000 French Protestants were killed. England's almost complete transformation to Protestantism involved several bloody civil wars.

It took a long time for the Protestants to digest the consequences of the Reformation. The Reformation essentially put the question of one's relationship to Christ's divinity in the hands of the individual Protestant. The Bible was the sole authority, much like the Qur'an and Hadith in Islam, and belief was the principal Religious Rule issue for Jesus. Different groups of the earliest Protestants fought over their particular scriptural interpretations of belief, orthopraxy, and heresy for a period. Dissident Protestants became so diverse that they rather quicky learned to form another sect rather than destroy the one that they were in.

The use of reason in religion is central to Jesus' teachings. He often taught in parables. These parables had to be interpreted by the listener using his/her reason. Jesus didn't give Religious Rules but emphasized the General Admonitions and reason, the combination of which demanded that one use one's head and one's heart. He required that each person reason in a context of compassion.

The emphasis on and the importance of reason and debate became paramount during the Reformation and the Western Enlightenment in the 17th and 18th centuries. Also, in line with Jesus' original teachings, the Enlightenment approach to politics effectively ejected the church from political power. Heresy and blasphemy disappeared as issues deserving punishment. As mentioned before, blasphemy became part of free speech, and heresy was reduced to a topic for dinner conversation.

The Christian church had punished heresy for centuries. It possibly stopped because Jesus never gave any support for this type of violence. The letters of Paul had some Religious Rules but recommended no punishments. The only supports for punishment were in the Old Testament.

The rise and success of the scientific method and the hard sciences in the West has contributed to the creation of a large secular population. In the 1500's no one claimed to be an "atheist". It wasn't until the Enlightenment in the 1700's that the first people openly identified themselves as atheists. Now secularist government is dominant in Western civilization, and there is no discrimination against atheism.

As mentioned before, it seems that Jesus gave almost no Religious Rules because he knew that humans would mess them up in numerous dangerous ways. It was a part of his genius. His primary interest was in telling us how to get along with each other and with God. If he had also given many rules, we would be irritating each other continually in trying to enforce them as we saw fit. Besides emphasizing the Moral Rules and the General Admonitions, Jesus was mainly interested in interpersonal harmony, forgiveness, healing the sick, helping the poor, and avoiding judgments of others (Luke 6:41). Religious Rules would help none of these. A good attitude was the best approach. As for salvation: you need to personally believe in Jesus' divinity, be kind to others, and actively help and sacrifice for others. The rest is a beautiful mystery, and if we are devout and forgiving, we may share in the joys of that mystery.

Jesus considered and treated everyone as an individual and an equal. The Old Testament had said that "all are created in the image of

God" (Genesis 1:27). Essentially, every individual is equally important. Additionally, one is not to judge others. In Matthew 7:1-3 Jesus said "Do not judge, or you too will be judged. For in the same way you judge others, you will be judged, and with the measure you use, it will be measured to you. "Why do you look at the speck of sawdust in your brother's eye and pay no attention to the plank in your own eye?" Jesus associated with tax collectors, soldiers, and prostitutes. He treated them all equally. There were no identifiable "others" in his teachings except hypocrites. About those who do not follow his admonitions to be kind he says, "He who is not with me is against me" Matthew 12:30. However, he prescribed no punishments for disagreements. Forgiveness is generally recommended. He let Rome take care of Moral Rules and Organizational Rules.

As mentioned earlier, Jesus even went so far as to separate church and state. "Render unto Caesar what is Caesar's and unto God what is God's" (Matthew 22:21. Luke 20:23-26). An eventual side effect of this separation was to allow Christians to identify with their nation state when dealing with political questions. Each of the Western nation states take care of the everyday issues of government, productivity, and security without church interference. They do not make policy with any concerns about Religious Rules.

Today in a world organized as "nation states", the selfishness of nationalism is blamed for many problems of exploitation, inequality, and hegemony. "Cosmopolitan" people and "Internationalists" and "globalists" want to work to decrease the importance of the nation state to bring about more worldwide equality to the distribution of goods and wealth. They would like some form of worldwide organization, possibly world government. This would inevitably involve many of the principals of socialism. Equality of opportunity and wealth is a noble goal, but until corruption can be controlled, rational humanitarian distribution of goods will not occur. Socialist or Marxist attempts have helped in certain ways, and they have produced some serious totalitarian governmental problems. They can control most corruption, but the economic and motivational problems in a strictly socialist state have yet to be solved. China's relaxation of socialist state control has produced "authoritarian capitalism". It is bringing marked economic success in many areas.

Jesus says that he comes not to destroy the Jewish law but to "fulfill it" in Matthew 5:17. "Do not think that I have come to abolish the Law or the Prophets; I have not come to abolish them but to fulfill them." It is not exactly clear what he means. How does one fulfill a law? If something is fulfilled, it is, in one sense, finished, and we can move on to a higher level. It appears that he fulfills the law by "transcending" it. To use an analogy, the laws that Jesus talks about fulfilling are like simple mathematics and geometry. Algebra, geometry, and trigonometry will get a lot done, but if you want to go to the stars or get to the deeper secrets of the universe, you must use calculus and higher math. Calculus fulfills the math issues by transcending them and moving to a higher level. Jesus transcends the limitations of being a militarily and politically heroic messiah by turning his role into a teacher telling us how to get along and reminding us that "The Kingdom of Heaven is within" Luke 17:21. Most of his teachings concern telling people how to be nice to each other. He fulfills the law by encouraging compassion, pointing out the spiritual possibilities, separating church/state, telling us not to judge others, recommending forgiveness, offering eternal life, and getting rid of Old Testament Religious Rules. Following his teachings would seem to describe how one "fulfills" the law. As usual, the miracles of healing and resurrection remain articles of faith.

In the West, the state is generally charged to provide Franklin D. Roosevelt's Four Freedoms: Freedom of Speech, Freedom of Religion, Freedom from Want, and Freedom from Fear. This is a huge task and requires economic success. With the passage of civil rights legislation Western democracies have recently become dedicated to keeping every individual safe, enfranchised, and free from personal fear. The Great Society was an attempt to overcome poverty which helped significantly.

The US Census bureau reports that the African American poverty rate went from 55% in 1950 to 30% in the 1980's and today is about 18.8%. The white poverty rate has been around 10% and in 2019 it was 7.8%. This would seem to indicate that 7% to 8% of all people will remain in poverty in US society since those whites had not been racially discriminated against. About 8% of African Americans would remain in poverty in this society even with no racism. We have a problem, but it is not insurmountable with better education. More government spending is proposed by the liberal administrations. There are moderates and radicals pushing the US to live up to its espoused principals of an equal chance for all. How much material wealth should the state guarantee? Enough to secure freedom from want but not so much as to stifle initiative. That is an elusive amount. Welfare can help the unlucky, but it won't solve the problem of equal opportunity. Only good equal education can provide a long-term solution to the inequality problems. Many schools in poor areas are not up to the task.

Everyone agrees that tight regulation of capitalism, equitable taxation, equal education, and adequate welfare are necessary. However, everyone also stays upset over the correct amounts. Even at its best, liberal democracy causes a permanent state of unhappiness in its participants because we would like it to be perfect. Importantly, without the regulated capitalist economic engine, the state might not have enough resources to provide good services or enough jobs. Adequate regulation of capitalism, equalizing taxation, fair treatment of workers, equal education, and sufficient welfare remain the big internal economic issues of liberal democracy today. "Our feet are always wet".

Today the most radical progressive agenda is associated, often wrongly, with issues such as defunding the police, leniency for vandalism, unchecked immigration, sanctuary cities, allowing shoplifting, stopping all evictions, teaching about gender fluidity in the primary schools, labeling small children as racist, and allowing people to live on the streets in large numbers. This mixture has made the progressive agenda look very suspect in the eyes of many well-meaning people. This broad based lack of will to uphold the law can be a sign that the society is losing its confidence and will soon come apart. Some areas of lax enforcement have always been occurring. Perhaps now the internet is making the exceptions seem more numerous and important than they really are. The vast amount of mis-information available to everyone may account for the feeling that our society is coming apart. Most people seem to be getting along well with each other, but the constant excessive hyperbole on the internet sometimes makes it seem that we cannot coexist. Increasing crime is a serious issue.

Equality, fairness, equity, and opportunity are constantly debated in a capitalist democracy. "That most fragile balance—between the freedom of markets and the prosperity of workers—must be sought and found." -Nouriel Roubini, prominent liberal economist. This balance will never be answered to everyone's satisfaction. However revolutionary violence is not necessary to change the balance in a functioning capitalist democracy. Just frame the issues in such a way as to win the elections. One problem in a democracy is that one party may corrupt the electoral process to maintain power. This could be the definition of fascism. On the other hand, unsubstantiated claims by prominent people that the system is corrupt can cause serious damage to the long term public faith in a democracy [82].

As mentioned previously, some try to turn Jesus into an advocate for socialism or "social justice" including equalities of income. The Gospel of Thomas, which was not included in the usual Bible, paints Jesus somewhat in this way. In one verse in the Bible, Paul recommends pooling money and resources, but Jesus never mentions it.

What about all the intolerance and problems supported by various Christian sects over time including: chattel slavery, racism, burning witches, inquisitions, etc.? Jesus offered no support for this intolerance, and he mentioned none of these issues. He does not mention slavery. Paul seems to support a less brutal kind of slavery. All slavery is brutal.

Jesus does not often have to be contextualized. He was not a political figure and was not actively organizing a tribe. He usually spoke about human interactions with each other and with God. These interactions have been taking place since the origins of humanity. He generally "spoke to the ages". Even though he wrote nothing, and all his quotes come from other's memory, his message does not get tangled up with a lot of Religious Rules or punishments. It is interesting that his biographers did not attribute dogmatic instructions to Jesus. I would think that his chroniclers, being compassionate but biased humans, would tend to push their biographies of Jesus to make him more dogmatically socialist. It seems that Jesus stayed "on message" as an advocate of kindness without an organizational or political agenda. He almost completely avoided any emphasis on Religious Rules. General Admonitions are most important. For Jesus enforcing Moral Rules and Organizational Rules is the state's responsibility. Jesus recommends treating every individual well, and he emphasizes forgiveness as a virtue.

Kenneth Clarke's previously mentioned *Civilisation* [sic] series on BBC, ended with an episode titled *Heroic Materialism*. In it, Clarke noted that it is now fashionable and common to value "kindness" highly in Western civilization. He noted that the emergence of humanitarian concerns occurred in Western politics for the first time in the 19th century. The welfare state and philanthropic institutions had their birth there. Socialist ideas put a lot of pressure on societies to help the unfortunate. All the monotheisms and Eastern religions have promoted care for the indigent. The intensely humanitarian interests in their teachings are beginning to be expressed in government. This is a quote from Clarke's last episode.

> "We are so much accustomed to the humanitarian outlook that we forget how little it counted in earlier ages of civilization. Ask any decent person in England or America today what he thinks matters most in human conduct: five to one his answer will be "Kindness." It's not a word that would have crossed the lips of any of the earlier heroes of this series. If you had asked St. Francis what mattered in life,

he would, we know, have answered "chastity, obedience and poverty"; if you had asked Dante or Michelangelo, they might have answered "disdain of baseness and injustice"; if you had asked Goethe, he would have said "to live in the whole and the beautiful." But kindness, never. Our ancestors didn't use the word, and they did not greatly value the quality — except perhaps insofar as they valued compassion."

The great monotheisms care. The socialists care. The great religions of the East care. The capitalists care. No one has a monopoly on caring. Developing viable programs is proving to be difficult.

Historical Islamic Issues with Religious Rules

A very brief, mostly political history of Islam

613 C.E. Muhammad begins receiving God's word with the help of the Angel Jabril (Gabriel), and he starts to instruct his people. He inspires and organizes his followers and unites Arabia. In 621 Muhammad takes his Night Journey to heaven and receives instructions on prayer. The ascending journey begins on Temple Mount in Jerusalem, the site of the Dome of the Rock and the Jewish Temple. It is also the site where Abraham was told to sacrifice his son, Ishmael, who is a prophet and ancestor of Muhammad. Muhammad dies in 632 CE.

632–661 C.E. Muhammad is succeeded by a series of four "Rightly Guided" Caliphs who rule until 661 C.E. when the Caliph Ali was killed, and the leadership was taken over by the Umayyad Caliphate. The Sunni / Shia schism occurred at this point. The Shia felt that the ruler should be descendent of Muhammad. The Sunni felt that the leader should be chosen by the elite. Sunni compose about 85% of Muslims today. Sometimes Sunni Islam is called Arab Islam even though includes Indonesia. Most of Sunni doctrine originated in the Arab world. The Shia are principally in Iran and Iraq.

661–750 C.E. The Umayyads moved the Caliphate to Damascus and expanded the empire. Their expansion in the West was stopped at the Battle of Tours in France in 732 C.E.

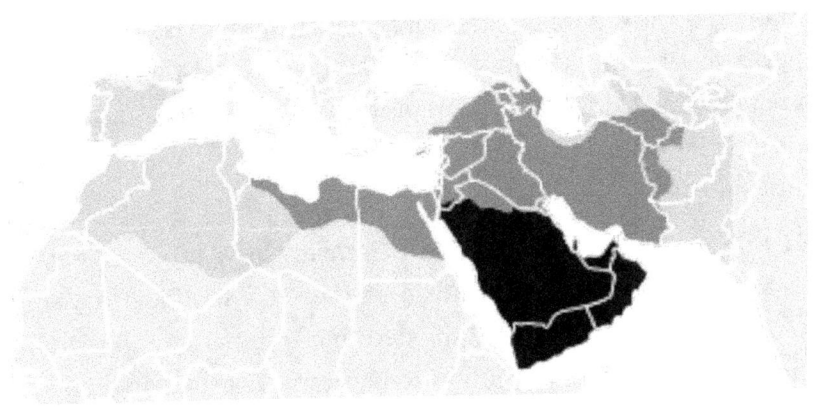

Map of Islam around 735 C.E. 100 yrs. after Muhammad's death.

750 C.E.–1258 C.E. The Abbasid family defeats the Umayyads, and the Abbasid Caliphate moves to Baghdad. The Golden Age of Islamic science, culture, and economics exists in Baghdad from around 750 until 1258. Abbasids thrived in Baghdad but later lost much political power in the western parts of the empire. In about 1019, the Seljuk Turks who had converted to Islam, took over the middle of the Muslim empire including Jerusalem. They provoked the Crusades when they denied Christian pilgrims access to Jerusalem. The Golden Age ended when the Mongols sacked Baghdad in 1258.

1096–1291 the Crusades occurred in Turkey, Syria, Palestine, and Egypt. The Seljuks, Fatimids, Mamluks, and Ayyubids fought the Crusaders and each other. After the sack of Baghdad, the Mamluks stopped the Mongols at the Battle of Ain Jalut just north of Jerusalem. That defeat and internal problems of succession in the Mongol empire stopped further westward Mongol conquests. The Mongols converted to Shia Islam and rebuilt Baghdad and Iran. The Mamluks ejected the remaining Crusaders in 1291 and ruled till taken over by the Ottomans in 1517.

1250–1517 C.E. During this period the Mamluks, Eurasian slave warriors, were in and out of power in the Middle East. In 1492 the Muslims were ejected from Spain.

1453–1916 The Ottoman Turks take the Balkans and Istanbul by 1453. After defeating the Mamluks in 1517, they moved the Caliphate to Istanbul. In attacking central Europe, the Ottomans got as far as Vienna twice in 1566 and 1683. Their navy was defeated in 1571 at the naval Battle of Lepanto.

1919–1940's The Ottoman's joined Germany in WWI and, after their defeat, the Empire was dismantled. The secret Sykes Picot Agreement between France and England divided the Arab parts of the Ottoman Empire into the nations we know today. It was poorly thought out, and the resulting boundaries have caused much difficulty. The British and French colonized the resulting nations except for Turkey. In Turkey Kemal Ataturk organized remnants of the Ottoman Army and held off the British. Ataturk became president and secularized Turkey. He dissolved the Caliphate in 1924.

1940's to now The colonized Muslim nations that had resulted from the partition of the Ottoman Empire gained their independence by the 1950's. They have tried various forms of government with varied amounts of democracy, socialism, capitalism, autocracy, and theocracy. Prominent political events since then include Israel, Iran-Iraq War, Arab Spring, 9/11, Afghanistan, invasion of Iraq, and ISIS. In sub-Saharan Africa numerous brutal fundamentalist Muslim organizations have formed and claimed large amounts of some countries. Concerning Religious Rules, conservative madrassa schools have been spread all over Sunni Islam.

Islam obviously has a long and glorious history. Within 100 years of Muhammad's death, an obscure tribe in Arabia conquered an empire that stretched from Spain all the way east to India. It included the entire North African coast and the Middle East except Turkey. The number of warriors and personnel required to subdue, rule, and administrate all these peoples and nations would have been enormous if the message and benefits of Islam had not been compatible with a secure and full life for many of the conquered peoples. The Muslim leaders reduced taxes, and put the economy in better condition. Sharia law created personal security and provided spiritual possibilities that resonated with large numbers of the citizens of the Byzantine and Sasanian Empires.

In the seventh century Muhammad promulgated the Moral Rules, General Admonitions, Organizational Rules, and Religious Rules in the Islamic legal system. In many places it was a significant improvement over what was happening at the time, particularly in Arabia. As mentioned previously, it restricted Muslims killing Muslims and put disputes in the courts, thereby ending the age-old rituals of tribal blood feuds. This allowed the Muslims to organize, and they became a powerful military force in the ancient world and a great civilization.

Islamic Organizational Rules offered some good protections to women and provided clear outlines for domestic law including inheritance, property, marriage, and divorce. The full spectrum of the Organizational Rules included some legal protections for the individual under habeas corpus. There were a few commercial and procedural rules including one rule forbidding usury. This prohibition made banking and finances difficult at times. Islam's strength and Sharia law provided a very powerful sense that, if a person followed the Rules, religious and otherwise, one's family and one's property were safe.

Bearable taxation and military service were important issues in ruling all the diverse peoples. *Jizya* was a tax on all non-Muslims. It was for protection and services. If one became a Muslim or volunteered for the army, the tax could be waved. Differing concerns over taxation and military service probably determined how various groups viewed conversion and cooperation.

Safety is the first and most important responsibility of government, and Islam's group-like society with its Sharia law established safety well. A close second is the feeling of community and family that Islam produces. There is nothing in Christianity like the Hajj where all Muslims go to Mecca, dress alike, participate together in the ceremonies, and treat each other as equals. In daily life, the ritual of five prayers, the wearing of prescribed dress, the fasting during Ramadan, the lack of stealing, and the hypnotic beauty of the spoken Qur'an create a deep sense of connectedness to others and to something larger than oneself. It is compelling and powerful. This sense of community can also create a feeling that everyone who is not a Muslim is an "other", an infidel. Seeing your neighbors as "others" rather than as your equals can create problems.

Islam was not universally forced on the conquered peoples, and for the most part those conquered could worship as they wished if they obeyed Islamic law. Non-Muslims were clearly identified as "others" (*mushrikun, kafir*). Christians and Jews were considered "People of the Book", and, as such, were not actively persecuted or forced to convert. In most cosmopolitan areas the Jews and Christians were taxed and had restrictions on their public actions and religious practices. The Jews and less orthodox Christian sects (Copts, Nestorians, etc.) were, in many cases, treated better than they had been as heretics under the Catholic Roman Church, the Byzantine Orthodox Christians, and the Zoroastrian Persians rule. They had to pay a tax, could only ride donkeys, had to stand when Muslims entered, were forbidden from praying loudly or displaying crosses, etc. but were not forced to convert and were not routinely persecuted.

Around the 8th century the concept of Dar al Islam, Dar al Ahd, and Dar al Harb was promulgated. The Dar al Islam was the "Land of peace" where Islam was the dominant religion, and Sharia law was in force. Dar al Ahd was the "land of treaty" agreements with nations in the Dar al Islam. Muslims could practice their faith there. Dar al Harb was the "land of war" where Muslims were not allowed the full expression of their religion which included Sharia law. Today these terms are usually used by fundamentalist groups when disparaging others. Bin Laden used them. In general, these terms and ideas reflect the conservative Muslim idea of world peace where everyone is a Muslim under Sharia law. The Western idea of world peace is when every country is a liberal democracy with individual rights and an uncorrupted judiciary.

Islam was considered the world center of learning and culture for hundreds of years. At that time the Islamic people were ruled by Caliphs who were political and religious leaders. The science of the time was done principally in Islamic lands. Viable economies thrived and cultural works flourished. The Muslim rulers enlisted the educated Zoroastrians, Jews, and Christians as civil servants, engineers, and teachers to supplement their own. Bagdad, Persia, Egypt, and Spain were the first-class world centers of learning. The years about 700 C.E. to 1258 C.E. were considered the Golden Age, and Baghdad was the largest and most learned city in the world. The age is said to have ended when the Mongols sacked Baghdad in 1258.

As mentioned above, in the 11th and 12th centuries many Islamic scholars, including Avicenna (Ibn Sina) in Persia and later Averroes (Ibn Rushd) in Spain, wrote works attempting to reconcile Islam with Greek reasoning and philosophy, principally Aristotle. Near the same time in Egypt the great Jewish physician and polymath, Maimonides, was trying to do the same with Judaism. In mainline Islam, Avicenna was opposed by more orthodox Islamic elements. One of the most prominent conservative scholars, Al-Ghazali of the Asharite school, wrote a book called *The Incoherence of the Philosophers* in which he attacked Avicenna and his school of thought for trying to introduce more Greek philosophy and reasoning into Islamic theology and practice. Al-Ghazali felt that it was inappropriate to equate human reasoning with God's message. He viewed their efforts as attmepts to put reason ahead of faith. Al-Ghazali firmly held the principle that faith was the most important issue in Islam. Also Al-Ghazali generally said that God did every individual act. God was omnipotent and active. This is called "Occasionalism".[83] Occasionalism is a complex position that generally says that God is the cause of everything. The classic example is the burring of cotton. Al-Ghazali held that when fire is put to cotton, God does the burning, not the fire. He said that he had no problems with physics, logic, or mathematics but that the final word could be found in the scriptures. Al-Ghazali implied that since God does everything, one must consider God's words first in every endeavor, even in politics and science. Al-Ghazali essentially stated that the most fundamental understandings could be gained by studying the Qur'an and the Hadith. Al-Ghazali's interpretation carried the day in the Caliph's courts and in the greater religious establishment. Although Al-Ghazali did not directly organize it, the formal study of and memorization of the Qur'an became the principal educational standards and goals for much teaching in Islam. Ultimately all debate, dialog, and science took place in a religious framework, requiring the blessing of theologians.

Shortly after this, Averroes, a great Muslim polymath and philosopher in Spain, wrote a book titled, *The Incoherence of the Incoherence*. He, like Avicenna, was attempting to reconcile Aristotle's teachings and reasoning with Islam. His commentaries were widely studied by the Scholastics in the Christian schools in Italy and France, but ultimately, had little effect in Islamic scholarship.

Occasionalism became the dominant theological position, and Islamic science, technology and political philosophy slowed significantly. [84] They have yet to recover fully. A form of this tradition is alive today in the *madrassas* subsidized by Saudi Arabia where the principal study consists of memorizing the Qur'an. Math, science, and philosophy are somewhat neglected. Later, the Ottoman Empire made efforts to develop a stronger scientific and somewhat democratic approach to education, but clerical intrusions continued to slow change.

The fact that an omnipotent God knows everything and does everything can create some areas of fatalism in religious followers. If everything is predestined to happen by God's actions, why should people worry about results or responsibility? This conundrum continues to be discussed when dealing with the complexities of predestination in theological reasoning.

The Arab word *Inshallah* means "If God wills it". It is frequently used to express opinion about the future. Some critics see it as an expression of fatalism which avoids responsibility for one's actions. Others just see it as a way of remembering God. Christians have long said, "God willing", which could be similarly interpreted. However, individual responsibility has been the Christian emphasis, and most Christians are felt to be responsible for their actions.

There is a strain of fatalism in Islam. For example, when 244 pilgrims were killed in a stampede during the Hajj in Mecca, the leader responsible for mosque organization said, "All precautions were taken to prevent such an incident, but this is God's will." On another occasion, after a building crane fell into Mecca's Grand Mosque on Sep. 11, 2015, killing 114 and injuring 394, the mosque's Imam, Abdul Rahman Al Sudais visited the injured and, as he met each one, told them, "This is God's will." These clerics are from the conservative Saudi branch of Islam. It is difficult to imagine a responsible Westerner or Christian making such statements.

I will leave this final question of free will vs. predestination for Calvinists and Muslim scholars to stress over. However, it seems that the emphasis on individual responsibility rather than on organized theological clerical opinions makes Protestants feel more responsible for their actions and less fatalistic.

In the 11th century, the Seljuk Turks, who had converted to Islam, conquered Islamic territory including most of Turkey, Iraq, Iran and southward to Jerusalem. Shortly afterwards, the Crusades involved Turkey, Lebanon, Syria, Egypt, and Palestine (Israel) for 200 years. As the Crusades were ending, the Mongols invaded from the east and captured most of eastern Islam, including Iran and Iraq and almost Jerusalem. The Fatimids and Mamluks ruled Egypt and Palestine and Egypt. In the mid 1300's the Ottomans rose out of Anatolia (modern Turkey). They took over Turkey, the Balkans, and the Arab nations, essentially all of Islam west of Iran. They took Constantinople and Greece in 1453. They invaded the West twice and both times were repulsed when defeated at Vienna in 1529 and 1683. As discussed before, they ruled northern Africa, the Balkans, and the Middle East until the end of World War I.

The Sykes Picot Treaty between France and England divided the Ottoman Empire into states that were colonized by the British and French. Unfortunately, the borders were drawn without sufficient attention to the ethnic and religious differences in the area. Bitter enemies were incorporated into the same nations. In other cases, ethnic groups were divided and became minorities in states ruled by hostile majorities. (Armenians, Kurds)

Mustafa Kemal Ataturk organized resistance and defeated French and British efforts to colonize Turkey. Ataturk maintained Turkish independence and worked seriously to change Turkey to a secular modern state. Ataturk eliminated the last semblance of central religious authority in Islam when he abolished the Caliphate in Turkey in 1924. Mosque and state were officially separated, and Islamic *ulemas* and *mullahs* were removed from all political activity in Turkey. Schools were opened for everyone, and the religious *madrassas* that had been educating the children in solely in religious studies were closed. A constitutional republic was established, and women got the vote. People were not allowed to wear the fez, a brimless hat that had been adopted by the Ottoman rulers in the early 1800s. Islamic references were banned in parliament. Ataturk was very instrumental in rejuvenating science and Turkish industry. Ataturk's liberal Jacobin-like policies marginalized Islamic and conservative groups.

There has been a resurgence of Islam in Turkish politics. Recently the conservative religious leadership and the conservative politicians who were marginalized by Ataturk's policies have combined to elect Recep Erdogan. Religious leaders have been put in administrative and judicial positions. Erdogan has introduced state funding for religious *madrassas*, forcing secular families to attend them in some areas. [85] He seems to feel that Islam is under attack, and he must be protector of Islam as a whole.

Almost all the Muslim nations coming out from under French,

English, or Italian colonial rule in the 20 years following WWII were politically established with some form of secular elected representative government. In Egypt the ideas of a secular Pan Arab Nationalism became prominent under Gamal Nassar in the 1950's. Egypt united with Syria for a brief period as the United Arab Republic. This dissolved after an army coup d'état in Syria. Ba'athism, a semi socialist Arab nationalist ideology, took over in Syria and Iraq. Iran was democratic until the US intervened to install the Shah, ostensibly to avoid communist takeover. Saudi Arabia was under the Saudi family who made a governing agreement with the Wahabis, a very conservative sect which thinks that there must be more enforced piety in government. Algeria fought a bloody, bitter war to get the French to leave. Pan Arabism, nationalism, constitutional democracy, Baathism, socialism, republicanism, and Islamism were all tried out in various countries. None have been very successful. Under the slogan, "Islam is the answer", a strong and generally reactionary clerisy has since recovered to play major roles in many states including Turkey, Iran, and Pakistan.

The establishment of Israel in Palestine with Western help has introduced its own serious set of problems. Many Palestinian Muslims were forced or terrorized into leaving their homes in Israel. This has created an unsolved refugee problem that has resulted in continuous friction and bloodshed. Israel's existence has destabilized Lebanon and polarized Lebanon's four major cultural groups to such a degree that the government of Lebanon is almost non-functional.

Today, codified domestic and inheritance law usually conforms to some forms of Sharia proposed by one of the principal Sharia law schools. Domestic and inheritance Sharia rulings are generally rational and not very contentious. The parts of Sharia concerning law concern Religious Rules about blasphemy, apostasy, and heresy are prominent features in the codified constitutions of many Muslim majority nations.

Islam's texts treat believers and nonbelievers differently. In several places the Qur'an tells believers not to associate with infidels. (Qur'an

3:118, 5:51) These restrictions probably addressed problems that occurred during the early tribal wars. Muslims are admonished by some Islamic scholars not to work under the authority of infidels or allow infidels to rule in majority Muslim areas. Again, contextualizing would be important in the relaxation of these prejudices.

Most people cannot perpetuate atrocities or hurt people unless they consider them to be lesser beings or threats because of their "otherness". Nazis-Jews, Settlers-Indians, Southern racist whites-African Americans, Islamic Fundamentalists-Westerners, colonialists-native peoples, one tribe-another tribe, etc. These represent situations in which one group felt that the other group was expendable in pursuit of some group goal. If the person is an "other", they are worth less and can be manipulated or eliminated. Otherness is ubiquitous in group-oriented societies. "Otherness" was also a large factor in the exploitation of native peoples during colonial imperialism.

In the Qur'an there are many verses or *suras* about killing, ambushing, punishing, and shunning infidels and enemies. These *suras* are quoted continuously by extremists from both sides. Western critics quote them to make Islam look bad. Islamic fundamentalists quote them to justify attacks against their enemies within Islam or elsewhere. These verses could be contextualized to the period when Muhammad's tribe was forming and was under serious threat. Today reform and modern Muslims can be dismayed when they are associated with these references to tribal warfare in the 7th century. Contextualizing can decrease the oppressive nature of the verses. However, appropriate contextualization of these warfare references requires a desire for harmony and cooperation. These efforts at cohabitation must be repeated in each generation and in all types of cultural and economic stress.

The Qur'an does not mention a punishment for blasphemy. It says to avoid people who do it, Qur'an 4:140. The Hadith are obscure on the subject and do not clearly recommend punishment for blasphemers. However, the five principal Islamic law schools are unanimous in recommending death for those who blaspheme God or Muhammad unless they repent. [86] Who decides what is heresy or blasphemy? Some Muslims feel that they can use violence in punishing what they consider blasphemy in such instances as the Charlie Hebdo killings, the Danish cartoon riots, and recently, the French teacher's beheading.

The rulers are expected to consult with the *ulema* (body of Islamic scholars) in all important decisions involving heresy, sacrilege, blasphemy, and apostasy, but the final authority is the Qur'an and the Hadith. Who interprets the Qur'an and Hadith? As with Protestant Christians there is no single authority outside of scripture, so everyone does their own interpretation of scripture. Muslims can go to the Islamic law schools or various scholars (*mufti*) and local mosque leaders (*imams*) for advice. All Islamic law schools want to impose concerns over Religious Rules on the civil law.

Judaism has schools of Jewish law called *yeshivas*. The *yeshivas* are only involved with rulings within the orthodox Jewish community. There are Christian schools of theology, but there is no such thing as a Christian law school with any influence in court proceedings.

For many, the security of knowing how to respond to almost all situations through following Sharia laws is one of the most attractive attributes of Islam. In a religious cultural exchange group setting, I recently asked two young female Muslims what they liked most about Islam. They responded, in unison, "We like it because it tells us what to do." A Christian could say the same words but would mean something different. Christian advice is usually vague and offers only General Admonitions such as forgiveness, patience, benevolence, and repentance for one's thoughtless acts. The average person usually knows how they have erred. Islamic advice frequently discusses Religious Rules and is often very much a legal opinion with a lot of references to the texts. There is a very specific "legal" way to do things. There are numerous websites from all branches of Islam where one can go to get legally "sanctioned" advice on almost everything. The Yaqeen Institute is one modern website giving advice on all sorts of issues. The leading paragraph of an article by Dr. Teesnem Alkiek, Director of Expanded Learning at the Yaqeem Institute concerns the hijab and begins with this paragraph. [87]

"When it comes to the obligation for a Muslim woman to cover her hair and body, many have expressed their confusion as to where this commandment is rooted. In order to address this topic, this book will explore how rulings in Islamic law are generally formed, while adopting the commandment for women to cover as a case study. We will explore the handful of sources jurists are presented with, and how they go about evaluating different texts to arrive at a legal conclusion."

In Islam even the clothes one wears are a <u>legal</u> question. Should these legal rulings be enforced?

Al-Islam.org is another website with some advice which seemingly suggests physical coercion for ongoing breaches of the prescribed dress and grooming codes. The following is some advice given when consulting Al-Islam.org, in the section "Interaction in Social Life". It is an example of an approach taught by some Muslim teachers.

"You might find someone among the women in your family not observing hijab, not concealing her hair; and you might find that she does not remove the nail polish at the time of ritual washing. You might even find among them someone who wears perfume for men other than her husband; and does not conceal her hair or body from the eyes of her cousins (maternal or paternal), brother-in-law, or husband's friend with the justification that they all live in the same house, and under the pretext that he is like her brother, or other similar groundless excuses. ...If you find any such situations, you should enjoin the good and forbid the evil by applying the first two methods: that is, expressing your displeasure at the situation, and then speaking about it. If these two methods do not work, then apply the third method (after asking the permission from a religious teacher): adopting practical [or physical] measures moving from softer to harsher ones." [88]

In essence, the woman will be physically forced to conform to their ideas of piety.

France has banned the hijab in its schools, and some workplaces in the EU forbid it. On the one hand, the rules forbidding it might be an attempt to take pressure off Muslim women. If the ban was not in place, conservative activists would be forcing young women to wear it as an expression of solidarity with a conservative Islamic religious and political agenda. The hijab is also an expression of piety. Is the public wearing of the hijab a sign of oppression or a sign of piety? It can obviously be either. How can anyone determine why it is being worn? Any public ritual or act of piety can be a sign of oppression. Modesty is recommended by all the monotheisms, but in modern Judaism and Christianity, the details are left up to the individual and the society. In Islam, piety is a legal question. Islam looks to Sharia law schools for the answer. In these schools many scholars condone forceful compliance.

Jesus specifically recommends that prayer and similar acts of piety be done in private. That avoids all these contentious questions about oppression and coercion. It also takes pressure off the women to conform or to serve as political statements.

"Justice" is one of the goals of *Sharia*, and today it is a prominent issue concerning Israel and the Palestinians. Justice is one of the words used in the name of many, if not all, of the political parties in the Middle East. It is on most of those banners that you see waving on TV in Arab lands. The problem is that people have different ideas about what justice is. Basically, it is fairness in dealing with others in political, contractual, legal, or historical contexts. Today, justice is often expanded to "social justice" which includes the distribution of wealth more equally. This adds a larger area of debate and conflict. Adequate taxation and welfare can resolve many of the economic issues without revolution.

Palestinian and Israeli definitions of "justice" differ greatly. The Palestinians have a compelling case in that in 1948 and 1967, they were removed from or terrorized into leaving their homes by European supported Jewish settlers. The Palestinians would like to return. The Geneva Conventions and the 1948 UN Declaration of Human Rights, both signed by Israel, support their "Right of Return". Their case for the justice of returning to their homes is strong. On the other hand, the vows of some Palestinian leaders to "destroy" Israel make for difficulty. Is a country required to welcome people who want to destroy the country or its people? The indiscriminate killing of Israeli civilians by extremist Palestinians weakens the emotional support for Palestinian return in the West. This conflict between two clearly identified religious groups has almost nothing to do with Religious Rules except where access to holy shrines is involved. There was considerable concern among some Jews about the formation of the state of Israel because of what they saw would be the moral costs of inserting themselves in the Palestinian territories. Their anxieties have proven to be prophetic.

Justice frequently comes with a historical context and sometimes involves revenge and retribution. Conditions were once good for a people, and they want them restored to that prior condition, or they want someone punished for a prior crime. Many want "Justice", but they may not get close to it without including some compromise and/ or forgiveness. We can only hope that a rational balance can be reached. I don't see it happening soon. The positions are so hardened on both sides that any Arab or Israeli leader who signs an agreement with any compromise will probably be swiftly assassinated. Egyptian leader Anwar Sadat and Israeli Prime Minister Ytzak Rabin were both killed by homegrown assassins who thought they compromised too much in the Egyptian/Israel peace treaty. These were political issues, not directly Religious Rules.

Some Muslims feel that the Golden Age of the Caliphate from about 650-1200 C.E. illustrates that Sharia law is an excellent way to run a government and an economy. They would like to reinstate a Caliphate to become prosperous again. They long for a "true" Islamic state under "true" Sharia law. They reject all current nation states claiming to be Islamic as impure or incorrect. They think that the correct reinstallation of sharia would solve many of their problems. ISIS (the Islamic State of Iraq and Syria) is an extremist attempt to create another Caliphate. It is thought to be supported mainly by private financing from Sunni Muslims in Saudi Arabia and Qatar. A secondary goal appears to be to take down the Shia dominated government in Syria. ISIS is incredibly brutal in imposing a fundamentalist Islam. It has practiced mass genocide, made sex slaves of women, burned opponents alive, inspired mass murderers, and committed countless other atrocities.

America seems to have many reform type Muslims. Pew Research did extensive polling of US Muslims and found that they practice the religious rituals at levels like other Americans who identify themselves as religious [89]. They are good neighbors and are almost universally against the violence and fanaticism associated with Islam. They like the tight warm Muslim family structure with its wonderful group rituals, clear instructions, and memories. Westerners (Muslims and Christians) as a whole say that the most meaningful and fulfilling things in their lives concern family (Pew Research).

The Qur'an, 2:190, says that one should only fight if attacked. One should not start a war. However, the term "attacked" is up for definition. What defines an attack? Bin Laden thought that Western cultural imports and soldiers on the holy soil of Arabia were attacks, and they represented existential threats to Islam. They had to be stopped.

In much of the Islamic world there is confusion about colonization, military defeat, violence, judgment, poverty, exploitation, punishment, lying, "otherness", strict pieties, and the imposition of Israel. These issues are all occurring simultaneously. In this atmosphere unscrupulous entities as well as sincere individuals, governments and religious communities can make some bad decisions. There are frequent attacks by lone gunners, suicide bombers, and religious mobs. Because of these attacks many people think that some of Islam supports violent solutions to religious differences. Compassionate contextualization of Muhammad's teachings would eliminate the need for much of this violence. [93] The possibility of Weapons of Mass Destruction (WMD) in the hands of fanatics adds a very serious dimension.

There is an underlying demand present in the essential statement of Islam, "There is but one God, Allah, and Muhammad is his prophet." We are told by Muhammad himself that he is a man; yet he is the last and paramount prophet of God. Many Muslims consider him the perfect man. Adherents have reasoned that if Muhammad is God's" final prophet", his words and deeds reported in the Hadith should certainly be consulted when deciding societal issues. The Hadith have some contradictory passages. The hearsay nature of many Hadiths statements, and the difficulty establishing authenticity, present problems concerning Religious Rules. As mentioned before, there are many prominent clerics who would like to eliminate the Hadith as a major influence.

As a political leader Muhammad also made treaties. Muhammad said that if he suspected treachery from others, that he could break the treaties with them Qur'an 8:55-58. This is entirely rational and reasonable. What would constitute treachery? Today ruthless zealots and gangsters seem to decide for themselves. This is another opportunity for scoundrels to subvert the peaceful and inclusive aspects of Islam.

There are Hadith that say that Muhammad would break agreements if they were unsatisfactory. "By Allah, and Allah willing, if I take an oath and later find something else better than that, then I do what is better and make up for my oath." (Hadith Bukhari, Volume 7, Book 67, Number 427). This is a rational approach to right an error. Sometimes the fanatical interpret this approach as permission to break almost any agreement if they "make up" in some way. The definition of "making up" also presents opportunities for mischief.

Generally, reform, modern, and less conservative Muslims have no interest in the punitive verses concerning Religious Rules. They do not even have a detailed awareness of many of them, particularly the Hadith. However, various *muftis* (religious scholars and leaders) give opinions and issue fatwas recommending punishments concerning the violations of Religious Rules. The results can be seen on the website *thereligionofpeace*. If the operative verse in the Qur'an was verse 2:256 "There should be no compulsion in religion", there would be many fewer problems.

Historical Eastern Religion's Relationship to Religious Rules

Eastern religions in their purest states are not faith based like the three great monotheisms. In them there is no central element of faith in some historical prophet who is giving us God's word. To them "God" is everywhere and available to those enlightened enough to experience this "truth". Hindus and Buddhists are essentially mystics trying to be enlightened as to this truth of the universe. If they achieve enlightenment, they will be completely fulfilled and merge with the "God" or essence of the universe. The wording is a little tricky but can be beautifully poetic. Faith and heresy have no meaning. For many this world is an illusion to be transcended. Piety is very important as a path for many, but not for all. Some moderates in the intellectual Eastern religious community feel that trying to maintain a pious environment is just "mood making", a pleasant form of fooling oneself into thinking that one is special.

The term "yoga" means "union". In one sense, enlightenment involves a union with the creative essence of the universe or "God". The various forms of union or yoga include almost everything, and they were discussed earlier under Chapter 8, "Mysticism". Some paths are more treacherous and confusing than others. Generally, piety is thought to be a good path, and sexuality a precarious path.

The *Bhagavad Gita* is a central text of Hinduism and is a small part of the *Mahabharata,* one of the two great Sanskrit epic poems of India. The other is the *Ramayana.* The *Bhagavad Gita* involves Krishna, a principal god, posing as a chariot driver for Arjuna, a warrior prince and the most famous archer. A great battle in a civil war is about to take place. As the two armies are lined up, Arjuna tells Krishna to take the chariot out between the armies. Arjuna wants to view the whole experience. After reaching the center and looking at the armies Arjuna sits down on the chariot and says that he cannot fight. He goes on to say that he has teachers, family, and friends in both armies. He cannot kill them. The battle is a metaphor for our inner struggle. At times we must rid ourselves of some things that we like or value. Krishna describes the options and finally says, "You must do your duty." Arjuna was given a role in this life, and he must fulfill it. His karma involves being an archer. Krishna also advises Arjuna to keep in mind that there are other simultaneous levels of fulfilling consciousness available at all times to everyone. Keep those in your consciousness while you do your duty. That wisdom will place one beyond fear and hope. It will put you in the best position to do the right thing.

In some areas, the East is very interested in levels of piety as personal discipline to reach a state of enlightenment. It is not enforced as a group obligation. For some, the more pious and purer that one is, the more likely to have a revelation and gain enlightenment. (Satori, moksha, or nirvana.). This piety is an individual act. It can be done in a group but is not usually enforced. Enlightenment is the primary goal. Enlightenment is accompanied with ending the suffering which is caused by attachment to the things of this world. However, in some of India, the less educated Hindu populace in the countryside can enforce a public religious piety and misogyny with threats, violence, and shunning. [94]

There is one prominent issue that can probably be considered Religious Rules: the caste system. One charitable theory of the caste system's origins holds that it is an extension of an obsessive focus on enlightenment. It theorizes that children were encouraged to do what their parents did because it would be the easiest occupation to follow. That would in turn give them more time to reach for enlightenment through pious or strenuous actions. Possibly this hardened into an insistence in staying in one's station from birth. In truth however, the caste system probably had a lot to do with protecting the privileges of the upper classes. The caste system presents serious social problems considering today's democratic standards. With the advent of Indian democracy, the caste system was outlawed in India in 1950, but it still has strong roots in Indian society. Many affirmative action laws and quotas have been enacted to solve the problems created by the caste system.

The status of cattle is said to have begun as an appreciation for their nature of giving without asking a lot in return. This appreciation has slowly solidified into today's unusually strict respect. The cow is venerated for its good nature. Some say it is worshiped. Others just say it is "venerated". It does not need to be a controversial issue. Many Hindus follow the doctrine of *ahimsa* which demands that one be kind to all living things. That has resulted in widespread vegetarianism and pacifism among Hindus.

Historically the treatment of women is ambivalent at best and occasionally very discriminatory. The Indian legal system was based on an ancient manuscript, the Manusmriti. The manuscript supposedly recorded the teachings of the "progenitor of mankind", Manu. The Manusmriti stated, "Where women are revered, there the gods rejoice; but where they are not, no sacred rite bears any fruit". But other parts the text say that good daughters and wives are dutiful and obedient. That has proven to be an opening for misogyny, abuse, Dowry Deaths, Honor Killings, and oppression. *Suttee* or *Sati* (the forced suicide of a woman on the death of her husband, usually by burning) was present and tolerated by the Manu-smriti but not widely practiced. When the British arrived, they permitted *suttee* for a brief while before outlawing it. [95]

Strictly speaking in the East there are no Religious Rules revealed from God. Heresies and blasphemies are not major issues because no prophet has given a particular revelation or "text" directly from God. All the authors of Hinduism's organizing texts are obscured by time and the Hindu lack of concern for history. The primary Hindu texts (the Upanishads, Vedas, Mahabharata, and Ramayana) do not have a collection of revealed rules.

Hindus and Buddhists were so unconcerned with time and events that they wrote no histories. Their goals were so abstract that events took on little importance. Besides no histories, they wrote no tragedies either. Fate and tragedies had little relevance when yoga, moksha, and enlightenment are the main issues. No histories and no tragedies.

The Vedas are the earliest of Hindu scriptures consisting of hymns and philosophy. In the *Rig Vedas* there is a passage praising God which expresses a very basic Hindu approach to God. "Only that god who sees in highest heaven: he only knows whence came this universe and whether it was made or uncreated. He only knows, or perhaps he knows not." This last phrase places the definition of "God" in a very different place. It is unlike the god of the great monotheisms.

Hindu and Buddhist writings consist of epic tales, philosophic musings of wise men, moral/ethical instructions, and observations about various gods. Some texts describe how a Brahmin (upper caste) should conduct an ethical and moral life. In Hinduism some harsh penalties for adultery were proposed on marriage across caste lines. When considering the present emphasis on democracy, these penalties are tainted by the strong bias given upper caste people and considerable misogyny.

India has had some political and religious fanatic groups, but they seem to have mainly coalesced due to perceived nationalist and existential threats, particularly from Muslim minorities. The Muslim population in India is the third largest in the world, behind Indonesia and Pakistan.

Hindus have no central religious authority and generally don't involve the state in punishment for infractions of piety. In their purest form, they tend to recognize that all ways of life are paths to enlightenment if done with a compassionate heart. As mentioned above, Jesus makes two very Eastern statements when he says; "You shall know the truth and the truth shall set you free," (John 8:32) and "The kingdom of heaven is among (or within) you" (Luke 17:22). Additionally, in the Book of Revelations 21:5 in the New Testament the author, John of Patmos, has Jesus saying, "Behold, I make all things new". Hindus and Buddhists would recognize these statements as fundamental expressions of their views.

In Thomas Mann's *Magic Mountain*, the humanist hero, Stetimbrini, says, "You cannot pay any attention to the religions of the East for they are all in love with death." I think that he means that the Hindus and Buddhists are interested in "killing" who they are, to become something else that is close to an abstraction. Ergo, no histories or tragedies. Mann's Westerners are interested in becoming as fully human as possible. They want to experience a large variety of earthly possibilities. It is a significant distinction and an important one.

Confucius says that "One cannot know about such things". Duty, proportion, family, and honor are what matter.

Chapter 10
Religious Rules Today

Religious Rules in Judaism today

Today Judaism is divided into Reform, Conservative, Orthodox and ultra-Orthodox depending on how many of the Religious Rules are observed. There are some groups of mystics. who deal with the Kabbalah, the Jewish mystical literature. Usually the issues of heresy, blasphemy, apostasy, and sacrilege are up to the individual and the extended family. Those who commit offenses can be shunned or excommunicated.

The Jewish scriptures have numerous Organizational Rules concerning government. These passages concern kings and were not examples of a voting democracy. The only Jewish state, Israel, has laws saying one can be jailed for up to three years for "crudely" offending another's faith. It was designed to decrease religious tension between Jews and Muslims. It was not meant to punish people for discussing religious issues.

Antisemitism is an unacceptable position in world culture. The most fundamental Jewish sects practice without significant threats or interference. Pockets of antisemitism exist only in the most extreme groups like the Proud Boys who have gotten some encouragement from President candidate Donald Trump who famously advised them to "Stand back and stand by".

Religious Rules in Christianity today

The Christian Religious Rules are mostly in the Old Testament part of the Bible. There are a few in Paul's letters and even fewer in Jesus' message in the New Testament.

Issues concerning punishment for heresy, blasphemy, sacrilege, and apostasy disappeared after the Enlightenment and the separation of the church and state. In Christianity, heresy and blasphemy are not issues for the government or fanatics. The Culture Wars in America today involve some religious issues concerning women's roles in the church, social justice (economic equality), gun possession, and sexual identity issues. Abortion is probably the most prominent issue. In reducing government's role in supporting abortion Supreme Court Justice Kenney speculated that "…it seems unexceptionable to conclude some women come to regret their choice to abort the infant life they once created and sustained," he wrote. "Severe depression and loss of esteem can follow." He was proven wrong on all counts. The two largest follow up studies on women who had had abortions revealed that close to 95% of them were happy with their decisions. [96]

As mentioned before, Paul and Peter give limitations to female roles. Jesus included women as equals and companions. There were no women disciples, but he conversed with the Samaritan woman at the well, and while teaching, Jesus was followed by several women in his travels. Some helped support him financially. Concerning LGBTQ issues, Paul recommends against homosexuality but no punishment. Jesus did not speak on homosexuality, slavery, contraception, social justice, or abortion. He did not limit women's roles in any way. He created no group of "others" to be treated differently. His Christianity was a "Big tent".

One evening, when I was thirteen or fourteen years old and leader of a youth group at our Presbyterian church, I was at the weekly Wednesday night church dinner. I was in one of the hallways and found myself alone with the preacher. For some reason or other, I told him that I didn't think that Jesus was the son of God. He said, "That is all right. A lot of good people don't think so." There was no attempt on his part to make this an important event. His calm unhurried response has, I think, colored my approach to religious issues ever since. He made it apparent that one's religion can be a "big tent" organization where lots of compassionate viewpoints are tolerated. We should be able to include a wide variety of belief in a moral, kind, and reasonable atmosphere. We don't need to bother people because of Religious Rules.

According to Pew Research about 70% of the US identifies as Christian of some sort. About 6% identify as non-Christian faiths including Jews (1.9%) and Muslims (0.9%). Europe is about 51% Christian and 4.5% Muslim. [97] Almost all the rest have no organized religious belief. In general, organized Christianity is declining very slowly in the US and the Western nations. The statistics show that the US is not producing a lot of new Christians. The Evangelical Christian churches are growing, but it is predominantly at the expense of the older mainline Protestant and Catholic churches. Christian believers are just changing denominations. Christianity is growing in Africa, Asia, and South America. Most of the growth is in the Evangelical Protestant community. In general, they are more socially and politically conservative, but the differences are generally not great.

Catholicism has some Religious Rules concerning its sacraments, but membership is voluntary, and the rules are no longer enforced by religious courts. For heretics and sacrilege there are no punishments on earth except excommunication. Shunning can be a powerful punishment in small, closed societies.

If someone with today's modern sensibilities is seeking spiritual community and approaches Jesus' teachings, they find a compassionate spiritual teacher who is interested in interpersonal forgiveness, avoids judgment, creates no "others", and offers salvation without requiring a lot of Religious Rules.

To a modern spiritual seeker encountering Jesus for the first time, the attachment of the Old Testament to Jesus' life and teachings can be confusing. The Religious Rules in the Old Testament add a lot of negative "baggage" to the public image of Jesus. Paul's comments about slavery, women's roles, and homosexuality are also problematic. Philosophically Jesus puts forgiveness, tolerance, and the Golden Rule front and center. Jesus' message is very approachable for someone with a modern philosophic inclination if Jesus is not attached firmly to the Old Testament or Paul.

It has been observed that, if someone is brought up in a home that does not speak about God, they are much less likely to become religious in the monotheistic sense. In my experience, rational moderate unchurched people interested in joining a spiritual community or church often avoid serious contact with the Bible because of the Old Testament and Paul. They tend to end up in something like Unitarianism, Transcendentalism, or some watered-down version of Buddhism or Hinduism. A focus purely on Jesus' philosophic teachings reveals a humanitarian, if demanding, set of admonitions encouraging compassion, forgiveness, and service. To repeat, G.K. Chesterton's observant comment, "Christianity has not been tried and found wanting. It has been found difficult and left untried." The forgiveness recommended by Jesus probably constitutes the most difficult part.

Approaching the Bible as a whole requires some sincere effort. If seekers do value reason, the Old Testament's punishments and the New Testament's emphasis on miracles sometimes seem to put off an appreciation of Jesus, the philosopher, spiritual guide, and possible savior.

Some people seem to feel that they must defend Jesus' image. However, it is almost impossible to negatively satirize or criticize Jesus. His stances are so universally benign or enlightened that hostility or criticism of the man makes one look superficial or uninformed.

He was not defending a tribe, creating "others", or suggesting punishments. One can certainly criticize the Catholic Church and

Protestant organizations that supported slavery and punished heretics but criticizing Jesus doesn't work very well.

Religious Rules in Islam Today

With the end of colonization of the Arab world in the 1950's, most of the newly formed predominantly Muslim nations installed secular governments. Generally, these economies are struggling somewhat. There has been a push to return to enforcement of Religious Rules. Sharia is very close to democratic norms today except in the enforcement of Religious Rules. Unfortunately, the adoption of Religious Rules interferes with individual rights of speech, press, and religion.

Charges of heresy, sacrilege or apostasy can be used to invalidate actions, discredit public figures, and maintain power. Public figures will have to conform to the opinions of religious bodies, especially Sharia law schools. The adoption of conservative Sharia standards has usually resulted in the need for everyone to display a more orthodox public image that conforms to Religious Rule standards of dress, prayer, and piety. People will be identified as those who follow the Rules and rituals and those who do not follow. If someone does not conform, they are "others", and they can be treated differently.

Fundamentalist militias are perpetrating atrocities in the name of Islam in Afghanistan, Africa, Indonesia, the Middle East, and the Philippines. Many see their local government as corrupt and ineffective and, as a solution, they want to impose their ideas of Sharia. This application of a brutalizing misogynist type of Sharia is unnerving to the rest of the world. It seems that those advocating Sharia are just fascist-like groups justifying their grasps for power and wealth. The fundamentalist's exploitation of women is particularly retrograde and distressing. Human Rights Watch documents much of the violence and oppression caused by these groups. [98]

The fact that various Muslims regularly kill rivals or infidels for "insulting" their prophet or "attacks on Islam" makes people think that large numbers of Muslims harbor at least a small number of fanatics in their midst. It can make non-Muslims cautious and unwilling to endorse anything that encourages special treatment for Muslim sensitivities. They also oppose increased Muslim immigration and any support for Muslim ideas of public piety. About 15% of US generally feels that if groups of Muslims are gathering and pushing for special privileges, dangerous fanatics will be among them. Another 20% say that most Muslims support extremist views (Pew Research). [99]

On the other hand, fundamentalist Muslims see Western nations (white Christians) as oppressive and insulting to them and/or Islam. The invasion of Iraq, the relatively recent history of colonization, and spread of lascivious Western cultural norms are seen as insults to Islam. They see these conflicts in religious terms. The West sees it in geopolitical terms.

Today, in countries with majority Muslim populations, religion still plays a significant role in politics. Religious Rules are discussed constantly and followed or imposed to varying degrees. Muhammad's texts mixing mercy and compassion with coercion, and punishment play out differently in different countries. Compassionate contextualization requires some sincere and effort, and some think it is offensive. Blasphemy and heresy are still serious issues in much of political Islam. As discussed above political figures like President Erdogan in Turkey and Prime Minister Imran Khan in Pakistan have been involved in very public international efforts to stifle satires and criticisms of Muhammad. In Pakistan President Khan supports the death penalty for those that disrespect their prophet with blasphemy. Erdogan claims that France's increased scrutiny of Islamic groups following religiously motivated murders is a display of French "Islamophobia." No Western politicians feel the need to defend Christianity or Christians from criticism.

Many Muslims think that Islam is under assault from the West, and they feel powerless. The most recent conflict involving the West was the Iraq War, and it was not religiously motivated. It involved no issues concerning religious matters. However, militant Islamists say that attacks on Muslim political groups or nations are attacks on Islam itself. "Defense of Islam" is often used as a powerful recruiting tool for soldiers and martyrs in diverse political groups and militias. The fact that many Muslims in the Middle East identify politically as Muslims rather than Iraqis, or Pakistanis or Jordanians explains some of the misunderstandings. Western news correspondents in the middle east report that continuous loops of pictures of dead Muslim children on various Arab TV channels have had an intense emotional effect. These continuous, "almost pornographic", showings are designed to vilify the West and recruit followers. They are so ubiquitous that one Western journalist calls them "the Muzak of the Arab world". [100] These distressing films and resentment of colonization have combined in the Muslim world to recruit violent followers such as the San Bernadino shooters.

Modern Muslims are possibly hoping for an Islamic "Reformation". They hope that Islam is going through a period of internal examination leading to a more tolerant and merciful approach to Religious Rule issues. Clear labeling of the various groups might be helpful but is not being proposed by any influential body. Given the single source of the Qur'an and Hadith, it may be a difficult journey. The Muslim scriptures do not have a variety of competing and contradictory authors to weigh in the balance when deciding issues. Reformers must depend on contextualization of Muhammad's advice and good will. Fortunately, they do have a long tradition of scholarship and commentary on the Qur'an, some of which contextualizes the scriptures in compassionate and flexible ways. They also have several very clear admonitions to tolerance in the Qur'an and Hadith. [102]

Some Muslims say that these groups claiming Islamic sanction for violence are the result of foreign colonialism and have no basis in Islam. They say that the colonizers should be blamed for disrupting the society and creating an environment of poverty and corruption that encourages the development of brutal religious militias with varying political agendas. However, many non-Muslim nations have been colonized without resulting in unending periods of terror and carnage by groups claiming religious sanction. [103]

The internet facilitated the creation of militant religious organizations and plays the major role in recruiting. It has connected groups of religious malcontents and fundamentalists that would not have been able to organize otherwise. This, combined with frequent uncontextualized support for armed struggle in the Islamic religious texts has facilitated growth of terrorist and revolutionary groups. Combine this with the almost continuous disturbing pictures of Muslim victims of violence in the media, and terrorism seems to be a reasonable option.

The Saudi's are a rentier state, dependent on oil. They have immense power due to the money. Saudi Arabia is an example of the accumulation of large amounts of power in the hands of a fundamentalist community, the conservative Wahabi. This does not often happen in history. In the 1970s the Wahabis began to use this wealth to set up fundamentalist madrassas all over Islam. As discussed elsewhere, this has had some oppressive effects in areas that were once more tolerant such as Indonesia. To its credit prominent members of the Saudi royal family have become broadly educated and are now working to improve the lot of the Saudi people and lessen the grip of extremism. Recently, the rulers have become less doctrinaire as they continue to deal with demands of greatness and power. There are signs that they are beginning to recognize a duty to use their wealth to bring more peace and harmony to the world. [104] This accumulation of wealth and power might have the opportunity to present an Islam to the world that is tolerant of human rights that are important in other cultures.

Many scholars, including Umar Faruk Abd-Allah, praise Islam's "unity in diversity". In his paper, "Islam and the Cultural Imperative", Abd-Allah sees recent Islamic history as glorious rather than backwards and oppressive. Sharia is the cornerstone of his glorious progressive history. Sharia was an improvement over other forms of law before 700, especially concerning the tribal blood feuds in Arabia. With Sharia law the Islamic empire had brought to its individual citizens a new level of personal safety and reasonable limits to authority. Sharia was the link that kept them all together. Islam flourished for a long time. Will Islam undergo a reformation to include democratic or tolerant norms?

Islamic scholar Mark Fathi Massoud's paper, "Don't blame Sharia for Islamic Extremism – Blame Colonialism" [105] says that colonialism influenced the emerging nation states to not fully adopt Sharia because it didn't protect individual rights. Massoud says that this rejection of Sharia left it in the hands of the extremists. He surmises that, if the emerging nations had adopted Sharia, Sharia would not have become so aggressive and would be held in higher esteem by others. Now with the subsequent failure of secular rule in the Muslim states, Sharia has been proposed as a road to economic and political success. Massoud states that, unfortunately, in the meantime Sharia had become radicalized, endorsing various militias who became parties to numerous and continuous atrocities. He blames Western interference and incompetent rulers, not Sharia. He says, "But there is no inherent tension between Sharia, human rights, and the rule of law. Like any use of religion in politics, Sharia's application depends on who is using it – and why." Many would say that is precisely why religions should not be in politics. Extremists can use the trust provided by faith and belief to encourage gullible violent men to harm or intimidate others. by 900 C.E

Another scholar noted that if Islam allowed for individual choice and worship, the varieties of the sects created by this would produce many beautiful, compassionate, creative, and friendly congregations. The resulting various sects would probably present a kaleidoscopic array of mosques that joyously welcomed visitors and tolerated differences in worship and piety. Celebrations would be numerous and delightful. Interpersonal communication would be easy and warm.

Massoud continues, "When it comes to Muslim-majority countries, however, Sharia takes the blame for regressive laws – not the people who pass those policies in the name of religion." Furthermore, he states, "For the Muslim world, finding a system of government that reflects Islamic values while promoting democracy will not be easy after more than 50 years of failed secular rule. But building peace may demand it." Is he describing a reformation? The assumption here is that the Sharia proposed by one religious group is superior to that proposed by another. Who decides which Religious Rules are enforced? Who decides what is Sharia? Everyone seems to have a different idea. The law schools want that role, and they differ a lot. However, all of them want to impose many Religious Rules of some sort or another. "Islam is the answer". Massoud finishes by making a caveat common to all fundamentalist assertions concerning laws in Islamic nations. He says that democratic laws and rights are acceptable "as long as they are not clearly repudiated in the revealed (Sharia) law". Ultimately, the law must agree with someone's idea of Sharia. Will Sharia be compassionately contextualized, or will it demand strict adherence to its favored Religious Rules?

The suicidal terrorism associated with Islamic fundamentalists is relatively new. It had a devastating entrance in the US on Sept 11, 2001. The West had dealt with terrorists such as the Baader Meinhof Gang and The Red Brigades, but the Japanese Kamikaze pilots were the only suicidal killers of recent memory. How are these people made? A source of information is: *Origins and Contexts of Terrorism*. National Research Council. 2002. "Terrorism: Perspectives from the Behavioral and Social Sciences". Washington, DC: The National Academies Press. doi: 10.17226/10570

In part the report states, "The search for identity is probably important, but so is the venting of anger, the power motive, and the glamour and aura of heroism and martyrdom."

The report notes that the typical ingredients of such suicidal movements are:

"A totalistic worldview rooted in a sacred religious system.

A profound sense of threat, angst, and apprehension about the destruction of their society, culture, and way of life.

A specification of certain agents who are assigned total responsibility for this deterioration.

An unqualified, and absolute, sense of rage that is felt to be morally legitimate.

A utopian view of their own culture and society—perhaps referring to an imagined, glorious past."

Fundamentalist and politically oriented teachers have also used verses from the Qur'an that extoll martyrdom, such as Qur'an 22:58–59. "Those who leave their homes in the cause of Allah, and are then slain or die, on them will Allah bestow verily a goodly Provision: Truly Allah is He Who bestows the best provision. Verily He will admit them to a place with which they shall be well pleased: for Allah is All-Knowing, Most Forbearing."—translated by Abdullah Yusuf Ali.

Islam's great appeal seems to lie in its warm family and community life and the safety of Sharia law in some very dangerous and corrupt places. It offers membership in a large community with many splendid people. It promotes a very tight warm extended family structure. It gives every Muslim a very clear identity. It is kind to the destitute, disadvantaged, or stranger. It has beautiful traditions, rituals, community gatherings, and art. It has clear compassionate instructions on many ethical issues. It is kind to animals. It provides for the aged. It defends its adherents. It promises a path to heaven where one is rewarded with beautiful young virginal women companions and youths as servants. (Qur'an 56:22-24).

Coincidentally, its Religious Rules include punishments for impieties such as apostasy, sin, violations of dress codes, homosexuality, adultery, and blasphemy. The definitions of several of these terms allow for wide discretion, for good and bad. The dependence on various forms of Sharia, which are not codified, allows for regional discrepancies and opportunities that use Sharia oppressively. Compassionate contextualizing that emphasizes individual rights would seem to be essential but does not seem to be imminent. Codifying (writing down) Sharia would seem to help. At least the parties would know what each other is talking about.

Like the other monotheists, every Muslim is responsible for his/her own fate. The final authorities in Islam are the texts, the Qur'an and Hadith. A follower may go to the scholars (*ulema*) for advice, but the individual must decide. The search for right answers goes always to the texts. Some important General Admonitions in the texts advocate mercy and compassion. However, there are very many clearly Religious Rules concerning various approaches to dress, food, rituals, heresies, blasphemy, apostasy, women, and sexuality. They condemn alcohol, adultery, usury, gambling, mixing with other religions, and mixed sex dancing and dating. Some tolerate more benign forms of slavery and sexual intercourse with one's slaves (Qur'an 23:5, 33:50). Some recommend freeing one's slaves. Others advocate punishment for disturbing or ignoring the piety of the religious community. Still others condone punishment for leaving and criticizing the religion. To properly contextualize these readings, Muslims are individually responsible. There are many scholars with very different agendas who want to tell them what to do or force them. Codifying Sharia might make things clearer.

The *ulema* gives answers based on intensive study and interpretation. However, they are not the final authority. The Qur'an and the Hadith are the final authority, and they are sometimes contradictory. The *ulema*'s opinion is just the *ulema*'s opinion. Compassionate and tolerant "Cherry Picking" may be increasing for the better. If the *ulema* is generally compassionate and tolerant, they can be ignored by those bent on confrontation. Anyone can read the text, and every Muslim can follow the texts with his/her opinion no matter what a particular *ulema* says. In a formal way this is very similar to Protestantism. Charitable contextualizing will be essential.

Orientalism

"Orientalism" and "Islamophobia" are two recently coined terms. Any discussion including religion today must address them.

"Orientalism" accuses most Western scholars and writers of having biased, stereotypically negative views of Muslim societies. [106] Dr. Edward Said, a Palestinian American professor at Colombia, developed the field of "post-colonial studies" and popularized the term "Orientalism". He feels that poorly informed depictions of Muslim culture and history have been used to justify Western colonialism in the Middle East. Dr. Said felt that negative essentialization (simplification) of the Muslim world merely served to justify Western imperial power and colonization. "Implicit in this fabrication," writes Said, "is the idea that Western society is developed, rational, flexible, and superior."

In 1798 Napoleon's France was the first Western culture to invade and seriously study Muslim culture and society. Scholars were sent with the French armies to study Ancient Egypt and the current culture. The backwardness of science, democracy, and technology made the Islamic Middle East seem inferior and very vulnerable. The strong family life, traditions, warm ceremonies, and community support in a dangerous world were treasured by many Muslims, but they seemed to be of minor interest to the French Orientalist historians. The superiority of Western technology and the freedoms proposed in the recent Western ideas of democracy aroused some of the Islamic intelligencia to defend Middle Eastern culture. A prominent Islamic scholar of the time, al-Jabarti, "wrote extensively to criticize Napoleon's pronouncement that 'all men are equal before God' as a 'lie and stupidity' and further proof that the West was vested in making the reasoning of man supreme to the will of God." [107] Westerners think that reason is a tool given by God, and that it is useful in science and politics, but most have found that they must be very careful with it. The fact that Al-Jabarti's defense of the Middle East's politics and achievements is theological illustrates the deep influence of religion in politics and public discourse. The French writers and scholars with Napoleon became the first of Dr, Said's Orientalists. They and the French painters of the time emphasized sex, violence, lassitude, and exoticism in their portrayals of the of the Middle East.

The harem with its sensuality, mystery, polygyny, and male possessiveness was such an exotic difference that it heavily influenced European views of Islamic social life in the 19th century. The male was completely in charge and the female was essentially a possession who had almost no role in society except sex and motherhood. Additionally having sex with one's female slaves was explicitly approved by the most holy of Islamic texts (Qur'an 23:5-6, 33:50). At the time the sexes in the Middle East were even excluded from being together socially except for family events. In the West at that time, queens ruled frequently, and gender mixed parties and celebrations were continuous. In actuality there had been numerous female rulers in Islamic nations. They were usually the wives of rulers, and they gained political control on the death of their husbands. On the other hand, Middle Eastern women at times had more enlightened power where divorce, inheritance, and land ownership were concerned. Divorce laws were much easier for men but did grant some financial help for the woman. Slavery in much of the Middle East was not officially ended until after WWI when many countries were colonized by European nations.

The Orientalist viewpoint today seems to see Islam as a failed political venture. To them Islam had a dynamic beginning and a very long run in the Middle East and East. It had developed algebra and was at the center of science and philosophy. Ultimately it produced almost nothing after its Golden Age around the 13th century. After A-Ghazali's push for occasionalism, it developed no significant science, or technology, and no political philosophic improvements leading to democracy. Much of Islam had a relatively long period of stability with the Ottoman Empire. The Ottoman Empire was ultimately defeated and broken up. Most nations formed from it were colonized by European powers. In the 1950's the Arab Islamic states emerged from colonialism into a group of marginally functional states. Today many blame colonialism for its woes. Is this just a cyclical historic process? Muslim conservatives think that the states failed because they lost the purity of Islam. Was it just the fact that Islamic lands were in a difficult geographic area open to pressure on all sides? The unfortunate boundaries that arose out of the Sykes Picot Agreement certainly did not make things easier.

Because almost all Muslims were of darker skin, white critics were also labeled as "racists". The label, "racist", adds a serious additional level of scorn. Dr. Said uses the term "racism" frequently in describing Orientalism. The charge of "racism" can be a superficial and misleading attempt to avoid scrutiny, or it can be a clear identification of bigotry and ignorance. The fact that all peoples outside the West are darker than the Westerners means that any interaction can be called racist. Accusations of racism can be an attempt to avoid difficult questions.

Islamophobia

The term "Islamophobe" became prominent in the 1990's. It is a label for someone who disliked Islam because they are poorly informed or bigoted. Like "Orientalism", the term "Islamophobe" is to be used to identify and discredit various critics of Islam. It is true that many critics are ignorant of the beauties and the truths in Islam. They are poorly informed and deal in negative stereotypes that do not reflect the depth and compassion of much Islamic culture. However, based on the recent obvious democratic and economic failures in post-colonial Islamic nations, the critics can claim to have some insight. In the other hand, many of the failures are blamed on Western colonialism's effects.

Compared to the West much of Islam has frequent mob violence in the name of blasphemy, and any openly moderate politicians are under constant pressure from conservative religious figures. Pointing out the problems presented by these groups does not mean that one is "Islamophobic".

Today the situation seems to be that many Muslims feel that they are misunderstood in the West. They feel that they are unfairly called on to "defend" their religion by critics that they label "Islamophobes". Some Muslim voices call on the religious community to reform itself. This requires internal debate and criticism. This is not easy in a culture which feels it is misunderstood and under pressure by the outside world.

It is difficult and potentially dangerous for moderate Muslims and external critics to speak out or define themselves well. If they openly and clearly say that public adherence to some Religious Rules is not necessary or confusing, then radicals may want to silence them in the name of unity. They are often accused of blasphemy to silence them. Some Islamic states are lax in suppressing or neutralizing the retrograde and dangerous elements that stifle reform. Many reform, moderate, or Western Muslims have no interest in being labeled as critics of "Islam". I certainly do not. I want Islam to succeed and provide for its people without allowing fundamentalists to excessively harass them over things that are of marginal importance.

Islamic unity would create more political power. More conservative Muslim activists will see any dissenters as undermining the unity that they desire. It can be very dangerous. In today's polarized environment, moderates can be vilified by both extremes. On the other hand, established, clearly labeled groups, might, like many Protestant sects, provide a group refuge for those who want a more tolerant Islam. The Muslims in the US are possibly safe enough to begin to make such distinctions. MRM (Muslim Reform Movement) is a North American group that is trying to decrease the fundamentalist approach supported by Saudi Arabian money for *madrassas*. EXMNA (Ex-Muslims of North America) is a group supporting apostates.

Chapter 11
American Muslims Today and Religious Rules

Parts of this book have to do with the visible problems in Middle Eastern, African and Asian Islam. To most American Muslims and reform or modern type Muslims everywhere, the "Muslims" who want to kill Westerners, issue violent fatwas, and punish apostates are not even remotely related to the Islam that they know and follow. To most American Muslims, Osama Bin Laden, Boston Marathon bombers, the Fort Hood killer, San Bernardino killers, suicidal terrorists, Philippine insurgents, ISIS, Boko Haram, and their proteges have no relationship to the Islam that they practice.

According to Pew Research and poling American Muslims are rather typical Americans in political questions. They have been immersed in a liberal democratic society and like its freedoms and benefits. They constitute about 1% of Americans. Pew Research concludes, "They (American Muslims) are anything but wholly apart; indeed, in important respects, Muslim Americans reflect the religious and political values held by most other Americans." (Pew Research. *Muslims and Islam: Key findings in the U.S. and around the world.* By Michael Lipka. August 9, 2017.) A majority says that there is more than one way to interpret Islam. They feel that unity is not obligatory. Will they openly define themselves as a different sect with a set of tolerant codified ideals and beliefs?

Western Muslims are probably not being heard correctly. The reform type Muslim community is fatigued at being stereotyped as backward, intolerant, and dangerous. The fact that reform type Muslims and dangerously fundamentalist Muslims share many religious texts and pious Religious Rules such as clothes, food, fasting, and prayer rituals makes for confusion on some public levels. The more moderate Muslims don't openly identify as moderate, and they can superficially look like they are sympathetic to fundamentalist groups. Does observation of the outward pieties imply agreement with conservative agendas? Also, it is distressing that every so often a Muslim in the West commits an atrocity in the name of Islam. It appears that Western Muslims will be asked to explain their positions repeatedly unless they label the different factions clearly.

Modern Muslims, Jews, and Christians all hope that female genital mutilation, honor killings, dowry deaths, and forced marriages will be eliminated.

Concerning Israel, Americans in general support the Israelis. In a 2021 Gallup Poll, 75% of Americans view Israel favorably, 30% viewed the Palestinians favorably. On the other hand, almost 90% of American Muslims support the Palestinians in the Israeli-Palestinian conflict. [107] However, a majority of American Muslims think that the state of Israel and the Palestinian can coexist. An article in Pew Research by Russel Heimlich, in Nov 2012, is available online and is titled *Most Muslim Americans Say that Israel, Palestinian Rights Can Coexist.*

"In a survey of Muslim American attitudes, 62% said that a way can be found for Israel to exist while also addressing the rights and needs of the Palestinian people. These views were virtually unchanged from 2007....

In contrast, majorities or pluralities in most predominantly Muslim nations surveyed by the Pew Global Attitudes Project in 2007 expressed the view that the rights and needs of the Palestinian people cannot be taken care of as long as the state of Israel even exists."

American Muslims seem to feel that the Palestinians have been treated badly and that the Palestinians have the stronger case for injustice. The Palestinian suicide bombers and random rockets are viewed as legitimate acts of war by a people who have no other way to fight. Some view the "terrorists" as freedom fighters. The randomness of the killing does not play well in the West. Problematically, the charges of anti-Semitism, colonialism, terrorism, Islamophobia, Orientalism, and imperialism are used in confusing and misleading ways by all parties. Forgiveness and compromise do not seem immanent. The clear identification of the various Islamic parties, like the Christian Protestants have done, may be central to any final agreement. As things stand, the desire for a powerful unified religious component to all the political issues seems to make any agreement almost impossible.

Chapter 12

Religious Rules in Confucianism, Hinduism, Buddhism and Taoism Today

India is democratizing and cleaning out most of the vestiges of the caste system which was deeply rooted in Indian culture. Women's rights are spreading to the rural areas. Illiteracy was widespread and is now about 20% in India. Religious Rules concerning heresy, blasphemy, and apostasy are not issues in the religion or the state. Hinduism, Buddhism and Taoism have essentially no enforced Religious Rules concerning heresy, blasphemy, apostasy, dress, sex, homosexuality, women's roles, or food. Public displays of affection are illegal if they are offensive. Kissing in public is frowned upon and those who do it can be jailed for up to 3 months. Local traditions impart various cultural values. In many but not all sects, one must remain celibate to be a Buddhist priest.

Confucius was interested in developing one's discernment and virtue. There are no revealed Religious Rules. Significantly, he valued the group (family, community, or state) over the individual. Principles, duty, and attitudes are important. "Do not do unto others what you do not want them to do to you" is the central tenet. In relations with others, consensus was to be desired over confrontation, and persuasion rather than victory. He had no problem with authority but thought that power should be in the hands of the "most virtuous". At certain points Confucian societies have functioned as true meritocracies in that promotion and status have been determined by examinations. He had no desire to follow a set of revealed Religious Rules to please a god.

Confucius did speak of "divine order", but, like science's secrets, this order was to be discovered by rational effort and discernment, not imposed by religious authority. The three leaders of the Chinese "religions", Buddhism, Confucianism, and Taoism are so compatible that they are often pictured together in Chinese art.

Conclusion

I said at the beginning that I wanted to create a viewpoint and a vocabulary that will allow people to communicate more clearly about religious differences. If we understand clearly where and why we differ, communication would be easier. Problematically, we must want to get along, and we must contextualize the messages of our prophets. Because of religious or cultural fervor, those prerequisites are not often met.

The principal differences between religions are determined by our attitudes toward the Religious Rules. Identifying the Religious Rules would, I hope, facilitate discourse. I assume that better definitions will improve relations by increasing moderation. Fundamentally the religious message in all the great religions is one of kindness, mercy, and inclusion as illustrated in the General Admonitions common to all. The Moral Rules are rational and generally agreed on. Everyone thinks that lying, stealing, murdering, and adultery are bad ideas. Issues around fornication are religious and cultural. Organizational Rules mainly differ along group/individual and capitalist/socialist lines of reasoning. Religious differences and problems center on the enforcement of Religious Rules.

The Moral Rules and the compassionate General Admonitions are all essentially the same in the great religions, and they make living in society much better. They require reasoning, tolerance, concern, and protection for every individual. They require that we listen carefully to the narratives of others. On the other hand, Religious Rules are revealed, not rational. They are revealed to and by prophets and are completely idiosyncratic. Because they are idiosyncratic, contextualization becomes very important. What matters greatly, and what doesn't?

Problematically, government adoption of Religious Rules usually involves eliminating individual human rights concerning speech, press, or religion. The Tanakh, the Talmud, the Bible, the Qur'an, and the Hadith create many confusing issues that require contextualization for compassionate applications. This is not always easy.

One can see why some charitable Jewish, Christian, and Muslim scholars don't want to focus on Religious Rules. Reform Jews usually see the Religious Rules as cultural folklore. To them charitable deeds are much more important than any creeds of belief or acts of piety. The moderate Christians prioritize Jesus' teachings about forgiveness, charity, and inclusion rather than orthodoxy. The more modern Muslims would like to focus on the mercy which is extolled in the Qur'an and limit the influence of the Hadith. Some Hadith are beautiful, but many are historically questionable and too easily manipulated to justify oppression.

Personal individual adherence to Religious Rules concerning piety gives a deep level of ritual satisfaction to many and a profound sense of belonging to something much larger. When the state, or various fanatics force the pious Religious Rules on the community, it can be totalitarian and oppressive. The Religious Rules create a "group" mentality. This can separate people from each other and open the door to nepotism, corruption, "otherness", conflict, and sometimes, genocide. It would seem to be best for religious people to concentrate on the Moral Rules and General Admonitions from their prophets and relax on the Religious Rules where others are concerned. In short, if you want to be pious, fine, but don't expect it of others. If you want a more pious atmosphere, convert the neighbors.

As for blasphemy, heresy, and apostasy surely God will eventually take care of those issues. We don't need to get involved. It would be generous and helpful if people would avoid offending the sensitivities of others. It would also be helpful if religious people would be less concerned by the sacrilege and apostasy of others.

I have suggested that religious groups identify themselves more clearly. The Jews use the words "reform", "conservative", and "orthodox".

It is very helpful that Protestants use thousands of names. These generally let others know how one stands on Religious Rules. Some Muslims use the term "Modern Muslim" to indicate tolerance. Sufis are generally tolerant. This can dissipate some of the awkward moments and more easily allow for conversation and understanding. This sort of labeling goes against the unity desired by religious groups wanting political power. It seems that the greater the demand for unity, the more oppressive the group.

Decreasing any emphasis on Religious Rules has allowed the West to develop societies that are proving to be the best yet known to the world despite their deeply flawed racist, colonial, and imperialistic histories. Many people, (except those who benefit substantially from the corrupt power structure in their nation,) want to live in the West or a democratic country that has benefited from Western influence such as Japan, South Korea, Taiwan, Singapore, etc. The West has recognized that emphasizing the individual rights of speech, press, religion, habeas corpus, and the vote is essential to progress in creating and maintaining a relatively honest and sociable society. The Western type nations have also separated church and state. Everyone is free to worship as they choose.

The West has valued reason within a predominantly moral framework provided by their religion's Moral Rules and General Admonitions. They have also produced extensive welfare benefits for the disadvantaged and are seriously working on the elimination of the residual effects of slavery and racism. The amount of this welfare and affirmative action is debated constantly. The economic inequity problems associated with capitalism are at the center of ongoing political discourse. Equality of economic status will be impossible without a totalitarian socialist type of state. Equity, meaning an equal opportunity, is only fully realized with a better educational system and home life for the disadvantaged. This equity is very desirable and possibly achievable. Can capitalism be compassionate enough to alleviate the problems of the poor and disadvantaged? Is socialism a useful step in controlling overwhelming corruption? China and Cuba have used socialism to control crime and benefit the poor.

Venezuela is trying to benefit the poor, but seemingly has made life worse because of its inability to control serious crime. It is rated as having the highest crime environment in the world.

Centralizing the individual's rights has made Western societies relatively tolerant, democratic, and, when combined with highly regulated capitalism, economically very successful. Most importantly, emphasis on individual rights allows them to progress toward less racism, and full civil rights, usually spurred on by the occasionally disruptive pressure of "progressives" who are today's radicals. The residual effects of slavery, lynching, and Jim Crow legislation have produced economic and educational inequalities. Recognition of these racially flawed outcomes is essential because they must be improved. Progress is occurring, but as usual, it is slow and incomplete.

On the negative side, many people believe the success of the West is based on the colonialization and exploitation of others. That, to some extent, is true. Historically it has been true of all powerful nations. However, it is not the only narrative. Western civilization's role in creating human rights and institutions such as the United Nations is unique and revolutionary. In the West, despite underlying prejudice and serious flaws, the liberal democracy has provided remarkable opportunity to its minorities. Even though the playing field was not equal, the African American minority has responded by creating the largest and richest Black population in the world. Much of this has come since the Great Society was begun in the 1960's. For the first time in history, many can improve their material wealth and safety without becoming corrupt, nepotistic, or brutal. Adequate taxation, sufficient welfare, efficient unions, fair elections, and capitalist economies work well if the countries are not too corrupt. Western interference in the attempts to employ socialist solutions in third world countries is controversial.

Economic and social equity are now goals of liberal Western governments. Education is, probably, the only long-term solution. Equity of opportunity can only come with equality of education. Much more must be done to provide the schools, the neighborhoods, the cultural values, and the home environment necessary to produce real racial equity. Very small school classes may be possible steps to any form of equity. Someone said, "To liberals, education is the answer to every problem." This may be true.

For the rational person, a religion teaching kindness, promoting honesty, endorsing compassionate reason, emphasizing forgiveness, separating church and state, and avoiding enforcement of Religious Rules would seem not only desirable, but also supportive of the best parts of liberal government and the General Admonitions. Contemporary Christianity, reform Judaism, and the modern Muslim are not searching for victory or a forced unity. They are all searching for a more joyous coexistence while they reach for salvation and understanding. Western Culture is dealing with some cultural issues involving the residuals of racism. Islamic culture is under stress and looking for better economies and stable government. Increased tolerance may be an essential ingredient. Already, large numbers of sincerely religious people, through compassionate contextualizing, find spiritual fulfillment and a sense of brother/sisterhood with all peoples. Hopefully a charitable reading and contextualization of all texts will spread.

"Our feet are always wet."

THE END.

Endnotes

(1)   1 Samuel 8:11-18. "So Samuel spoke all the words of the Lord to the people who had asked of him a king. He said, 'This will be the procedure of the king who will reign over you: he will take your sons and place them for himself in his chariots and among his horsemen and they will run before his chariots. He will appoint for himself commanders of thousands and of fifties, and some to do his plowing and to reap his harvest and to make his weapons of war and equipment for his chariots. He will also take your daughters for perfumers and cooks and bakers. He will take the best of your fields and your vineyards and your olive groves and give them to his servants. He will take a tenth of your seed and of your vineyards and give to his officers and to his servants. He will also take your male servants and your female servants and your best young men and your donkeys and use them for his work. He will take a tenth of your flocks, and you yourselves will become his servants. Then you will cry out in that day because of your king whom you have chosen for yourselves, but the Lord will not answer you in that day.'"

(2)   Jesus said, "Render unto Caesar what is Caesar's and unto God what is God's." Matthew 22:21.

Paul's letter to the Romans 13:1. "Let everyone be subject to the governing authorities, for there is no authority except that which God has established. The authorities that exist have been established by God."

1 Peter 2:13. "Submit yourselves for the Lord's sake to every human authority: whether to the emperor, as the supreme authority." Qur'an chapter 4:59. "O ye who have believed, obey Allah and obey His Messenger and the people of authority amongst you."

(3)   "Pakistan journalism student latest victim of blasphemy vigilantes." *Deutsche Welle*. April 15, 2017. Subsequently, over 50 people were convicted in the murder. One was sentenced to death, three to life imprisonment. It was determined that this was planned, not a spontaneous act. A website labeled *thereligionofpeace* keeps a tally of these events.

In May of 2022, Deborah Yakubu, a college student in Nigeria, was beaten to death by other students for supposed blaspheming Muhammad. In Nigeria in 1994 Gideon Akaluka was killed by a mob for blaspheming the Qur'an.

(4)   Ahi al-Kalam was a movement in early Islam (around 800 C.E..) that rejected the importance and validity of the Hadith. Shortly thereafter, a group named Mu'tazili worked to reconcile Greek reason with Islam. At that time, they too felt that the Hadith were too subject to prejudice and error to be authentic guides.

Recent proponents of using the Qur'an alone, include Aslam Jairajpuri, Distinguished Professor of Arabic and Persian, and Ghulam Ahmad Parwez, a pioneer of Qur'anic doctrine from pre-Independence India. They attempted to rationally interpret Qur'anic themes, by challenging the established Sunni doctrine that considers the Hadith to be important. These recent Islamic scholars hold the position that the Hadith should not be considered canonical since Muhammad did not write them down. Many others reported them at various later dates. These scholars feel that the Hadith are too subject to distortion and manipulation.

(5)   Manzoor, Sarfraz "Can we drop the term 'moderate Muslim'? Its meaningless".
        The Guardian. (16 March 2015) Retrieved 12 September 2017. Manzoor says that
        "moderate" is an offensive label to most Muslims in that it implies that they are not
        devout.

        One's stance relative to the seriousness of the different Religious Rules probably
        separates the Muslims into groups ranging from modern/reform to fundamentalist.
        All people who call themselves Muslims believe that Muhammad is the prophet
        appointed by God to bring the Qur'an, the word of God, to the people of the world.
        The reform or moderate Muslims probably think that the adherence to the Religious
        Rules should be more of an individual matter. Not a group issue. The "traditional"
        (orthodox and conservative) Muslims are more interested in adhering to the Reli-
        gious Rules and wanting to enforce them to some extent or other. Some Muslims see
        all Islam as one. Manzoor thinks that further labeling implies that there are multiple
        Islams, some of them dysfunctional. They see the labels "moderate" or "modern" as
        criticism which implies that they are not devout or that the message is not clear or,
        even worse, impure.

        "Moderate Muslim" is also a label used in US counterterrorist discourse. It sepa-
        rates Muslims into "moderates" or "extremists". It implies that the support of Islamic
        terrorism is the characteristic of a "radical" faction within Islam, and that there is a
        "moderate" or reform faction of Muslims who denounce terrorism.

(6)   *Sola scriptura* means that Christians are justified in their actions and by scripture
        alone. It can be accompanied by two other "solas". *Sola gratia*, Christians are saved
        by grace or God's beneficence alone. *Sola fide*, Christians are justified by faith alone.
        For the purposes of this book *Sola scriptura* generally means that the Bible itself,
        gives the only valid instructions.

(7)   Matthew 6:1-8, "Be careful not to practice your righteousness in front of others to
        be seen by them. If you do, you will have no reward from your Father in heaven. "So
        when you give to the needy, do not announce it with trumpets, as the hypocrites do
        in the synagogues and on the streets, to be honored by others. Truly I tell you, they
        have received their reward in full. But when you give to the needy, do not let your
        left hand know what your right hand is doing, so that your giving may be in secret.
        Then your Father, who sees what is done in secret, will reward you. And when you
        pray, do not be like the hypocrites, for they love to pray standing in the synagogues
        and on the street corners to be seen by others. Truly I tell you, they have received
        their reward in full. But when you pray, go into your room, close the door and pray
        to your Father, who is unseen. Then your Father, who sees what is done in secret,
        will reward you. And when you pray, do not keep on babbling like pagans, for they
        think they will be heard because of their many words."

        Matthew 6:16-18. "When you fast, do not look somber as the hypocrites do, for
        they disfigure their faces to show others they are fasting. Truly I tell you, they have
        received their reward in full. But when you fast, put oil on your head and wash your
        face, so that it will not be obvious to others that you are fasting, but only to your
        Father, who is unseen; and your Father, who sees what is done in secret, will reward
        you."

(8)   Besides his contributions to government, Jefferson is known to have had many
        slaves. He is generally thought to have had an ongoing sexual relationship with one
        of his slaves, Sally Hemmings. His writings and this quote from him in the Jefferson
        Memorial in Washington, D.C. show that he was profoundly conflicted and deeply
        concerned about slavery, but he did not free his slaves.

"God who gave us life gave us liberty. Can the liberties of a nation be secure when we have removed a conviction that these liberties are the gift of God? Indeed, I tremble for my country when I reflect that God is just, that his justice cannot sleep forever. Commerce between master and slave is despotism. Nothing is more certainly written in the book of fate than that these people are to be free. Establish a law for educating the common people. This it is the business of the state and on a general plan."

(9) The "Curse of Ham" in Genesis 9:25 was used by racists to support slavery and racism. It states that "Cursed be Canaan; lowest of slaves shall he be to his brothers." Ham was Noah's son, and Canaan was Ham's son. Ham found his father drunk and naked and went to tell his brothers. Noah cursed his son Ham and grandson, Canaan. Racist scholars held that Canaan had dark skin. There are numerous mentions of Ethiopians in the Bible. They were most assuredly Black, but it is not mentioned. No one cared about race then.

(12) Here are some quotes from the Bible, the Qur'an, and Hadith. One can string them together to make religion look violent and oppressive or one can put together a list to emphasize the compassionate and tolerant aspects. Concerning the violent quotes and punishments, context is very important.

It is easy for Christians to pick and choose because there are over 40 authors to the Bible. One must pick and choose because they bring different messages. Jesus never mentions punishments on earth.

Deuteronomy 7:1-2. "When the LORD your God brings you into the land you are entering to possess and drives out before you many nations—the Hittites, Girgashites, Amorites, Canaanites, Perizzites, Hivites and Jebusites, seven nations larger and stronger than you—and when the LORD your God has delivered them over to you and you have defeated them, then you must destroy them totally. Make no treaty with them and show them no mercy."

Jeremiah 47:4 "For the day has come to destroy all the Philistines and to remove all survivors who could help Tyre and Sidon. The LORD is about to destroy the Philistines, the remnant from the coasts of Caphtor."

Psalm 144:1 "Praise be to the LORD my Rock, who trains my hands for war, my fingers for battle."

Genesis 9:5-6 "And for your lifeblood I will surely demand an accounting. I will demand an accounting from every animal. And from each human being, too, I will demand an accounting for the life of another human being. "Whoever sheds human blood, by humans shall their blood be shed; for in the image of God has God made mankind."

Muhammad is the only source of the Islamic texts. He must be contextualized because sometimes he speaks of the importance of tolerance and sometimes he is defending his tribe.

These quotes from the Qur'an are from the Penguin Classic publication, *The Koran*. Translation by N. J. Dawood, 1990, unless noted otherwise.

The compassionate references can look like this:

Qur'an 2:256 "There shall be no compulsion in religion."

Qur'an 23:95 "Requite evil with good."

Hadith, Bukhari 1:2:13 "None of you [truly] believes until he wishes for his brother what he wishes for himself."

Hadith, "The proof of a Muslim's sincerity is that he pays no attention to that which is not his business."

Hadith, Abu Dawud, Tirmidhi "Women are the twin halves of men.".

Hadith: Musnad Ahmad 23494. "That person is nearest to God, who pardons... him who would have injured him."

The forceful emphasis can look something like this: (These translations can be compared with various others, or you can go online.) It is often said that the only real way to understand the Qur'an is to read it in Arabic.

Qur'an 2:190 "And kill those who fought against you wherever you encounter them."

Qur'an 2:194 "If you are oppressed, oppress those who oppress you to the same degree."

Qur'an 2:285 "Can you believe in one part of the scripture and deny another?"

Qur'an 3:228 "Those who believe should not take unbelievers as friends."

Qur'an 4:34 "But as for those wives from whom you fear disobedience, first admonish them.... then hit them."

Qur'an 4:104 "Seek out your enemies relentlessly."

Qur'an 5:32 "The penalty for those who wage war against Allah and His Messenger and strive on earth to cause corruption...they be killed or crucified or that their hands and feet be cut off from opposite sides..."

Qur'an 9:39 "If you do not fight, He will punish you sternly and replace you by other men."

Qur'an 48:29 "Muhammad is the Prophet of God; those who are with him are severe with infidels but compassionate among themselves."

(13)   Here is an enigmatic quote from the Encyclopedia Britannica concerning Taoism. "Adepts often search for their divine teacher in all the holy mountains of China until they finally discover him in one of the "palaces" inside their heads."

(14)   Tzvi Freeman. "Do Jews Believe in Heaven?" *Chabad.org*. "An overview of fundamental Jewish beliefs concerning reward and the afterlife."

(15)   Study of the present Egyptian Constitution and the law articles that conflict with minority Rights. – *UN Human Rights Office of the High Commissioner*.

"..., by attaching a qualification to the adoption of International Laws and Treaties which states "taking into consideration the provisions of the Islamic Sharia and the fact that they do not conflict with the text annexed to the instrument, we accept, support and ratify it." This has rendered the adoption of the international law useless. A similar qualification was also made to the adoption of international law in Egypt on ratification of the "International Covenant on Civil and Political Rights" which was signed by Egypt in 1982".

(16)   Turan Kayaoglu, "Giving an Inch Only to Lose a Mile: Muslim States, Liberalism, and Human Rights in the United Nations." *Human Rights Quarterly* 36, no.1 (February 2014: 61-91).

Heini Skorini, Chapter 5. "The OIC and Freedom of Expression: Justifying Religious Censorship Norms with Human Rights Language." From the book, *The Organization of Islamic Cooperation and Human Rights*. Petersen and Kayaoglu. In the series *Pennsylvania Studies in Human Rights*, 2019.

(17)   Speech reported in *Los Angeles Daily News*, November 10, 2017.

Hakan Yavuz and Ahmet Erdi Ozturk, "Turkish secularism and Islam under the reign of Erdoğan." *Informa. Taylor and Francis Online.* 18 Feb 2019.

(18) This is a quote from 28 Too Many, an organization attempting to end FGM.

"The 4 main Islamic schools of jurisprudence differ in their interpretations of the teachings and provisions of Islamic law and guidance regarding Female Genital Mutilation. Shafi'i school of Islamic thoughts considers FGM to be obligatory. While the Hanbali, Maliki and Hanafi school of Islamic laws consider FGM to be recommended (or preferred). Although there is no mention of FGM in the Qur'an. A Hadith (saying of the prophet, Fiqh-us-Sunnah Volume 1, Purification and Prayer, Fiqh 1.021A) conveys a discussion between prophet Muhammed and a woman (Um Habiba) who was known for being a practitioner of FGM. Having seen her, Muhammad asked her if she kept practicing FGM. She answered "yes", adding: "unless it is forbidden, and you order me to stop doing it." Muhammed replied: "Yes, it is allowed. Come closer so I can teach you: if you cut, do not overdo it, because it brings more radiance to the face, and it is more pleasant for the husband." This is a very questionable Hadith that Shia Muslims think is not truly part of Muhammad's message.

(19a) Sami A. Aldeeb Abu Sahlieh, "To Mutilate in the Name of Jehovah or Allah: Legitimization of Male and Female Circumcision," *Medicine and Law*, July 1994, pp. 575-622

(19) Kecia Ali. "Honor Killings, Illicit Sex, and Islamic Law." *The Feminist Sexual Ethics Project.* Brandeis University. June 10, 2003.

Saroop Ijaz. "Honor Killings Continue in Pakistan Despite New Law." *Human Rights Watch*

September 27, 2017.

(20) Between 1987 and 2017 at least 1,500 people were charged under Pakistan's blasphemy law and at least 75 people involved in accusations of blasphemy were killed by vigilantes in Pakistan. *Center for Social Justice*

"Iranian Pastor Youcef Nadarkhani Arrested After Police Raid His Home". *Iran Human Rights Monitor.* 23 July 2018. " Will spend 6 years in jail for blasphemy."

-Majid Rafizadeh. "Biden Admin and EU Silent on Iran's Increasing Persecution of 'Religious Minorities." *Gatestone Institute.* Feb 9, 2022.

(21) Many people thought that even if the US found no WMD that the elimination of Saddam, the most murderous dictator since Mao, was reason enough. An article in the NYT by a senior editor before the invasion clearly espoused this opinion.

NYT. "The World: How Many People Has Hussein Killed?" By John Burns, NYT, January 26, 2003.

"In the end, if an American-led invasion ousts Mr. Hussein, and especially if an attack is launched without convincing proof that Iraq is still harboring forbidden arms, history may judge that the stronger case was the one that needed no inspectors to confirm: that Saddam Hussein, in his 23 years in power, plunged this country into a bloodbath of medieval proportions, and exported some of that terror to his neighbors."

There was enormous pressure on the US to try to avoid the invasion. The US and 31 other countries had put an Army in the desert in Kuwait to persuade Saddam to allow full inspection for WMD. Saddam seemed about to give in and allow more indepth inspections for nuclear WMD. France, Germany, and Russia had initially supported a forceful solution if there was no inspection. They were very much against invasion and wanted more time. With their support, Saddam seemed to feel that he could get away without the inspections and the US would not invade. He refused to abdicate. Summer was coming and the US could not leave an army in the desert indefinitely. The invasion was on, and a long period of instability in the area has been the result.

The US leaders viewed the Iraq war as an attack on a dangerous and brutal dictator, Saddam Hussein, who they thought was developing WMD to facilitate terrorism. Coincidentally, the invasion was an attempt by the US to establish a liberal democracy in the Middle East. It always seemed that the US would someday try to create a democracy in the Middle East. Iraq had oil wealth and a large educated middle class. It seemed possible.

Many Muslims viewed the war as an attack on Islam in general. From that perspective the whole world changes. The US felt that the invasion was not an attack on Islam but an operation to depose the world's most violent, oppressive dictator of the last 45 years to ensure that he did not spread WMD's to terrorist organizations. Simultaneously, the US also attempted to establish a democracy in the Middle East. The war was over quickly, but the resulting civil war between the disenfranchised Sunni minority and the formerly repressed Shiite majority has resulted in many deaths (400,000) and much turmoil. Saddam Hussein had been responsible for the violent deaths of an average of about 42,000 of his citizens yearly for the 20+ years of his power. His brutality was legendary. Yet, many Muslims classified the US invasion as an attack on Islam rather than a liberation of the Iraqi people.

(21a) Osama Bin Laden's "Letter to the America" in 2002 explaining why he attacked on 9/11. Full text available in numerous internet sites. It begins with a long rant about America's injustices including everything from supporting Jewish capitalists, to invading Iraq, to dropping the atomic bomb on Japan, and many more. He makes seven demands. First that Americans convert to Islam. Second that they stop the immoral acts of fornication, usury, gambling, drinking, homosexuality, and capitalism. If the US does not do these things, "then prepare to fight with the Islamic nation."

(22) Elizabeth Suicpac. "US Muslims are observant but open to multiple interpretations of Islam." *Pew Research*. August 2, 2017.

Michael Lipka.. "Muslims and Islam: Key findings in the U.S. and around the world." *Pew Research*. August 9, 2017

"Living in a religiously pluralistic society, Muslim Americans are more likely than Muslims in many other largely Muslim-majority nations to have a lot of non-Muslim friends. Only about a third (36%) of U.S. Muslims say all or most of their close friends are also Muslims, compared with a global median of 95% in the 39 countries we surveyed.

Roughly two-thirds of U.S. Muslims (65%) say religion is very important in their lives. About six-in-ten (59%) report praying at least daily and 43% say they attend religious services at least weekly. By some of these traditional measures, Muslims in the U.S. are roughly as religious as U.S. Christians, although they are less religious than Muslims in many other nations."

(22a) Patrick Winn. *The World*, March 8, 2019. Recently a Christian named Ahok had served as the elected governor of Jakarta. When running a second time, he was arrested and jailed for 2 years for blasphemy when he said that if was acceptable for

Muslims to live under politicians who were of other religions. The parliament also passed a law making extramarital sex illegal and punishable by the government. Since gays cannot marry in Indonesia, this also criminalized homosexuality.

Krithika Varagur. "Indonesia's Moderate Islam is Slowly Crumbling. Liberal Muslims are fretting as fundamentalists seize the popular moment." *Foreign Policy*. Feb 14, 2017.

Jonthon Coulson. "Saudi 'philanthrocapitalism' in Indonesian educational spaces." *Institute of Current Word Affairs*. Oct 5, 2017.

Tavleen Tarrant, Joseph Sipalan. "Worries about Malaysia's 'Arabisation' grow as Saudi ties strengthen." *Reuters*. "A string of recent events has fueled the concern. Hostility toward atheists, non-believers and the gay community has risen. Two annual beer festivals were canceled after Islamic leaders objected. A hardline preacher, accused of spreading hatred in India, has received official patronage. The government has backed a parliamentary bill that would allow the shariah court wider criminal jurisdiction over Muslims in the state of Kelantan. And after religious officials supported a Muslim-only laundromat, Malaysia's mostly ceremonial royalty made a rare public intervention, calling for religious harmony

Atika Shubert, CNN Correspondent, "Fatwa on vocal Indonesian moderate". Jan 22, 2003.

(23)   Antonia Ward. "ISIS's use of Social Media Still Poses a Threat to Stability in the Middle East and Africa". *Georgetown Security Studies Review. The Rand Blog*. December 11, 2018

(24)   Three points of the Amman Message.

(Number 1) Whosoever is an adherent to one of the four *Sunni* schools (*Mathahib*) of Islamic jurisprudence (*Hanafi, Maliki, Shafi`i* and *Hanbali*), the two *Shi'i* schools of Islamic jurisprudence (*Ja`fari* and *Zaydi*), the *Ibadi* school of Islamic jurisprudence and the *Thahiri* school of Islamic jurisprudence, is a Muslim. Declaring that person an apostate is impossible and impermissible. Verily his (or her) blood, honor, and property are inviolable. Moreover, in accordance with the Shaykh Al-Azhar's *fatwa*, it is neither possible nor permissible to declare whosoever subscribes to the *Ash`ari* creed or whoever practices real *Tasawwuf* (Sufism) an apostate. Likewise, it is neither possible nor permissible to declare whosoever subscribes to true *Salafi* thought an apostate.
Equally, it is neither possible nor permissible to declare as apostates any group of Muslims who believes in God, Glorified and Exalted be He, and His Messenger (may peace and blessings be upon him) and the pillars of faith, and acknowledges the five pillars of Islam, and does not deny any necessarily self-evident tenet of religion.

(Number 2) There exists more in common between the various schools of Islamic jurisprudence than there is difference between them. The adherents to the eight schools of Islamic jurisprudence are in agreement as regards the basic principles of Islam. All believe in Allah (God), Glorified and Exalted be He, the One and the Unique; that the Noble Qur'an is the Revealed Word of God; and that our master Muhammad, may blessings and peace be upon him, is a Prophet and Messenger unto all mankind. All are in agreement about the Five Pillars of Islam: the two testaments of faith (*shahadatayn*); the ritual prayer (*salat*); almsgiving (*zakat*); fasting the month of Ramadan (*sawm*), and the *Hajj* to the sacred house of God (in Mecca). All are also in agreement about the foundations of belief: belief in Allah (God), His angels, His scriptures, His messengers, and in the Day of Judgment, in Divine Providence in good and in evil. Disagreements between the *'ulama* (scholars) of the eight schools of Islamic jurisprudence are only with respect to the ancillary branches of religion (*furu*') and not as regards the principles and fundamentals (*usul*) [of the religion of Islam]. Disagreement with respect to the ancillary branches of religion (*furu*) is a mercy. Long ago it was said that variance in opinion among the *'ulama* (scholars) "is a good affair".

(Number 3) Acknowledgement of the schools of Islamic jurisprudence (*Mathahib*) within Islam means adhering to a fundamental methodology in the issuance of *fatwas*: no one may issue a *fatwa* without the requisite personal qualifications which each school of Islamic jurisprudence determines [for its own adherents]. No one may issue a *fatwa* without adhering to the methodology of the schools of Islamic jurisprudence. No one may claim to do unlimited *Ijtihad* and create a new school of Islamic jurisprudence or to issue unacceptable *fatwas* that take Muslims out of the principles and certainties of the *Shari'ah* and what has been established in respect of its schools of jurisprudence.

(25) Qur'an 17:22-39 "Do not set up another god with God, lest you become condemned and damned. Your Lord has commanded that you worship none but Him, and that you be good to your parents. 23. If either. of them or both of them reach old age with you, do not say to them a word of disrespect, nor scold them, but say to them kind words. 24. And lower to them the wing of humility, out of mercy, and say, "My Lord, have mercy on them, as they raised me when I was a child." 25. Your Lord knows best what is in your minds. If you are righteous—He is Forgiving to the obedient. 26. And give the relative his rights, and the poor, and the wayfarer, and do not squander wastefully. 27. The extravagant are brethren of the devils, and the devil is ever ungrateful to his Lord. 28. But if you turn away from them, seeking mercy from your Lord which you hope for, then say to them words of comfort. 29. And do not keep your hand tied to your neck, nor spread it out fully, lest you end up liable and regretful. 30. Your Lord expands the provision for whomever He wills, and restricts it. He is fully Informed, Observant of His servants. 31. And do not kill your children for fear of poverty. We provide for them, and for you. Killing them is a grave sin. 32. And do not come near adultery. It is immoral, and an evil way. 33. And do not kill the soul which God has made sacred, except in the course of justice. If someone is killed unjustly, We have given his next of kin certain authority. But he should not be excessive in killing, for he will be supported. 34. And do not go near the orphan's property, except with the best of intentions, until he has reached his maturity. And honor your pledge, because the pledge involves responsibility. 35. And give full measure when you measure, and weigh with accurate scales. That is fair, and the best determination. 36. And do not occupy yourself with what you have no knowledge of. The hearing, and the sight, and the brains—all these will be questioned. 37. And do not walk proudly on earth. You can neither pierce the earth, nor can you match the mountains in height. 38. The evil of all these is disliked by your Lord.

(26) Hadith: -Bukhari 9:83:50. "What is on this paper?" He replied, "The legal regulations of Diya (Blood money) and the (ransom for) releasing of captives, and the judgment that no Muslim should be killed in retribution for killing a Kafir (disbeliever)."

(28) After signing a peace treaty with Israel, Yasir Arafat, in addressing critics in a mosque in South Africa said that the signing was only *taqiyya*, a pause until they were more powerful and able to defeat Israel.

(29) Matthew 12:30-32. "Whoever is not with me is against me, and whoever does not gather with me scatters. And so I tell you, every kind of sin and slander can be forgiven, but blasphemy against the Spirit will not be forgiven. Anyone who speaks a word against the Son of Man will be forgiven, but anyone who speaks against the Holy Spirit will not be forgiven, either in this age or in the age to come."

(29a) A.A. Mansour. "Hudud Crimes (From Islamic Criminal Justice System, P 195-201, 1982, M Cherif Bassiouni, ed. - See NCJ-87479)" *US Department of Justice. Office of Justice Programs Library.* 1982

Jonathan Brown. "Stoning and Hand Cutting- Understanding the Hudud and the Sharia in Islam" *The Yaqeen Institute.* Sept. 2021

(30) Nafees Takar and Paul Alexander. "Pakistan University Mob Kills Fellow Student Over Blasphemy Allegations". *Voice of America.* East Asia Pacific. April 13, 2017.

Farhat Haq. "Sharia and the State in Pakistan, Blasphemy Politics." Copyright Year 2019. Between 1987 and 2017 at least 1,500 people were charged under Pakistan's blasphemy law and at least 75 people involved in accusations of blasphemy were killed by vigilantes in Pakistan.

(31) Michael Lipka. "Muslims and Islam: Key findings in the U.S. and around the world." *Pew Research.* August 9, 2017.

(32) Mark 16:15-16. "And he said to them, 'Go into all the world and proclaim the gospel to the whole creation. Whoever believes and is baptized will be saved, but whoever does not believe will be condemned.'"

Matthew 28:19. "Go therefore and make disciples of all nations, baptizing them in the name of the Father and the Son and the Holy Spirit, teaching them to observe all that I have commanded you. And behold, I am with you always, to the end of the age."

(33) Qur'an 4:74. "Let those who would exchange the life of this world for the hereafter, fight for the cause of God, whoever fights for the cause of God, whether he dies or triumphs, We shall richly reward him."

Qur'an 4:76. "The true believer fights for the cause of God, but the infidels fight for the devil."

-Penguin Classics translation by N. J. Dawood.

Qur'an 9:39. "If you do not fight, He will punish you sternly and replace you by other men."

(34) Exodus 22:25–27. "Making a profit off a loan from a poor person is exploiting that person."

Qur'an 2:275. "Those who consume interest cannot stand [on the Day of Resurrection] except as one stands who is being beaten by Satan into insanity. That is because they say, 'Trade is [just] like interest.' But Allah has permitted trade and has forbidden interest. So whoever has received an admonition from his Lord and desists may have what is past, and his affair rests with Allah . But whoever returns to [dealing in interest or usury] - those are the companions of the Fire; they will abide eternally therein."

(35) Matthew 25:14-30. English Standard Version. "For it will be like a man going on a journey, who called his servants and entrusted to them his property. To one he gave five talents, to another two, to another one, to each according to his ability. Then

he went away. He who had received the five talents went at once and traded with them, and he made five talents more. [17] So also he who had the two talents made two talents more. [18] But he who had received the one talent went and dug in the ground and hid his master's money. [19] Now after a long time the master of those servants came and settled accounts with them. [20] And he who had received the five talents came forward, bringing five talents more, saying, 'Master, you delivered to me five talents; here, I have made five talents more.' [21] His master said to him, 'Well done, good and faithful servant. You have been faithful over a little; I will set you over much. Enter into the joy of your master.' [22] And he also who had the two talents came forward, saying, 'Master, you delivered to me two talents; here, I have made two talents more.' [23] His master said to him, 'Well done, good and faithful servant. You have been faithful over a little; I will set you over much. Enter into the joy of your master.' [24] He also who had received the one talent came forward, saying, 'Master, I knew you to be a hard man, reaping where you did not sow, and gathering where you scattered no seed, [25] so I was afraid, and I went and hid your talent in the ground. Here, you have what is yours.' [26] But his master answered him, 'You wicked and slothful servant! You knew that I reap where I have not sown and gather where I scattered no seed? [27] Then you ought to have invested my money with the bankers, and at my coming I should have received what was my own with interest.[28] So take the talent from him and give it to him who has the ten talents.[29] For to everyone who has will more be given, and he will have an abundance. But from the one who has not, even what he has will be taken away. [30] And cast the worthless servant into the outer darkness. In that place there will be weeping and gnashing of teeth.'

(36)   Jewish Tanakh. Exodus 20:17. "You shall not covet your neighbor's house; you shall not covet your neighbor's wife or his male servant or his female servant or his ox or his donkey or anything that belongs to your neighbor."

Jewish Tanakh, Deuteronomy 19:14 "You shall not move your neighbor's boundary mark, which the ancestors have set...."

Matthew 25:14-30. Jesus' parable of the talents recognizes private property.

Hadith: Bukhari: Volume 3, Book 43, Number 660: Narrated 'Abdullah bin 'Amr bin Al-'As: "I heard the Prophet saying, 'Whoever is killed while protecting his property then he is a martyr'".

(37)   Hebrew Scriptures, Genesis 3:16 describes Adam's role over Eve: "...thy desire shall be to thy husband, and he shall rule over thee." Genesis 4:19 continues in the same vein.

Christian Bible New Testament: Paul's letter to a church in 1 Timothy 2:11-12, "Let a woman learn in silence with all submissiveness. I permit no woman to teach or have authority above men; she is to keep silent."

Jesus treats women as equals. He makes no statements about lesser roles or rights. His followers were said to be amazed when they found him speaking to a strange Samaritan woman at a well. He ate with tax collectors, prostitutes, Pharisees, sinners, and soldiers.

Muslim quotes:

Qur'an 2:228 "Women shall with justice have rights similar to those exercised against them, although men have a status above women. God is mighty and wise."

Qur'an 4:34   "Men have authority over women because God has made one superior to the other, and because they spend their wealth to maintain them. Good women are obedient. They guard their unseen parts because God has guarded them. As for those from whom you fear disobedience, admonish them, and send them to beds apart and hit them. Then if they obey you, take no further action against them."

(38) Tanakh (Old Testament.) Leviticus 18;22. "Thou shalt not lie with mankind as with womankind: it is abomination."

New Testament, Paul's letter to the Romans 1:26-27. "For this reason God gave them up to dishonorable passions. Their women exchanged natural relations for unnatural, [27] and the men likewise gave up natural relations with women and were consumed with passion for one another, men committing shameless acts with men and receiving in their own persons the due penalty for their error."

Paul's First letter to the 1 Corinthians 6:9. "Do you not know that the unrighteous will not inherit the kingdom of God? Do not be deceived; neither the immoral, nor idolaters, nor adulterers, nor sexual perverts,"

Qur'an 7:80. In the Qur'an's story of Lot's visit to Sodom and Gomorrah and the subsequent destruction by Allah, Lot says, "You lust after men instead of women. You are truly a degenerate people."

Dawood Hadith 4447, Narrated Abdullah ibn Abbas: The Prophet said: If you find anyone doing as Lot's people did, kill the one who does it, and the one to whom it is done.

(39) Angelina E. Theodorou. "In 30 countries, heads of state must belong to a certain religion." *Pew Research Center*. July 22, 2014.

(39a) Meir Kahane (1981). *They Must Go*. Those who refuse to accept noncitizen status shall be compensated for property, but not given a bonus, and shall be transferred only to Arab – not Western – lands. The transfer shall be effected peacefully, if possible, but if the Arab still refuses, then forcibly and without compensation.

(40) Edward Gibbon, "Rules for Christians living under Islamic Empire". From *The Decline and Fall of the Roman Empire.*. 1789. Internet Medieval Source Book. "In the name of God, the Merciful, the Compassionate! This is a writing to Umar from the Christians of such and such a city. When You [Muslims] marched against us [Christians], we asked of you protection for ourselves, our posterity, our possessions, and our co-religionists; and we made this stipulation with you, that we will not erect in our city or the suburbs any new monastery [place where monks live], church, cell or hermitage [secluded retreat];that we will not repair any of such buildings that may fall into ruins, or renew those that may be situated in the Muslim quarters of the town; that we will not refuse the Muslims entry into our churches either by night or by day; that we will open the gates wide to passengers and travelers; that we will receive any Muslim traveler into our houses and give him food and lodging for three nights. that we will not harbor any spy in our churches or houses or conceal any enemy of the Muslims. That we will not teach our children the Qur'an; that we will not make a show of the Christian religion nor invite anyone to embrace it; that we will not prevent any of our kinsmen from embracing Islam, if they so desire. That we will honor the Muslims and rise up in our assemblies when they wish to take their seats; that we will not imitate them in our dress, either in the cap, turban, sandals, or parting of the hair; that we will not make use of their expressions of speech, nor adopt their surnames... that we will not sell wine; That we will not display the cross upon our churches or display our crosses or our sacred books in the streets of the Muslims, or in their marketplaces; that we will not recite our services in a loud voice when a Muslim is present; that we will not carry Palm branches [on Palm Sunday] or our images in procession in the streets; that at the burial of our dead we will not chant loudly or carry lighted candles in the streets

of the Muslims or their marketplaces; and that we will not strike any Muslim. All this we promise to observe, on behalf of ourselves and our co-religionists, and receive protection from you in exchange; and if we violate any of the conditions of this agreement, then we forfeit your protection, and you are at liberty to treat us as enemies and rebels."

(41)   "A Study of the present Egyptian Constitution and the law articles that conflict with minority Rights."– *UN Human Rights Office of the High Commissioner.*

"Non-Muslim witness in court: A "Just" witness has to be a "free Muslim, i.e., not a slave Muslim; non-Muslims witness in court is not admissible according to Islamic Shari law. The Arabic Tafseer (interpretation of the Qur'an) of Jalaleen, Ibn-Katheer, Al- Tabaree and Al-Kortobi, all agree that a witness must be a free Muslim. "

https://www.ohchr.org/Documents/Issues/Minorities/WG/11/Al-Kalema-3A.pdf

(42)   "Prohibition of Interfaith Marriage". *Law Library of Congress*, This article is in Library of Congress website. This report provides information on the laws of twenty-nine countries, plus the West Bank and the Gaza Strip, that prohibit marriages between people of two different religions. In most of the countries identified for this report, the prohibition of interfaith marriage arises from the implementation of Islamic personal status laws, either in codified or uncodified form, with respect to marriages involving Muslims. These countries either do not have separate civil marriage laws or do not allow Muslim individuals to marry under such laws.

(43)   Tanakh, Deuteronomy 13:5. "But that prophet or that dreamer of dreams shall be put to death, because he has spoken in order to turn you away from the Lord your God."

Hadith Bukhari 9:84:57. "It is acceptable to kill anyone who leaves the faith. I would have killed them according to the statement of Allah's Apostle, 'Whoever changed his Islamic religion, then kill him.'"

(44)   Sarah Bond. "Innovation Philanthropy in ancient times: some early examples from the Mediterranean." *Showcase of Fundraising Innovation and Inspiration (SOFII).* April 2, 2011.

(45a)   Analisa Merelli. "The US has a lot of money, but it does not look like a developed country." *Quartz.* March 10, 2017. The US is behind most developed nations in multiple areas including amount of poverty, food security, provision of health care, child care, education, and dangerous crime. It does well in employment, infrastructure, energy access, and gender equality.

(46)   National Vital Statistics System Reports published by the CDC National Center for Health Statistics. 1940-2014.

(46a)   When handgun control is mentioned many opponents say one of two things. "If we get rid of handguns, only criminals will have guns," or "It is impossible. There are too many handguns out there." In the first place, every successful liberal democratic nation in the world except the US has strict handgun control, and it works very well. Yes, it will take a long time for handguns to be removed from the culture. We need to begin now so our grand children can live in a handgun free environment.

(47)   EdBuild, an institution exploring school funding in the US, reports that African American, Latinx, and Asian school districts receive $23 billion less in funding than

predominantly white districts. This happens because the schools are funded locally. If we are interested in a fair and equitable education system that produces a true meritocracy, these funding disparities need to be addressed.

(48) Roger Annis. "Criticism of Aristide is Misplaced." *The Socialist Worker.* Feb 2, 2010.

Aristide's accomplishments included; "Building more schools than all of Haiti's preceding governments combined Expanding Haiti's medical cooperation with Cuba, including opening the country's first medical school in 2003. (The school was taken over by U.S. Marines in March of 2004 to be used as a barracks, and then passed over to the UN troops for the same purpose. Only recently was it evacuated by the jackboots.) Creating the country's first-ever ministry of women's affairs. Building social housing on a scale never seen in Haiti. I saw some of this housing, most of its construction interrupted by the 2004 coup d'etat, during my first and only visit to Haiti in 2007.Improving the country's historical patrimony--monuments, public buildings, etc. Doubling the minimum wage. Bringing reforms to Haiti's agriculture that would make it possible for peasants to survive and grow food. Resisting the international pressures to privatize the state telephone, electricity companies and the Port-au-Prince docks. Initiating an action at the World Court in 2003 to recover the $21 billion (current dollars) in funds that were extorted from Haiti by France from 1825 to 1947."

(49) Thomas Cahill. How the Irish Saved Civilization.

(49a) There are various ways in which this statement by Napoleon is interpreted. Many think that he was saying that Europe was different and Washington's rejection of royalty stance was not possible in Europe.

(50) Claire McInerny. "AISD Parents Weigh In On When Kids Should Learn About Sex, Pregnancy And Gender Identity", *Austin Texas Public Radio. Station UT 90.5.* December 7, 2018.

(50a) Glenn Loury. "The False God of Antiracism. A Conversation with Michael Fortner." *The Glenn Loury Blog.* Jan 8, 2023. "When are we going to recognize that it's time to man up and woman up, to face the realities of life. No one said life was fair. There's no guarantee anywhere that life is fair. It is what it is, and we'd better get busy making the best of it right now.

Now, let me just say this. That's not the political speech that I would give. I'm saying that here because I've been asked a question by my friend who was so generous in his introduction, I feel like I owe him an answer. I wouldn't run for Congress on that speech. But I would damn sure run my family on that speech. That's what I would tell my kids."

(51) Thomas Hogan. *City Journal.* March 21, 2022. "Will Business Fight Back?" The Chamber of Commerce addresses the nation's shoplifting outbreak, but its members need a more active strategy to combat the problem. Recently, San Francisco recalled its ultra-liberal district attorney who was allowing shoplifting up to $1000.

(52) Abraham Lincoln's Second Inaugural Address, 1865. "With malice toward none; with charity for all; with firmness in the right, as God gives us to see the right, let us strive on to finish the work we are in; to bind up the nation's wounds; to care for him who shall have borne the battle, and for his widow, and his orphan—to do all which may achieve and cherish a just, and a lasting peace, among ourselves, and with all nations."

Martin Luther King's "I Have a Dream speech". August 28, 1963 "And when this happens, and when we allow freedom ring, when we let it ring from every village and every hamlet, from every state and every city, we will be able to speed up that day when all of God's children, black men and white men, Jews and Gentiles, Protestants and Catholics, will be able to join hands and sing in the words of the old Negro spiritual: Free at last. Free at last. Thank God almighty, we are free at last."

(54) Vanessa Williamson "Americans Love Paying Taxes." *The Atlantic,* April 15, 2015. Based on "Culture differences and tax morals in the United States and in Europe". *Journal of Economic Psychology.* Vol 27, Issue 2, April 2006. Pages 224-246

"Residents of the United States are unusually likely to see chipping in their share as a civic duty, a moral obligation, and a patriotic act." "You might wonder if these attitudes are nothing more than a nice sentiment, but Americans put their money where their mouths are, so to speak. Compared to 14 European countries, Americans report the highest willingness to pay taxes, and the United States has one of the highest rates of tax compliance in the developed world. One might credit this to fear of the IRS, but economists have concluded that high-compliance rates in the U.S. cannot be explained solely by the level of enforcement."

(55) A Canadian government website https://www.publicsafety "Brief 48, Definitions of Corruption" states "Corruption can be defined and categorized in different ways. The most common types or categories of corruption are supply versus demand corruption, grand versus petty corruption, conventional versus unconventional corruption and public versus private corruption." It then goes on to give a three page breakdown of these different types.

(56) Henry Louis Gates. "How many slaves landed in the US?". *The African Americans. Many Rivers to Cross.* PBS.

"BBC News/ Africa/ Focus on the slave trade" May" 25, 2017. Archived from the original on May 25, 2017. Retrieved July 21, 2019.

(56a) Nasiruddin Hamid, Qadian. "How Islam Abolished slavery." *LightofIslam.in* Aug. 23, 2020. Muhammad quote from Sahih Bukhari, Kitab al-Buyu' (The Book on Sales and Trade) "Allah the Exalted addressed me saying, 'There are three types of people who I shall be at war against on the day of resurrection. Firstly, a person who makes a covenant in My name but does not fulfill his agreement. Secondly, a person who enslaves a free person, sells him, and consumes his value. Thirdly, a person who employs an individual, benefits from his labor, but does not pay him his wage."

Sahih Bukhari, Kitab al-Itq (The Book on Manumission of Slaves) Muhammad said, "Your slaves are your brethren. Hence, if an individual has a slave under his control, then he should feed him what he eats himself and he should clothe him with what he wears himself. Do not burden your slaves with a task that is beyond their capacity and if you do, then assist them in this task yourselves."

(57) *Global Estimates of Modern Slavery: Forced Labour and Forced Marriage.* International Labour Organization (ILO), Walk Free, and International Organization for Migration (IOM), Geneva, 2022

(58) There is an ongoing discussion about predestination and free will in many religious groups. They would seem to be incompatible except in the most abstract terms. I will offer an approach suggested fifty years ago. It is as follows:

1. Free will and predestination only apply to persons who are spiritually pure or fully enlightened beings (saints? mystics?).

2. Because they are not driven by personal desires, anxieties, or prejudices, the enlightened have the "free will" to pick any alternative in a situation. And, because they are not prejudicially influenced by anxiety or favoritism, they are "predestined" to choose the right or best solution.

Ordinary humans are very influenced by desires and prejudices. Consequently, many decisions are neither useful nor spiritually beneficial.

(59) "The US Commission on International Religious Freedom report for 2017" **lists 71 countries** that have blasphemy laws, in some cases punishable by death.

(60) A website, *thereligionofpeace,* keeps a list of the violent acts done in the world in the name of Islam since 2001. Over 42,000 so far.

(61) "Search: Laws Criminalizing Apostasy in Selected Jurisdictions". *Library of Congress.* This gives a list of countries criminalizing apostasy.

"Death for apostasy is only applicable in case of apostasy by men; in case of women, the punishment is not death but life imprisonment. And if such a woman repents, then her repentance is accepted, and the punishment is lifted."

Ayesja Ishtiaq. "The Grip of Fanaticism on Pakistan's Law", *Davis Political Review. UC Davis.* Nov 15, 2018.

"Pakistan seemed well on its way to establishing successful social and political re-forms in the past two years when it came face to face with one of its long-standing adversaries. Section 295-C of the Penal Code of Pakistan, most commonly known as the 'anti-blasphemy law', has been a subject of controversy ever since the process of Islamization enacted by the military dictatorship of Zia-ul-Haq. Under this law, whoever 'defiles the sacred name of the Holy Prophet' can be punished by death or sentenced to life in prison. Encouraged by this law, a large number of Islamic groups have made it their duty to accuse other religious minorities of blasphemy. In a coun-try where 96 percent of the population is Muslim, this situation has created a dev-astating repression of freedom of religion and speech for non-Muslim minorities. There have been countless cases of intolerance leading to mob lynching and mas-sive public furor against almost anyone belonging to a religion other than Islam."

(62) Hebrew Scriptures, Genesis 3:16 describes Adam's role over Eve: "...thy desire shall be to thy husband, and he shall rule over thee."

Christian Bible, New Testament: Paul writing in 1 Timothy 2:11-12, "Let a woman learn in silence with all submissiveness. I permit no woman to teach or have author-ity above men; she is to keep silent."

Jesus treats women as equals. He makes no statements about lesser roles or rights.

Muslim Texts: Qur'an 2:228   "Women shall with justice have rights similar to those exercised against them, although men have a status above women. God is mighty and wise."

Qur'an 4:34 "Men have authority over women because God has made one superior to the other, and because they spend their wealth to maintain them. Good women are obedient. They guard their unseen parts because God has guarded them. As for those from whom you fear disobedience, admonish them and send them to beds apart and hit them. Then if they obey you, take no further action against them."

(63) Eltahawy, Mona "Egypt's Cruelty to Christians", *NYT.* Dec 22, 2016. .

Moheb Zaki. "Egypt's Persecuted Christians" *The Wall Street Journal.* May 18, 2010.

Many other references recounting bombings and abduction of Coptic women.

(64) "India's Caste System Remains Entrenched 75 years after Independence." *The Economist.*. September 11, 2021.

(65) Matthew D. Walker (2019): "Punishment and Ethical Self-cultivation in Confucius and Aristotle". *Taylor and Francis Group.* Law & Literature

(66) Brian Whitaker. "Everything you need to know about being gay in Muslim countries" *The Guardian.*, June 21, 2016

(67) Alean Al-Krenaw," Mental health and polygamy: the Syrian Case". *World Journal of Psychiatry.* March 22, 2013. "RESULTS: Findings revealed that women in polygamous marriages experienced lower Self Esteem, less life satisfaction, less marital satisfaction and more mental health symptomatology than women in monogamous marriages. Many of the mental health symptoms were different; noteworthy were elevated somatization, depression, hostility and psychoticism and their general severity index was higher. Furthermore, "first wife syndrome" was examined in polygamous families, comparing first with second and third wives in polygamous marriages. Findings indicated that first wives reported on more family problems, less Self Esteem, more anxiety, more paranoid ideation, and more psychoticism than second and third wives."

(68) Hijab. There is much controversy about the wearing of the head scarf, probably because it is such an obvious event. Many wonderful intelligent women wear them as an expression of piety. Unfortunately, hijab wearing is forced on other women in oppressive societies. Problematically, all extreme elements demand that women wear the hijab. Jews have numerous rules about dress. Paul mentions modesty in dress. Jesus doesn't mention dress or any outward signs of piety. He encourages one to be pray, worship, and give money in private

(Matthew 6:1-8). "Be careful not to practice your righteousness in front of others to be seen by them. If you do, you will have no reward from your Father in heaven." So when you give to the needy, do not announce it with trumpets, as the hypocrites do in the synagogues and on the streets, to be honored by others. Truly I tell you, they have received their reward in full. But when you give to the needy, do not let your left hand know what your right hand is doing, so that your giving may be in secret. Then your Father, who sees what is done in secret, will reward you. And when you pray, do not be like the hypocrites, for they love to pray standing in the synagogues and on the street corners to be seen by others. Truly I tell you, they have received their reward in full. But when you pray, go into your room, close the door and pray to your Father, who is unseen. Then your Father, who sees what is done in secret, will reward you. And when you pray, do not keep on babbling like pagans, for they think they will be heard because of their many words."

Jesus seems to know that outward signs of religiosity and piety create confusion and can easily be misunderstood.

(69) Hadith Sahih Bukhari 9:83:17 Allah's Apostle Muhammad said, "The blood of a Muslim who confesses that none has the right to be worshipped but Allah and that I am His Apostle, cannot be shed except in three cases: In punishment for murder, a married person who commits illegal sexual intercourse and the one who reverts from Islam (apostate) and leaves the Muslims."

Sahih al-Bukhari 9:84:57. "It is acceptable to kill anyone who leaves the faith. I would have killed them according to the statement of Allah's Apostle, 'Whoever changed his Islamic religion, then kill him.'"

(70)   Mariz Tedros, "Mutilating bodies: the Muslim Brotherhood's gift to Egyptian women." *openDemocracy,* (24 May 2012). "FGM, although practiced for thousands of years, has been on the decline in the past decade thanks to a socially sensitive and nationwide campaign to show that FGM is neither religiously prescribed, nor linked to a woman's moral behavior. Because the Muslim Brotherhood and the Salafists support it, the progress made in eliciting positive social change on curbing the practice now risks being reversed."

(72)   "Hurting sentiments" can mean most anything. Between 1987 and 2017 at least 1,500 people were charged under Pakistan's blasphemy law and at least 75 people involved in accusations of blasphemy were killed by vigilantes in Pakistan according to the Center for Social Justice.

(73)   Mark Woodward and Muhammad Sani Umar. "Culture as Counter Extremism: West African, European, and Southeast Asian Cases". *Minerva Research Initiative. The Owl in the Olive Tree.* July 9, 2019

(74)   Etgar Lefkovits. "Priests: Remove anti-Semitic Liturgy." *Jerusalem Post.* April 20, 2007

"… the anti-Semitic passages were most conspicuous during Easter services, and included statements such as 'the Jewish tribe which condemned you to crucifixion, repay them, Oh Lord,' which is repeated half a dozen times, and 'Christ has risen but the Jewish seed has perished,' as well as references to Jews as 'God-killers.'"

(75)   Seven Rules of Noah

1. Do not worship false gods.

2. Do not curse God.

3. Do not murder.

4. Do not be sexually immoral.

5. Do not steal.

6. Do not eat a limb taken from a live animal.

7. Set up courts and bring offenders to justice.

The last one would imply that one should not lie, but it is not explicit,

(76)   There have been several murderous attacks on Muslims by ultra-Zionist figures and groups associated with the formation of and preservation of the state of Israel. Some attacks have been efforts to drive Muslims from Israel. Others have been labeled as revenge for the killing of Jews. Baruch Goldstein, who killed 29 Muslims in the Cave of the Patriarchs Massacre, 1994, said it was an effort to drive Muslims out of Israel and revenge for the killing of Meir Kahane, the founder of the Jewish Defense League. This was a Jewish organization labeled "terrorist" by the US government. The state of Israel condemned his actions as "insanity" and an affront to Jewish sentiments everywhere.

(77)   Matthew 10:33-37. [33] "But whoever disowns me before others, I will disown before my Father in heaven.[34]" Do not suppose that I have come to bring peace to the earth. I did not come to bring peace, but a sword. [35] For I have come to turn a man against his father, a daughter against her mother, a daughter-in-law against her mother-in-law. [36] A man's enemies will be the members of his own household.' [37] Anyone who loves their father or mother more than me is not worthy of me; anyone who loves their son or daughter more than me is not worthy of me."

(78) The Lord's prayer (King James Version):

Our Father who art in heaven,

Hallowed be your name.

Your kingdom come,

your will be done,

on earth, as it is in heaven.

Give us this day our daily bread,

and forgive us our debts,

as we also have forgiven our debtors.

And lead us not into temptation,

And deliver us from evil,

For thine is the kingdom and the power and the glory forever.

Amen

(79) The Eight Beatitudes from the Sermon on the Mount in the Book of Matthew 5:3-12

Blessed are the poor in spirit: for theirs is the kingdom of Heaven.

Blessed are those who mourn: for they will be comforted.

Blessed are the meek: for they will inherit the earth.

Blessed are those who hunger and thirst for righteousness: for they will be filled.

Blessed are the merciful: for they will be shown mercy.

Blessed are the pure in heart: for they will see God.

Blessed are the peacemakers: for they will be called the children of God.
Blessed are those who are persecuted because of righteousness: for theirs is the Kingdom of Heaven.
Blessed are you when people insult you, persecute you and falsely say all kinds of evil against you because of me.
Rejoice and be glad, because great is your reward in heaven, for in the same way they persecuted the prophets who were before you.

(80) John 2:1-11 (NRSV) On the third day there was a wedding in Cana of Galilee, and the mother of Jesus was there. [2] Jesus and his disciples had also been invited to the wedding. [3] When the wine gave out, the mother of Jesus said to him, "They have no wine." [4] And Jesus said to her, "Woman, what concern is that to you and to me? My hour has not yet come." [5] His mother said to the servants, "Do whatever he tells you." [6] Now standing there were six stone water jars for the Jewish rites of purification, each holding twenty or thirty gallons. [7] Jesus said to them, "Fill the jars with water." And they filled them up to the brim. [8] He said to them, "Now draw some out, and take it to the chief steward." So they took it. [9] When the steward tasted the water that had become wine, and did not know where it came from (though the servants who had drawn the water knew), the steward called the bridegroom [10] and said to him, "Everyone serves the good wine first, and then the inferior wine after the guests have become drunk. But you have kept the good wine until now." [11] Jesus did this, the first of his signs, in Cana of Galilee, and revealed his glory; and his disciples believed in him."

(81) Inquisitions were prolonged and intensive interrogations or investigations about doctrinal beliefs conducted by the Catholic Church. They were often conducted under torture of various kinds and frequently resulted in death. Begun in the 1200's

they continued in Spain until the 1830's. The Cathars were labeled heretics who emphasized the humanity of Christ, rejecting his identity as God on earth. They were very Gnostic in their thinking. Very pious, they tended toward chastity and austerity. They thought that the Catholic Church's sacraments and government were corrupt. They were subject to the first "Inquisition" and were obliterated in a Catholic "Crusade" in 1209.

(82)   Assuring that everyone has the vote is the job of government. In the US the methods used to produce an accurate vote have recently come under scrutiny and are being debated. Audits, recounts, and statistical evaluations of the results have revealed no significant abnormalities that would alter the outcome. Conservative news outlets stated that a PhD statistician, Charles Cicchetti, offered numerous mathematical and statistical scenarios that purported to prove that the election was fraudulent. Several statisticians from the National Academy of Science (NAS) were appointed to review these statistical approaches. They concluded that Cicchetti proved no statistical evidence of fraud at all. The National Academy of Science was chartered by Abraham Lincoln and is the most prominent collection of scientists in the world including over 190 Nobel Prize winners.

Andrew C. Eggers, Haritz Garro, and Justin Grimmer. "No evidence for systematic voter fraud: A guide to statistical claims about the 2020 election." *Proceedings of the National Academy of Sciences*. November 9, 2021.

(83)   Occasionalism is a philosophical theory about causation which says that created substances cannot be efficient causes of events. Instead, all events are caused directly by God. For many Muslim scholars and clerics this seemed to mean that the most relevant information on how nature works comes directly from study God's message in the Qur'an and Hadith. Education focused on the Islamic holy texts as the best way to learn and explore. After this Islam generally reduced the importance of the Greek uses of reason and empiricism in the scientific study of nature, technology, and political philosophy. Islam has yet to recover educationally.

(84)   Bernard Lewis. "Muslims, Christians, and Jews: The Dream of Coexistence" *The New York Review of Books*. March 26, 1992 issue. Lewis said, "Al-Ghazali made a career for himself in thirteenth century Islam by attacking the rationalist approach of Ibn Sina (Avicenna) and thereby severely damaged Islamic scholasticism."

(85)   Ceylan Yeginsu, "Turkey Promotes Religious Schools, often defying Parents." *New York Times*. Dec. 16, 2014,

(86)   "Islam and Blasphemy" in Wikipedia. I do not like to use Wikipedia as a source, but it does make good lists. View of the various prominent Islamic Sharia law schools are outlined here.

Hanafi – views blasphemy as synonymous with apostasy, and therefore, accepts the repentance of apostates. Those who refuse to repent, their punishment is death if the blasphemer is a Muslim man. If the blasphemer is a woman, she must be imprisoned with coercion (beating) till she repents and returns to Islam. If a non-Muslim commits blasphemy, his punishment must be a *tazir* (discretionary, can be death, arrest, caning, etc.).

Maliki – view blasphemy as an offense distinct from, and more severe than apostasy. Death is mandatory in cases of blasphemy for Muslim men, and repentance is not accepted. For women, death is not the punishment suggested, but she is arrested and punished till she repents and returns to Islam or dies in custody. A non-Muslim who commits blasphemy against Islam must be punished; however, the blasphemer can escape punishment by converting and becoming a devout Muslim.

Hanbali – view blasphemy as an offense distinct from, and more severe than apostasy. Death is mandatory in cases of blasphemy, for both Muslim men and women, and repentance is not accepted.

Shafi'i – recognizes blasphemy as a separate offense from apostasy but accepts the repentance of blasphemers. If the blasphemer does not repent, the punishment is death.

Ja'fari (Shia) – views blasphemy against Islam, the Prophet, or any of the Imams, to be punishable with death, if the blasphemer is a Muslim. In case the blasphemer is a non-Muslim, he is given a chance to convert to Islam, or else killed.

(87) Tasneem Alkie. "Is the Hijab Religious or Cultural? How Islamic Rulings are Formed". *Yaqeen Institute.*

(88) This quote is from "Islam Questions and Answers" on the Internet. There are numerous similar sites giving similar advice about all aspects of dress and behavior.

(89) Religious Beliefs and Practices. *Pew Research*, July 2917. While Americans overall have become somewhat less religious in recent years, measures of various beliefs and practices have been relatively stable among those who identify with a religion (e.g., Protestants, Catholics). The current survey shows a similar pattern among U.S. Muslims. About four-in-ten Muslims say they attend religious services at least weekly, and a similar share say they perform five daily prayers (*salah*). These numbers have changed little since 2007. In addition, about four-in-ten Muslim women say they always wear hijab in public, almost identical to the share who said this in previous surveys.

If there is one measure that shows a modest decline in religious observance among U.S. Muslims over the past decade, it is in the share who say religion is very important in their lives: 65% now say this, compared with 69% in 2011 and 72% in 2007.

Eight-in-ten U.S. Muslims say they fast during the Islamic holy month of Ramadan, and most are satisfied with the quality of mosques available to them – though few see the mosque as central to their spiritual life.

Beyond these measures of religious practice, many Muslim Americans see room for multiple and more contemporary interpretations of their faith. A majority of U.S. Muslims say there is more than one true way to interpret Islam, and about half say traditional understandings of the faith need to be reinterpreted to address current issues. Protestant Christians have similar outlooks.

(94) Leeza Mangaldas. "Misogyny in India: We are all guilty". *Special to CNN.* Jan 3, 2013.

(95) *History Of General Sir Charles Napier's Administration of Scinde.* (p. 35). London: Chapman and Hall [1] at books.google.com. Retrieved 10 July 2011. The British banned anything like *sati* in 1829. "After the ban, Balochi priests in the Sindh region complained to the British Governor, Charles Napier about what they claimed was a meddlement in a sacred custom of their nation. Napier replied: 'Be it so. This burning of widows is your custom; prepare the funeral pile. But my nation has also a custom. When men burn women alive, we hang them, and confiscate all their property. My carpenters shall therefore erect gibbets on which to hang all concerned when the widow is consumed. Let us all act according to national customs!' Thereafter, the account goes, no suttee took place

(96)   Annie Lowrey. Titled "The Most Important Study in the Abortion Debate", *The Atlantic Magazine*. June 11, 2022. It explored women's responses, feelings, and economic well-being. It evaluated a set of over 1000 women and interviewed them every 6 months for 5 years. Half had had abortions. Half came in too late for the abortion. It found that women who had abortions were happier, economically better off, and, in general, more pleased with every aspect of their lives. In a previous case limiting abortion, Supreme Court Justice Kenney had speculated that "…it seems unexceptionable to conclude some women come to regret their choice to abort the infant life they once created and sustained," he wrote. "Severe depression and loss of esteem can follow." He was proven wrong on all counts.

   Social Science and Medicine. Volume 248, March 2020, 112704. "Emotions and decision rightness over five years following an abortion: An examination of decision difficulty and abortion stigma." Rocca, Samari, et al. Over 95% were pleased with their decision 3 years later.

   The debate over abortion is unsolvable. It is not addressed in any of the religious texts. Medicine was primitive. The facts around pregnancy were unknown, and the process too dangerous. In democratic states the predominant cultural opinion on abortion will generally be the prevailing practice even though working it out will be confusing and disruptive. Where in that chain of circumstances does the woman lose the option to control her destiny? Should we make criminals out of women who want control over reproduction? When does a fetus have rights? When does "life begin"? If the state doesn't provide abortion, the poor and working women's choices will be limited. Working women and poor women will be the people who bear the brunt of restrictions. Aesthetics, morals, and cultural tolerance will combine to set the line, and it will change over time. Contraception certainly eliminates many more children than abortion.

(97)   France is about 54% Christian, 5% Muslim, and 40% no religion. England is similar with 60% Christian, 4.4% Muslim and about 32% no religion. Australia is 52% Christian. Canada is 55%. South Korea 29%, Singapore 20% and Germany is about 55% Christian

(98)   "Muslims and Islam: Key findings in the US and around the world." *Pew Research*, August 19, 2017.

   "Nearly all Muslims in Afghanistan (99%) and most in Iraq (91%) and Pakistan (84%) support sharia law as official law. But in some other countries, especially in Eastern Europe and Central Asia – including Turkey (12%), Kazakhstan (10%) and Azerbaijan (8%) – relatively few favor the implementation of sharia law." Significant majorities of Muslims in almost every country in Africa, the Middle East and Southeast Asia would like some form of Sharia law.

   Human Rights Watch. April 5, 2016. "Iraq: Women Suffer Under ISIS."

   Human Rights Watch. April 2, 2022. "Indonesia Military Finally Ends Abusive 'Virginity Test'.

(99)   Michael Lupka, "Muslims and Islam: Key findings in the US and around the World." *Pew Research*, Aug 9, 2017 "About a quarter of Americans say there is a fair amount of support (24%) for extremism among U.S. Muslims; 11% say there is a great deal of support."

(100) Susan Linfield, Cruel Radiance: Photography and Political Violence. P 162

   "The former group of images is meant to establish Muslims as the world's greatest victims; the later, as the world's greatest warriors. Does the circulation of such also perform "a profound public service"? These are not underground images; though Westerners often describe them as pornographic, they operate in an entirely public sphere. Documentary footage of war---of heads exploding, eyes blowing out, corpses disintegrating---runs in continuous loops on popular Arabic TV stations such as Qatar's Al-Jazeera, Dubai's Al-Arabiya, etc.---: New York Times columnist Thomas Friedman has described this visual carnage as "the Muzak of the Arab world..." In particular, there is a focus on images of babies and children who are bleeding, screaming, maimed, dying and dead. "It's pretty hard to adequately describe the level of bloodiness during an average Al Jazeera newscast," Michael Wolff, then the media critic for New York Magazine, wrote. "It's mesmerizing bloodiness...It's snuff-film caliber."

(101) Lists of fatwas are available from many sites including:

Critical Muslim is a project of the Muslim Institute, London, which is a learned society of Fellows. It is published by C. Hurst and Co. (www.hurstpublishers.com), a highly respectable publisher of books on Islam and the Muslim world, as a paperback book; and co-published by Oxford University Press (Pakistan) and distributed in the United States by Oxford University Press (USA). Each issue is devoted to a single theme, which also serves as the title of the individual book.

Patrick Winn. "Moderate Malaysia has so many fatwas, that there is a website to keep track of them." *The World* . Global Post, January 5, 2015.

(102) The compassionate references can look like this:

Qur'an 2:256 "There shall be no compulsion in religion."

Qur'an 23:95. "Requite evil with good."

Hadith: Bukhari 1:2:13. "None of you [truly] believes until he wishes for his brother what he wishes for himself."

Hadith: "The proof of a Muslim's sincerity is that he pays no attention to that which is not his business."

Hadith: "Women are the twin halves of men."

Hadith: "That person is nearest to God, who pardons... him who would have injured him."

(103) India, Botswana, Jamaica, Bahamas, Cuba, Kenya, Rhodesia, Tanganyika, Singapore, Hong Kong, etc...

(104) Yasmine Farouk, Nathan J. Brown. "Saudi Arabia's Religious Reforms Are Touching Nothing but Changing Everything". *Carnegie Endowment for International Peace.* June 7, 2021.

Saudi Arabia's Islamic institutions have undergone massive reform as the monarchy consolidates its vision for the country's future. These reforms are incremental and reversible but together represent a systematic restructuring of religion's role in Saudi politics and society.

(105) Mark Fathi Massoud. Associate Professor Univ. of California, Santa Cruz. "Don't blame Sharia for Islamic extremism – blame colonialism." *The Conversation*. April 8, 2019. Massoud says that Post-colonial Arab leaders "...avoided resolving tough questions about religious identity and the law by refusing to adopt Sharia law. That created a disconnect between the people and their governments. Muslim-majority countries stunted the democratic potential of Sharia by rejecting it as a mainstream

legal concept in the 1950s and 1960s. This left Sharia in the hands of extremists. But there is no inherent tension between Sharia, human rights, and the rule of law. Like any use of religion in politics (my bold letters), Sharia's application depends on who is using it – and why." Many would say that is precisely why religions should not be in politics.

He concludes, "Fundamentalism and violence, in other words, are a post-colonial problem (due to rejection of Sharia)– not a religious inevitability."

(106) Concerning "Orientalism" Winston Churchill was a noted "Orientalist" according to Dr Said's criteria. Churchill commented (*The River War,* first edition, Vol II pages 248-250, 1899)

"How dreadful are the curses, which Mohammedanism lays on its votaries!

Besides the fanatical frenzy, which is as dangerous in a man as hydrophobia in a dog, there is this fearful fatalistic apathy. The effects are apparent in many countries. Improvident habits, slovenly systems of agriculture, sluggish methods of commerce, and insecurity of property exist wherever the followers of the prophet rule or live.

A degraded sensualism deprives this life of its grace and refinement, the next of its dignity and sanctity. The fact that in Mohammedan law every woman must belong to some man as his absolute property, either as child, a wife, or a concubine, must delay the final extinction of slavery until the faith of Islam has ceased to be a great power among men.

Individual Muslims may show splendid qualities, but the influence of the religion paralyses the social development of those who follow it.

No stronger retrograde force exists in the world. Far from being moribund, Mohammedanism is a militant and proselytizing faith. It has already spread throughout Central Africa, raising fearless warriors at every step' and were it not that Christianity is sheltered in the strong arms of science, the civilization of modern Europe might fall, as fell the civilization of ancient Rome."

(107) Frank Newport. "Americans' Religion and Their Sympathies in the Middle East" A Gallup article in May of 2021. Limited polling indicates about 90% of US Muslims support the Palestinians.

Appendix

Examples of the Tanakh and the Talmud

The Tanakh is the same as the Christian Old Testament and is composed of several different themes. The major part of it is a history of the Jews with the 613 rules of Jewish law mixed in. The first five books, The Torah, are possibly written by Moses. They relate the early history of mankind and the Jews before they take over the Promised Land. These books are the source of most of the Jewish law and rules. The next 12 books continue the history of the Jews. The last 22 books are a mixture of proverbs, songs, and the prophesies of greater and lesser prophets. The Tanakh covers Jewish history from the beginning of mankind until about 350 B.C.E. Generally, the Jews are not told to conquer or convert the world. They are told to be a good example to other nations. The Ten Commandments are at the foundation of the religion.

A divinely inspired leader, teacher, and savior of the Jews is first predicted in the Torah. The term Messiah is not used until the book of Samuel. His coming is prophesized by several of the later prophets. Most Jews do not think that he has arrived. Christians think that Jesus is the Messiah.

The Talmud is a very extensive study of the Tanakh done over roughly 250 years from 200 C.E. to 450 C.E. It consists of about 2711 pages of the writings of several famous rabbis and essentially tells the faithful how to follow the Jewish laws on a day to day basis.

The God of the Jews has many facets. His actions and demands are by turns protective, demanding, forgiving, angry, vengeful, merciful, fatherly, and motherly.

Some quotes from the Tanakh:

Book of Genesis 12:2-3 "And I will make of you a great nation, and I will bless you and make your name great, so that you will be a blessing. I will bless those who bless you, and him who dishonors you I will curse, and in you all the families of the earth shall be blessed."

Deuteronomy 7:2 "And when the Lord thy God shall deliver the Canaanites before thee; thou shalt smite them, and utterly destroy them; thou shalt make no covenant with them, nor shew mercy unto them: Neither shalt thou make marriages with them; thy daughter thou shalt not give unto his son, nor his daughter shalt thou take unto thy son.." King James Version.

Canaanites is the name given to the various people who occupied the Promised Land when Moses arrived after 40 years in the wilderness.

Leviticus 19:18 "Do not seek revenge or bear a grudge against anyone among your people but love your neighbor as yourself. I am the Lord."

Micah 6:8 "What does the Lord require of you? To act justly, and to love mercy and to walk humbly with your God."

Exodus 34:6-7. "The Lord then passed in front of him [Moses] and called out, 'I, the Lord, am a God who is full of compassion [mercy]1 and pity, who is not easily angered and who shows great love and faithfulness. I keep my promise for thousands of generations3 and forgive evil and sin'".

Examples of God's vengeance include the worldwide flood, the destruction of Sodom, and the defeat at the hands of the Assyrians.

The flood is recounted in Genesis 6:7. "So the LORD said, "I will wipe from the face of the earth the human race I have created—and with them the animals, the birds and the creatures that move along the ground—for I regret that I have made them."

Genesis 20:24 "Then the LORD rained down burning sulfur on Sodom and Gomorrah—from the LORD out of the heavens."

Isaiah 66:13. "As a mother comforts her child, so will I comfort you; and you will be comforted over Jerusalem."

The Talmud

The word Talmud roughly means "study". It is generally a record of the rabbinical debates in the 2nd to the 5th century concerning the Torah, particular the laws. It is central to the education of students of Jewish law and tradition. A brief description is in the text in Chapter 2, of this book.

Examples:

The prohibition of reciting an unnecessary berakhah (blessing formulated with G-d's name) violates the verse "Thou shalt not take the name of the Lord thy G-d in vain"

The liar's punishment is that even when he speaks the truth, no one believes him

A person's true character is ascertained by three parameters: his cup (i.e., his behavior when he drinks), his pocket (i.e., his financial dealings), and his anger.

Do not appease a person while he is still angry.

Silence is beautiful for wise people; it is all the more beautiful for fools.

Like the Hadith, there are some very controversial inclusions. Scholars defending these inclusions point out that in recording the debates, all positions are mentioned and explored. They are not necessarily agreed with. Some of the more controversial include:

Rabbi Ila'i said: If a Jew is tempted to do evil he should go to a city where he is not known, dress in black clothes, cover his head in black, and do what his heart desires so that G-d's name will not be desecrated.

"A goy (Gentile) who pries into The Law (Talmud) is guilty of death."

A Jew need not pay a gentile the wages owed him for work.

The New Testament

The New Testament consists of 25 books. The first four are the story of Jesus by Matthew, Mark, Luke, and John. The 5th is the history of the disciples of Jesus called the Acts of the Disciples. The next 19 are letters mostly by Saint Paul to various churches. The last is a mystical chapter called Revelations.

The stories of Jesus include his birth, days in the wilderness, his baptism, his 3 year ministry of teaching and healing, his crucifixion, and his rising from the dead, 3 days later. Some of his most prominent teachings include:

Mark 12:29-3. "The most important Commandment," answered Jesus, is this: 'Hear, O Israel: The Lord our God, the Lord is one. Love the Lord your God with all your heart and with all your soul and with all your mind and with all your strength. The second is this: 'Love your neighbor as yourself.' There is no commandment greater than these."

Matthew 7:12 and Luke 6:31 "Do unto others as you would have them do unto you."

Luke 17:20-21 Jesus says, "The kingdom of heaven is within you."

John 8:32. Jesus says, "You shall know the truth, and the truth shall set you free."

Matthew 12:31-32 Jesus says, "Therefore I tell you, people will be forgiven for every sin and blasphemy, but blasphemy against the Spirit will not be forgiven.

Matthew 10 34-36 Jesus says, "Do not think that I have come to bring peace to the earth. I have not come to bring peace, but a sword. For I have come to set a man against his father, and a daughter against her mother, and a daughter-in-law against her mother-in-law. And a man's enemies will be those within his own household."

(This is not a command. It is an observation concerning what will happen.)

John 14:6 "I am the way and the truth and the life. No one comes to the Father except through me"

John 11:25-26. "Jesus said to her, 'I am the resurrection and the life, he who believes in me, though he die, yet shall he live, and whoever lives and believes in me shall never die.'"

The letters in the rest of the New Testament are mostly from Paul concerning how to run a church and teach. Several verses of his advice are in the text of this book.

Examples of the Qur'an

Whereas the Christian Bible is very historical, tracing the events of the Jews and Jesus in a story telling framework, the Qur'an, although referencing 24 prophets from the Bible in small vignettes, is more a series of instructions and observations. It is clear that God is interested in mercy and justice. The Qur'an employs examples telling us how to interact with God and others. Optimistically it emphasizes God's mercy to his backsliding people.

These are some selected quotes from the Qur'an. The Qur'an is the word of God given to Muhammad after the angel Gabriel visited him in his meditations. Gabriel pressured him, forcing Muhammad to speak God's word to inform and instruct mankind. The Qur'an was given over a period of several years. The quotes cover most of the central issues about Islam today. The Qur'an is divided into 114 *Suras* or chapters. They are placed in order from the longest to the shortest. They are not in the order in which they were revealed. That order is not definitively known.

Arabic is difficult to translate, and translators tend to take sides. To try to give an even-handed example here I have used parts of four different sources.

1. -Al-Qur'an translated by Ahmed Ali, Princeton Press

2. -The Koran translated by N. J. Dawood, published in 1956 by Penguin Classics and revised several times since.

3. -Qur'an.com

4. -Thenoblequran.com

Those from Ahmed Ali have an "AA" at the end.

Those from Dawood have a "D" at the end.

Those from the Quran.com will have a "Q" by them.

Those from thenoblequran.com will have "NQ" after them.

All Suras begin with the following statement:

In the Name of God, The Compassionate, the Merciful.

2: 2-6. This is The Book free of doubt and involution, a guidance for those who preserve themselves from evil and follow the straight path, who believe in the Unknown and fulfil their devotional obligations, and spend in charity of what We have given them; Who believe in what has been revealed to you and what was revealed to those before you, and are certain of the Hereafter. They have found the guidance of their Lord and will be successful. As for those who deny, it is all the same if you warn them or not, they will not believe. AA

2:176-177 Righteousness is not that you turn your faces toward the east or the west, but [true] righteousness is [in] one who believes in Allah, the Last Day, the angels, the Book, and the prophets and gives wealth, in spite of love for it, to relatives, orphans, the needy, the traveler, those who ask [for help], and for freeing slaves; [and who] establishes prayer and gives zakat; [those who] fulfill their promise when they promise; and [those who] are patient in poverty and hardship and during battle. Those are the ones who have been true, and it is those who are the righteous. - Q

2:190 Fight for the sake of God those that fight you, but do not attack first. God does not love the aggressors. Slay them wherever you find them. Drive them out of the places from which they drove you. Idolatry is worse than carnage. -D

Fight in the way of Allah those who fight you but do not transgress. Indeed. Allah does not like transgressors. And kill them wherever you overtake them and expel them from wherever they have expelled you, and fitnah (trials and tribulations) is worse than killing. And do not fight them at al-Masjid al- Haram until they fight you there. But if they fight you, then kill them. Such is the recompense of the disbelievers. - Q

And kill (those who fought against you) wherever you encounter them and expel them from wherever they have expelled you. Tribulation is worse than killing. Do not fight against them by the Sacred Mosque until they fight you therein. If they fight you, then kill them and such is the recompense of the disbelievers. - NQ

2:285 So do you believe in part of the Scripture and disbelieve in part? Then what is the recompense for those who do that among you except disgrace in worldly life; and on the Day of Resurrection they will be sent back to the severest of punishment. And Allah is not unaware of what you do. –Q

The Messenger has believed in what was revealed to him from his Lord, and [so have] the believers. All of them have believed in Allah and His angels and His books and His messengers, [saying], "We make no distinction between any of His messengers." And they say, "We hear and we obey. [We seek] Your forgiveness, our Lord, and to You is the [final] destination." NQ

2:228 …And due to the wives is similar to what is expected of them, according to what is reasonable. But the men have a degree over them [in responsibility and authority]. And Allah is Exalted in Might and Wise. Q

…Women shall with justice have rights similar to those exercised against them, although men have a status above women. God is mighty and wise.- D

… And due to the wives is similar to what is expected of them, according to what is reasonable. But the men have a degree over them [in responsibility and authority]. And Allah is Exalted in Might and

Wise. NQ

2:256 There shall be no compulsion in religion- Q, NQ and D

3:28 Those who believe should not take unbelievers as their friends. AA

Let believers not make friends with infidels in preference to the faithful. - D

3:118 Believers do not make friends with any but your own people. They will spare no pains to corrupt you. - D

Oh you who have believed, do not take as intimates those other than yourselves, for they will not spare you [any] ruin. They wish you would have hardship. Hatred has already appeared from their mouths, and what their breasts conceal is greater. We have certainly made clear to you the signs, if you will use reason. - Q.NQ

4:34 Men are in charge of women by [right of] what Allah has given one over the other and what they spend [for maintenance] from their wealth. So righteous women are devoutly obedient, guarding in [the husband's] absence what Allah would have them guard. But those [wives] from whom you fear arrogance - [first] advise them; [then if they persist], forsake them in bed; and [finally], strike them. But if they obey you [once more], seek no means against them. Indeed, Allah is ever Exalted and Grand.-Q

Men have authority over women because God has made one superior to the other, and because they spend their wealth to maintain them. Good women are obedient. They guard their unseen parts because God has guarded them. As for those from whom you fear disobedience, admonish them and send them to beds apart and hit them. Then if they obey you, take no further action against them.- D

Men are protectors and maintainers of women by (right of) what Allah has made some of them to excel over others and also by (right of) what they spend from their wealth (upon women). Hence, righteous women are devoutly obedient (to Allah and their husbands) and guard in (the husband's) absence what Allah (wants to be) guarded (of their chastity and husband's property). But as for those (women) from whom you fear (further) rebellious disobedience, then (first) admonish them. (If they do not desist), then refuse to share their beds. (And if they continue in defiance), then hit them lightly (as a means of discipline, without causing pain or harm). However, if they obey you, then seek no means (of harm or annoyance) against them. Indeed, Allāh has ever been Most High, Most Great- NQ

4:91 You will find others who wish to obtain security from you and [to] obtain security from their people. Every time they are returned to [the influence of] disbelief, they fall back into it. So, if they do not withdraw from you or offer you peace or restrain their hands, then seize them and kill them wherever you overtake them. And those - We have made for you against them a clear authorization. NQ

4:151 Indeed, those who disbelieve in Allah and His messengers and wish to discriminate between Allah and His messengers and say, "We believe in some and disbelieve in others," and wish to adopt a way in between. Those are the disbelievers, truly. And We have prepared for the disbelievers a humiliating punishment. - Q 4:151 Those that deny God and His apostles, and those that draw a line between God and His apostles, saying' "We believe in some, but deny others" – thus seeking a middle way – these indeed are the unbelievers. For the unbelievers We have prepared a shameful punishment. D. 4:151- Verily, those who disbelieve in Allah and His Messengers and wish to make distinction between Allah and His Messengers (by believing in Allah and disbelieving in His Messengers) saying, "We believe in some but reject others," and wish to adopt a way in between. Those are the disbelievers, truly. And We have prepared for the disbelievers a humiliating punishment. NQ

5:9 Do not allow your hatred for other men to turn you away from justice. Deal justly; that is nearer to true piety.- D

Allah has promised those who believe and do righteous deeds [that] for them there is forgiveness and great reward. - Q and NQ

9:5 When the sacred months are over, slay the idolaters wherever you find them. Arrest them, besiege them, and lie in ambush everywhere for them. D

And when the sacred months have passed, then kill the polytheists wherever you find them and capture them and besiege them and sit in wait for them at every place of ambush. But if they should repent, establish prayer, and give zakat, let them [go] on their way. Indeed, Allah is Forgiving and Merciful – Q and NQ

9:39 If you do not fight, He will punish you sternly and replace you by other men. - D

10:21 God is swifter at contriving. (strategy) – D

And when We let mankind taste of mercy after some adversity has afflicted them, behold! They take to plotting against Our Signs! Say: "Allah is more Swift in planning!" Certainly, Our Messengers (angels) record all of that which you plot. NQ

23:1-6 Blessed are the believers…who restrain their carnal desires (except with their wives and slave girls, for these are lawful to them.)- D

… and they who guard their private parts, except from their wives or those their right hands possess, for indeed they will not be blamed. Q and NQ

23:95 Requite evil with good. -D

Repel, by [means of] what is best, [their] evil. We are most knowing…- Q and NQ

25:68 …do not kill except for a just cause. -D

And those who do not invoke with Allah another deity or kill the soul which Allah has forbidden [to be killed], except by right, and do not commit unlawful sexual intercourse. And whoever should do that will meet a penalty- Q and NQ

42:40 "And the retribution for an evil act is an evil one like it, but whoever pardons and makes reconciliation – his reward is [due] from Allah." NQ

"But he that forgives and seeks reconcilement shall be rewarded by God." D

48:29 Muhammad is the Prophet of God; and those who are with him are severe with infidels but compassionate among themselves-AA, D

60:4 "Enmity and hate have come between us forever unless you worship the one God." AA, D

Examples of Hadith-

The Hadith are the sayings and rulings of the prophet Muhammad as related from those around him at the time. Many reflect the compassionate and insightful side of Muhammad as the ruler of a tribe. Muhammad did not write them down. Certain of his followers reported as an oral tradition. Clerics wrote them at various times for the next 200 years. About 200 to 300 years after Muhammad's death they were first gathered into the different collections that we have today. His third and youngest wife is supposed to have contributed about 2000 of them.

There is some debate within Islam concerning which are really Muhammad's sayings. Different sects of Islam use different lists of Hadith as authentic. *Sahih* Bukhari (*Sahih* means "collection") and *Sahih* Muslim are two prominent lists. Sunni, Shia, and the other sects have different lists of the sayings. The lists range from about 4,000 to 16,000 Hadith.

The list below begins with several "attributed" sayings. The Hadith are in quotation marks and are numbered. They are mostly Bukhari Hadith and Muslim Hadith.

1. The ink of the scholar is more precious than the blood of the martyr.
2. The first thing created by God was the intellect.
3. One learned man is harder on the devil than a thousand worshippers.

4. Riches are not from an abundance of worldly goods, but from a contented mind.

5. He who wishes to enter paradise at the best door must please his mother and father.

6. Sahih Bukhari 1:2:13 "None of you [truly] believes until he wishes for his brother what he wishes for himself." This is very similar to the Golden Rule, "Do unto others as you would have them do unto you."

7. The thing which is lawful but disliked by God is divorce.

8. Women are the twin halves of men.

9. Actions will be judged according to intentions.

10. That which is lawful is clear and that which is unlawful likewise, but there are certain doubtful things between the two from which it is well to abstain.

11. The proof of a Muslim's sincerity is that he pays no attention to that which is not his business.

12. That person is nearest to God, who pardons... him who would have injured him.

13. .... yield obedience to my successor, although he may be an Abyssinian slave.

14. The creation is like God's family.... The most beloved unto God is the person who does good to God's family.

15. Modesty and chastity are parts of the Faith.

16. Sahih Bukhari 1:2:25. "I have been ordered to fight against people until they testify that there is no god but Allah and that Muhammad is the messenger of Allah and until they perform the prayers and pay the zakat, and if they do so, they will have gained protection from me for their lives and property, unless [they do acts that are punishable] in accordance with Islam, and their reckoning will be with Allah the Almighty."

17. Sahih Bukhari 6502. "Allah the Almighty has said: 'Whosoever shows enmity to a friend of Mine, I shall be at war with him.'"

18. "Allah has pardoned for me my people for [their] mistakes and [their] forgetfulness and for what they have done under duress."

19. Hadith by Al Tirmidhi - Whoever suffers an injury and forgives (the person responsible), Allah will raise his status to a higher degree and remove one of his sins

20. Sahih Dawud 4362. "A Jewess used to abuse the Prophet and disparage him. A man strangled her till she died. The Messenger of Allah declared that no recompense was payable for her blood."

21. Oaths and Treaties.

    Sahih Bukhari, Volume 7, Book 67, Number 427: "By Allah, and Allah willing, if I take an oath and later find something else better than that. Then I do what is better and make up for my erroneous oath.' "

22. **Apostasy**

    Sahih Bukhari 9:84:57. Narrated 'Ikrima: Some Zanadiqa (atheists) were brought to 'Ali and he burnt them. The news of this event, reached Ibn 'Abbas who said, "If I had been in his place, I would not have burnt them, as Allah's Apostle forbade it, saying, 'Do not punish anybody with Allah's punishment (fire).' I would have killed them according to the statement of Allah's Apostle, 'Whoever changed his Islamic religion, then kill him.'"

    Sahih al-Bukhari 9:83:17 " Allah's Apostle (Muhammad said, "The blood of a Muslim who confesses that none has the right to be worshipped but Allah and that I am His Apostle, cannot be shed except in three cases: In Qisas (retribution) for murder, a married person who commits illegal sexual intercourse, and the one who reverts from Islam (apostate) and leaves the Muslims."

23. **Stoning for adultery**

    The Qur'an does not recommend stoning. It recommends 100 lashes. Several Hadith recommend stoning.

    Sahih Bukhari 8:82:803-806. Stoning for adultery.

Sahih Bukhari 2:23:413. Narrated 'Abdullah bin 'Umar: The Jew brought to the Prophet a man and a woman from amongst them who have committed (adultery) illegal sexual intercourse. He ordered both of them to be stoned (to death), near the place of offering the Funeral prayers beside the mosque."

Sahih Bukhari 3:49:860. Narrated Abu Huraira and Zaid bin Khalid Al-Juhani: A Bedouin came and said, "O Allah's Apostle! Judge between us according to Allah's Laws." His opponent got up and said, "He is right. Judge between us according to Allah's Laws." The Bedouin said, "My son was a laborer working for this man, and he committed illegal sexual intercourse with his wife. The people told me that my son should be stoned to death; so, in lieu of that, I paid a ransom of one hundred sheep and a slave girl to save my son. Then I asked the learned scholars who said, "Your son has to be lashed one-hundred lashes and has to be exiled for one year." The Prophet said, "No doubt I will judge between you according to Allah's Laws. The slave-girl and the sheep are to go back to you, and your son will get a hundred lashes and one year exile." He then addressed somebody, "O Unais! go to the wife of this (man) and stone her to death" So, Unais went and stoned her to death.

24. Drinking alcohol

Sahih Bukhari *Book 17, Number 4226* Anas b. Malik reported that a person who had drunk wine was brought to Allah's Apostle (may peace be upon him). He gave him forty stripes with two lashes."

About the author

I am an optimist and political independent who thinks that religion has much to offer and does not have to increase the violence and misunderstanding in the world. I have an MD and a Bachelor of Fine Arts in painting. I am board certified in Emergency Medicine and practiced for 51 years. I am happily married to the love of my life, Tina. We have three wonderful children married to equally wonderful spouses. We have five delightful grandchildren. I was raised in middle class comfort and was brought up in a liberal Presbyterian Church. I have lived principally in Tennessee and California.

I have attended all sorts of religious revivals, retreats, ceremonies, and sermons including Jewish, Christian, Islamic, Hindu, and Buddhist groups. I have given talks on religious, cultural, and historical topics to small groups interested in discussion, debate, and dialectic. I believe that there is an intelligence underlying the universe. I think that "God", whatever form he/she takes, is not greatly concerned with abstract acts of religious piety and has designed a world that works best when we are more interested in tolerance and kindness toward each other. I hope this book expresses the important shared concern for tolerance, mercy, and kindness in the General Admonitions of the three great monotheisms.

www.ingramcontent.com/pod-product-compliance
Lightning Source LLC
Chambersburg PA
CBHW071142130626
46553CB00004B/1486